The Art of Marriage Maintenance

SYLVIA R. KARASU M.D. AND
T. BYRAM KARASU M.D.

JASON ARONSON
Lanham • Boulder • New York • Toronto • Oxford

Published in the United States of America
by Jason Aronson
An Imprint of Rowman & Littlefield Publishers, Inc.

A wholly owned subsidiary of
The Rowman & Littlefield Publishing Group
4501 Forbes Boulevard, Suite 200, Lanham, Maryland 20706
www.rowmanlittlefield.com

PO Box 317
Oxford
OX2 9RU, UK

British Library Cataloguing in Publication Information Available

Library of Congress Cataloging-in-Publication Data

Karasu, Sylvia R., 1949–
  The art of marriage maintenance / Sylvia R. Karasu and T. Byram Karasu.
    p. cm.
  Includes bibliographical references and index.
  ISBN 0-7657-0376-9 (alk. paper) — ISBN 0-7657-0377-7 (pbk. : alk. paper)
  1. Marriage. 2. Married people—Psychology. I. Karasu, Toksoz B. II. Title.

HQ734.K254 2005   2004029254
306.872—dc22

Printed in the United States of America

♾™ The paper used in this publication meets the minimum requirements of American
National Standard for Information Sciences—Permanence of Paper for Printed Library
Materials, ANSI/NISO Z39.48-1992.

The Art of Marriage Maintenance

Contents

Acknowledgments   vii

Credits   ix

Introduction   1

1   The Relationship in Marriage   5
2   Sex in Marriage   29
3   The Power Play in Marriage   51
4   Communication in Marriage   65
5   Pregnancy and Infants in Marriage   91
6   Children and Adolescents in Marriage   125
7   Midlife in Marriage   153
8   Marriage as a Cause of Illness   177
9   Redefining Marriage   195

Epilogue   221

Bibliography   225

Index   239

Acknowledgments

In a book such as this, we are grateful to so many people who have contributed their talents. Most importantly, we offer special personal thanks to Dr. Jason Aronson, whose company is now an imprint of Rowman & Littlefield Publishers, Inc. Dr. Aronson saw the potential and value in our project immediately and supported us throughout. We also offer special thanks to Ms. Melaina Balbo-Phipps, who helped us with our initial contract negotiations. We could not have had such a streamlined project without the conscientiousness of our editorial assistant, Ms. Sonya Kolba, who diligently and expeditiously saw us through the entire process. Mr. Stephen Driver expertly shepherded us through copyediting, typesetting, and production and insured that our manuscript was read thoughtfully and with extraordinary attention to detail. Ms. Linda Evans was an unusually intelligent and respectful copyeditor, and Ms. Julie Grady did a careful and attentive job proofreading our final manuscript. We are also especially grateful to Mr. Robert Dorman for his preparation of our index so that our information is more easily accessible to our readers and to Ms. Allison Nealon, who designed, with particular thought and sensitivity to the mood we wished to convey, our book cover. We are appreciative to all those others at Rowman & Littlefield Publishers who worked on our manuscript.

Mrs. Hilda Cuesta worked tirelessly and pleasantly on our manuscript for months. She typed and copied more drafts than we care to count and remained so completely identified with our project throughout this arduous process. Mrs. Josephine Costa diligently and enthusiastically helped us with all our correspondence and permission requests. Both Hilda and Josephine were a delight to work with and were extraordinarily competent and thorough in their efforts on our behalf.

We are most grateful to Dr. Peter Kramer, Ms. Judith Viorst, and Dr. Judith Wallerstein who gave generously of their time and expertise to review earlier drafts of our manuscript and offer their comments.

Inasmuch as there were many references to obtain and verify, we want to thank the staff at several libraries, most notably the Weill Medical College Library of Cornell University. In particular, we want to acknowledge the reference and information service librarians, Ms. Helen-ann Brown; Mr. Kevin Pain; and Mr. Daniel E. Cleary, who is the Head, Information and Access Services, all of whom helped in our references searches. We want to offer additional thanks to Mr. Bruce Silberman and Mr. Edsel Watkins, Library Assistants in the Inter-Library Loan Department there for tracking down particularly esoteric references that even Weill did not have as part of its collection. We also offer thanks to the Director of the Weill Medical College Library, Ms. Carolyn Anne Reid, who patiently listened to suggestions regarding the inter-library loan process.

We are also especially grateful to Ms. Cynthia Rosado, Assistant Chief, Access and Reader Service, Stack Maintenance and Delivery Division at the Center for Humanities and Social Sciences of the New York Public Library. This main New York branch of the library is a daunting place, whose sources are so well protected that it often takes considerable time to access them. Mrs. Rosado made that process so much easier for us.

Finally, we want to thank our many patients, both married and not, who have shared with us, over the years, their experiences, often poignant and painful, and helped us hone in our skills in dealing with the complexities of marriage.

Credits

Introduction

Billy Graham was once asked in an interview how his wife would describe her life with him. "Well," he said, "someone once asked her if she ever thought of divorce and she said, 'No, I've never thought of divorce, but I have thought of murder.'" Graham added, "And she was kidding, of course, because we have a wonderful relationship."[1]

If you have not thought of killing your spouse, as Ruth Graham jocularly stated she had, you are, indeed, an unusual person. Most likely, you may not have wanted to admit such a horrible idea consciously. If, by a remote chance, however, you truly have never thought of murder, your spouse probably has. Of course, actual spousal murder occurs only occasionally. The more common "offing" of a spouse is divorce, with many small "soul" murders occurring along the way.

Here is an example of how feelings change dramatically over the course of a marriage and lead to thoughts of divorce. This example demonstrates the evolution of one marriage, that of Albert Einstein. The following are two letters from him to his first wife, Mileva Marić. The first letter was written during their courtship and several years before they married in 1903. The second letter was written years later, in 1914, which was the year of their separation:

This first letter, from 1900, was one of forty-three extant letters between Einstein and Mileva:

> Without the thought of you I would no longer want to live among this sorry herd of humans. But having you makes me proud; and your love makes me happy. I will be doubly happy when I . . . kiss your sweet mouth which trembles blissfully for me alone.

The second letter, from 1914, was written the year of their separation:

> A. You will see to it (1) that my clothes and linen are kept in order, (2) that I am served three regular meals a day *in my room*, (3) that my bedroom and study are always kept in good order and that my *desk is not touched by anyone other than me.*
>   B. You will renounce all personal relations with me, except when these are required to keep up social appearances.
>   C. . . . (1) you will expect no affection from me and you will not reproach me for this, (2) you must answer me at once when I speak to you.

By the time of this second letter, Einstein was well into his affair with his cousin Elsa Lowenthal, who would become his second wife. By now, Einstein was describing Mileva as "an unfriendly, humorless creature who does not get anything out of life and who, by her mere presence, extinguishes other people's joy of living." He added, "I treat my wife as an employee whom I cannot fire."[2]

Many marriages do not even last as long as Einstein's. Unfortunately, these venomous interchanges are common enough to make us wonder what happens to the great love professed by both sides at the beginning and how that love so dramatically converts years later to hate and even murderous rage.

Over two million people marry each year in the United States. Some of these people are marrying for the first time; others are marrying for the second or more time. During that same year, about a million people will divorce. This number includes those who are divorcing for the first time, as well as those who have married and divorced before. Accurate statistics on divorce are difficult to access for many reasons, including that some states, like California, do not even report their data. Whatever the divorce rate, whether it is 40 percent or 50 percent or higher, depending on what demographics we study, we probably can all agree that divorce is far too common today.

Given that the type of evolution we saw in Einstein's marriage is not so unusual, we would imagine that marriage is an unpopular event. Clearly, it is not. In fact, getting married is one of the most popular of all life events. Barbara DaFoe Whitehead, in *Why There Are No Good Men Left*, notes that when a sample of single women, ages twenty to twenty-nine, was asked just how important it was for them to have a good marriage, 89 percent chose "extremely important." Some people even admit that they so much want to be married that they would rather marry and risk divorce than cancel their weddings.

Jennifer Bayot reported in July 2003 that new couples were often willing to go into substantial debt for the wedding alone. If anything, our wedding obsession has grown even worse, said Cathy Horyn, in an article in June 2004. Wedding plans often take on a life of their own. Horyn explains that in 2002 the average American couple spent over $22,000 for a wedding. Caterers in New York thought the number was closer to $50,000! She notes that while the number of marriages in the United States has remained fairly constant over the past twenty years, the number of wedding planners has risen 25 percent! With more services and more media coverage available, couples find themselves with greater choices for their weddings and more likely with credit cards charged to their limit even before they walk down the aisle.

Even same-sex couples want the right to get married. And they want *marriage* specifically, not *civil unions* or *domestic partnerships.* It is marriage that confers certain privileges, status, and rights.

Most people would not willingly invest their time and money in some endeavor or enterprise that has a chance of failing about 50 percent of the time. When it comes to marriage, however, we often put the odds aside. We assume divorce will not happen to us. More than sometimes, however, it does. Are we simply getting married for the myth and dream of marriage, and when we awaken to its reality, do we desperately want out? As Cyril Connolly has said, "Only by avoiding the beginnings of things, can we escape their endings."

Like any endeavor, marriage requires competence and knowledge. Mostly, we have relegated skills like becoming a spouse and a parent to a kind of on-the-job training. Marriage requires what we call *MarriageSense,* by which we mean an understanding and appreciation of what marriage entails for each spouse. We write it as one word to convey the importance of the bond between marriage and sense. Not many people enter marriage with well-thought-out ideas beyond the wedding arrangements, let alone with *MarriageSense.*

The Art of Marriage Maintenance is about *MarriageSense,* that is, marital life after the wedding. It is about the psychological and biological differences between men and women that make marriage so challenging. It is about why passion is in danger of fading within marriage, how hormones exacerbate behavior, and how our brains confound us. It is also about how pregnancy and having young children and adolescents often catapult a marriage to its breaking point and how the stresses of midlife, such as affairs and illness, contribute to marital discord. It is, in effect, how to ensure a happy and enduring marriage: the art of marriage maintenance.

Notes

1. In an e-mail to the authors, October 13, 2003, Mr. Stephen G. Scholle, vice president of administration, Billy Graham Evangelistic Association, stated: Billy Graham was interviewed by Mary Hart in 1990 and gave this response in reply to Mary Hart's question, "If I were sitting here with her [Ruth, Mrs. Billy Graham], how would she describe life with Billy Graham?"

2. Einstein's letters to Mileva Marić: Lot 3 (Letter 20), August 30 or September 6, 1900, and Lot 11, July 1914, *Einstein Family Correspondence* (New York: *Christie's Catalogue,* 1996); Einstein's description of Mileva Maric: Letter 489:365, "To Elsa Lowenthal" (Zurich, after December 2, 1913) and Letter 488:364–65, "To Elsa Lowenthal" (Zurich, before December 2, 1913), *Collected Papers of Einstein,* vol. 5, *The Swiss Years: Correspondence, 1912–1914,* trans. Anna Beck (Princeton: Princeton University Press, 1995).

CHAPTER 1

The Relationship in Marriage

Men and women exasperate each other as they are unwilling to understand, accept, and learn how to live with, if not to celebrate, their incompatibilities.

What Is It about Marriage?

Perhaps the most cogent understanding of what it means to be married comes, ironically, from the literature on the case for same-sex marriage. Jonathan Rauch, in *Gay Marriage*, says that the four words "Will you marry me?" are the four most ennobling words in the English language. Why is that so? Rauch emphasizes that marriage is not only a contract between two people; it also involves a pact with the community. It not only implies certain rights and privileges but also certain responsibilities in the eyes of the society. It is by virtue of this community support and its laws, both state and federal, that it confers on the two people a certain status unlike any other. In fact, by recent count, marriage empowers couples with over one thousand federal and another three hundred state rights and privileges, notes Davina Kotulski.

Most important, however, marriage implies and encourages a special relationship to develop between husband and wife. Marriage vows, in fact, state that the couple has promised to care and be there for each other, regardless of circumstances, as long as they both shall live. In one episode of the popular television show *Curb Your Enthusiasm*, husband Larry and wife Cheryl are planning to renew their vows after ten years of marriage. Cheryl insists that Larry include the line that he would love her "for all eternity." Larry, known to regular viewers for his selfishness, says, "I kind of thought I would be single in eternity."

For some, even the idea of "till death do us part" seems beyond comprehension and far too long. Think of your spouse, though, as your "life-witness," and you may think differently. Life-witness is a concept from Robert Louis Stevenson, who gave us *Treasure Island* and *A Child's Garden of Verses* and, most famously, *Dr. Jekyll and Mr. Hyde*. In one of his essays, Stevenson says that by marrying, "You have willfully introduced a witness into your life." We take life-witness to mean that your spouse is someone who experiences your life with you. Unlike the tree falling in the forest with no one to hear it, your spouse is there, amplifies the sound, and even sometimes gives it meaning. Couples who have lost a spouse often say the hardest part of life alone is no longer having that audience, no longer having someone with whom to share life. An unmarried person spoke of coming home hours later after an accident. It mattered to no one; no one was there to notice his lateness. Your spouse, however, will notice.

Why Can't You Be Like Me? A Spouse's Determination to Change the Other Is Negating and Dispiriting.

Those who marry may consider themselves badly cheated when they realize how different their spouse is from themselves. Inevitably, spouses enter marriage with unrealistic expectations of the other. Sometimes a spouse is actually seeking a psychological clone within the marriage. Each spouse may then naturally experience disappointment and disillusionment and tend to blame the other, as well as the institution of marriage, and wonder whether that other person really will be there "till death do us part."

Most people seem to have a powerful, innate need to change another person, especially their spouse. "Why can't you be like *me?*" is sung to many tunes. Interestingly enough, those who ask this question rarely want to change themselves; rather, they want their spouse to be like them. Can people really change? Will any change ever satisfy a spouse? Our focus highlights mainly male-female differences that permeate marriage and make the heterosexual marital relationship so fraught with conflict. Once spouses recognize that their partners have genuine and natural differences, they can better accept them. A major mistake, and the one that can do considerable damage to a couple, is the belief that there is only one way—their way.

When people do not comprehend these differences, they draw their own conclusions about someone else's personality, such as viewing the other as illogical or self-centered. Further, they can misconstrue the other's intentions, believing that the other doesn't listen, is uninterested, uncaring, controlling, or has some other personal agenda.

Ironically, perhaps, the more you come to accept your partner's traits—especially the shortcomings—the more undesirable qualities he or she will reveal: self-pity, jealousy, ambitions, pettiness, inadequacy, prejudices. Learning about these traits in your spouse requires more understanding and tolerance but also establishes even stronger intimacy.

> A man and a woman in an intimate relationship, especially a marriage, treat one another with cruelty that they would never consider directing toward anyone who meant less to them.
>
> —Michael Vincent Miller

Beth: *"You know, you are not normal. You should be on some sort of medication," she said.*

Ken: *"Oh, yeah? You are the norm? After ten years of analysis with four different therapists, you still blame your parents for everything that you do wrong in life. It is in your genes; look at your daughter, she is as unreasonable and hysterical as you are," he replied tersely.*

Beth: *"My daughter? Not our daughter? She has half of your fucking genes."*

Such cruelties have little to do with the intent to hurt the other. Rather, they occur in the context of severe disappointments we experience when a partner fails us empathically. We yearn for empathy from our spouses that mirrors the empathy an ideal mother has for her child. Michael Vincent Miller narrates a charming anecdote: "First God made Adam. But Adam complained that he was lonely. So God put him to sleep and made Eve from Adam's rib. When Adam awoke, he beheld a gorgeous female standing before him. Yet he still looked miserable, so God reappeared and asked him, 'What's bothering you now, Adam?' Look at the beautiful wife I made for you!" Adam replied, 'Yes, but first I need a mother.'"

That wish for the unconditional love we may have experienced or wished we had experienced from a mother primes us for disappointments. What makes matters worse is that our personality traits and temperament are at best modifiable. In his book of the same name, Matt Ridley speaks of "nature *via* nurture." No psychoanalyses, no doses of Prozac, and no marital demands can significantly alter that basic temperament dramatically, although they may help the individual's capacity to moderate its excesses. In other words our temperament is what we are born with genetically. Given that bedrock, we develop our personality in the context of our environment and our genetics.

The word "temperament" is related to the word "temper," the hardness imparted to a metal. Its intractable quality was expressed in Lewis Carroll's *Through the Looking-Glass,* when the Red Queen meanly interrogated Alice about her inability to do division, addition, and subtraction. Making sure that she fails, she demands of Alice to try another subtraction sum.

> "Take a bone from a dog: what remains?" Alice considered. "The bone wouldn't remain, of course, if I took it—and the dog wouldn't remain: it would come to bite me—and I'm sure I shouldn't remain!" "Then you think nothing would remain?" said the Red Queen. "I think that's the answer." "Wrong as usual," said the Red Queen— "the dog's temper would remain."

So will the temperament of your spouse, even after being stripped of all defenses.

Your temperament and personality traits obviously affect the way you relate to your spouse. So does what you experienced as a child yourself. If you find yourself making much ado about nothing, you may want to examine your own psychological predispositions that developed from your earlier experiences. We all relate to people in our current life with the contaminated feelings from past relationships, particularly from those of our parents and siblings.

Sometimes, a spouse is a stand-in for someone else within our original family. For example, one woman, who had a stormy relationship with her own mother, once got so angry at her husband, she actually, completely unaware of what she was doing, screamed at him, "MOTHER!" Unless spouses appreciate what conflicts they bring to the marriage, they will perpetuate and suffer from them chronically and repetitively in marriage. In *The Good Marriage*, Judith Wallerstein and Sandra Blakeslee go so far as to say that the first task of marriage is to separate psychologically from your family of origin. The next step is to establish a new connectedness with your parents.

When one spouse targets another because of unfinished business (i.e., unresolved conflicts) from the past, he or she engages in a chronic litany against the partner. This spouse usually has no intention of leaving the marriage, unless encouraged by a third party, such as a lover, family member, or therapist. Instead, that spouse continues the litany against the other. What brings spouses together initially is not always what keeps them there. One of the reasons we marry is to perpetuate these old feelings within our present relationship. In other words, we maintain the comfort of familiarity, regardless of how negative it may be. We call this "staying in our emotional home." If a spouse is a stand-in for the other's original source of complaint, such as a parent, he or she can stay married without having to stop complaining. Inexperienced marriage counselors are puzzled by that fact. They may wonder silently, or even directly, to one spouse or the couple, why they stay together when they have so many complaints. What these therapists fail to realize is that the complaining spouse is in her or his "emotional home."

Man Is Reluctantly, Woman Enthusiastically, Engaged in Intimate Relations.

Beth: *"How come you never hold my hand at the movies? I am the one who always reaches out, and you pull your hand away after a few minutes,"* she complained.

Ken: *"Why hold hands at the movies? I am watching the movie, engaged in a story. It has nothing to do with us. You distract me by squeezing my hand when characters kiss each other or whisper some romantic stuff. Plus, it is uncomfortable to reach over the divider of the chairs,"* he protested.

Deborah Blum in *Sex on the Brain* explains that women are genetically pre-programmed to touch, to caress, to hug literally and metaphorically, to be more affiliative (i.e., to build stronger attachments). Men may experience these needs as clinging. Attachment is a more significant issue for women than for men. This observation, in fact, has been true in virtually all cultures throughout history. Blum quotes researcher Ellen Frank that the importance of attachment for women obviously has an adaptive significance for the survival of the species: if women were not to attach, babies simply wouldn't survive. An extraordinary preprogramming may be seen in puberty, which, for girls, can be viewed as biological preparation for childbearing and rearing. For example, as a girl's estradiol (the main estrogen) rises, so does the intensity of her emotional connection. More specifically, estradiol apparently signals oxytocin, the hormone believed to be very influential in bonding behavior and emotional connection in women. Interestingly, events that precipitate depressive disorders tend in women to be about interpersonal loss and severing of relationships.

Women are genetically preprogrammed to be more affiliative (i.e., build stronger attachments) than men:

- Their need for strong attachments is true for all cultures and through history and has an adaptive significance.
- If women were not to attach, babies would not survive.
- As estradiol, the main estrogen, rises, so does the intensity of emotion and connection.

Women socialize more than men during working hours. They laugh and bring family pictures or food to work. They often know a great deal about their coworkers' home lives. Men and women often tend to use the telephone differently. For most men, the telephone, as well as e-mail, is a means to convey information, such as about plans. For many women, however, these devices of communication are an essential way they feel metaphorically connected to their men. They are means to convey feelings and engage in the relationship. Women often complain that men do not call or e-mail as frequently as they would like. Men seem not to understand that: even when women directly express the importance of calls or e-mails, men fail to comply.

Men, on the other hand, are more pragmatic and goal oriented; women may experience these traits as emotionally distancing. Men tend to isolate home from their work. They need not have a close relationship in the manner or degree of women. In fact, they relate better at some self-protective distance. The strength, control, and power that maleness typically implies require at least a partial disengagement from other people.

Men are genetically programmed to be less affiliative. They seem to strive for independence, at least on the surface. In the context of a responsive relationship, women see this independence as an undesirable trait, and they attempt to abolish it. This may become another source of conflict within marriage. For women, everything, from watching a movie, eating, having sex, working, or playing sports, is primarily based on the need to relate. Blum contrasts the sexual woman-to-woman relationship—the ultimate match of affiliative needs—with male-to-male relations with the observation, "Lesbians don't have bathhouses." Blum notes that more than others, lesbians establish long-term relationships, though they apparently engage in sex less often than heterosexual couples.

Sexual relations seem to thrive best in the homosexual male relationship. Blum quotes an interview she had with Daryl Bem, a Cornell professor, who repeats to her this joke:

> What does a lesbian bring on her second date?
> A U-Haul.

> And what does a gay man bring on his second date?
> What second date?

What Does Woman Really Want?

> The great question . . . which I have not been able to answer, despite my thirty years of research into the feminine soul, is "What does a woman want?"
>
> —Freud, *Sigmund Freud, Life and Work*, Ernest Jones

Millimant in Congreve's play "The Way of the World" wants not to be called by any name that is associated with her pending marriage.

> Millimant: *"D'ye hear, I won't be called names after I'm married; positively, I won't be called names."*
>
> Mirabell: *"Names!"*
>
> Millimant: *"Ay, as wife, spouse, my dear, joy, jewel, love, sweetheart, and the rest of the nauseous cant in which men and their wives are so fulsomely familiar. I shall never bear that."*

Women, at least, don't want to be men's "something." They don't want to lose their own identity. Susan Choi explores the personal conflicts she had in determining which name—her or her new husband's, or some hyphenated combination of the two—to use when she married. It was her mother, she explains, who brought those conflicts to her attention when, without any discussion, she created a new hyphenated name for her daughter on an envelope she mailed to her. Choi notes that we want our names to perpetuate our own history after we are gone; obviously, newly created hyphenated names cannot do that. Choi says she started realizing how random our names really are and how they cannot really reflect everything about ourselves. Sometimes, she even admitted, women choose names on the basis of sound and aesthetics, saying it is a "very nice name," rather than with some conviction about their identity.

One woman, who began using her husband's name when she married and paid taxes under her married name for twenty-eight years, had apparently not changed her name on her Social Security record. It was not until the New York Department of Motor Vehicles sent her a letter threatening to suspend her driver's license because the name on her Social Security record did not match the name on her license that she realized her failure to make the name change.

What does a woman want? In Sarah Ban Breathnach's *Simple Abundance,* she answers that complex question of Freud's with a deceptively simple answer: "a nap, Dr. Freud, a nap." Every mother is a working mother. Some have two jobs. That is why a mother is chronically tired and sleep deprived. Some women even support a husband's education. Years ago, Betty Friedan aptly popularized a new degree for these women, "'Ph.T.' (Putting Husband Through)."[1] A woman's fatigue, and perhaps resentment, usually manifests with vacillating moods and emotional overreactions, and sometimes with unpredictable behaviors. Even a woman herself can get confused with her own natural, fluctuating feelings and behaviors, as if she isn't exactly the same person, especially at different stages of her menstrual cycle (which itself is not synchronous with the calendar since ovulation occurs on a twenty-eight-day interval). A woman's subjective experience is influenced, if not regulated, by powerful hormones—estrogens (primarily estradiol) and progesterone. Their rise and fall cyclically may lead to various moods such as euphoria and dysphoria. This recognition, conveyed through works of art, is exemplified in Botticelli's famous painting *Primavera,* which displays the world of Venus. In *Soul Mates,* Thomas Moore notes the painting depicts the multifaceted female as the blended embodiment of extreme emotions.

Edward Shorter explains that as late as the last century pelvic lesions were considered responsible for women's instability and even insanity. In fact, an operation to remove normal ovaries was so popular that it was known as to "Battey-ize" a woman. The procedure was named after an American surgeon, Robert Battey, who devised it in the 1870s to treat mental and physical suffering in women. Some American mental institutions even hired gynecologists to remain on staff so that they could perform this surgery in order to calm their psychiatric patients. Physicians in Britain and America were also removing the clitoris as well as performing ovariectomies. This preoccupation of American physicians obviously affected how both doctors and their patients viewed a woman's body: women saw their pelvic organs as a cause of emotional and physical symptoms and sought out surgery as a cure, emphasizes Shorter. Remember, of course, the word "hysteria" comes from the Greek word for "womb."

A woman's hormonal changes are partly responsible for her almost daily fluctuation of mood. But it is women's patterns of dealing with these fluctuations that puzzles men.

> Ken: *"Why do you need so many outfits?"*
>
> Beth: *"One for each mood."*
>
> Ken: *"Oh! How many moods are there?"*
>
> Beth: *"You mean in any given day?"*

If a man goes to his "cave" when under stress, as John Gray explains in *Men Are from Mars, Women Are from Venus,* and isolates himself in his own sanctuary, a woman, under duress, goes to her "well" where she seeks nurturing and companionship, usually from other women, such as by telephone or e-mail. Sometimes, shopping has the same purpose, though temporarily at times, as short as one shopping spree.

Any woman, therefore, who preserves her two or three faces (or more) is a healthy woman, with all her hormones and corresponding effects fluctuating according to their natural cycles. Women are whole in their many faces, seemingly conflicted and contradictory, but in fact normal and complementary.

What Does Woman Really Want from Man? For Him to Be Domestic, Monogamous, and Powerful, but under Her Control.

> Male had become man. And man was on his way to becoming daddy.
>
> —Kalman Glantz and John K. Pearce

In general, domestication of man generates anger. The domestication of men is related to a man's wish to be selected by women, while women are interested in men who are interested in producing children. Men's domestication, therefore, is part forced, part forced upon. Men tend to simulate a disposition and an attitude that women value. Men are expected to be successful and active in seduction in the courting phase and to quiet down into greater passivity as fathers afterwards. Most men are unnatural in this family man role, however, and see themselves as relegated to the status of a henpecked or pussy-whipped husband. In the contemporary world of overlapping (or even reversed) roles of husbands and wives, society may now expect men to share household chores such as taking out the garbage, or helping with the children, as well as put in more than full-time jobs. When, for example, a wife goes to classes or to a job, or even has a "ladies' night out," and she comes home, though, she may encounter either a hormonally castrated, depressed man or a testosterone-fueled, enraged one. In other words, the more a man is domesticated and expected to help with chores and children, as well as perform his full-time job, the more resentful, angry, and impotent he may become. Most men, for example, will not automatically wash their own dirty dishes, despite how obvious they are, and especially not after working a ten-hour day.

The sexual revolution, while correcting the inequality between men and women, has had some unintended repercussions, including women's changed expectations of men. No more is there an automatic, sentimental adoration of the man. This, in turn, has become a challenge to male potency. With greater free play and increased demands by liberated women, sex has sometimes become a form of competition. Women more openly have begun to compare their experiences with other women, asking such questions as how strong and long is his erection, how big or long his penis, or how often can he make love? Nowhere was this more evident than in the explicit sexual behavior of the character Samantha and the overtly sexual conversations among Carrie and her three friends on the widely popular television show *Sex and the City*. In this sexual revolution, men were not expecting women's newfound assertiveness and the accompanying intimidation, rejection, aggression, or ridicule. In many instances, this assertiveness has resulted in psychological impotence for a man.

Psychological impotence in men, largely attributed to the aggression of their women, is on the rise. Note, for example, the popularity of Viagra in the last few years and now Cialis, a medication that lasts for an entire weekend. To regain their potency, men sometimes seek other sexual partners, especially submissive or easily orgasmic women, outside of marriage. Controlling a powerful man is the best aphrodisiac for women. Although recently women have independently sought to possess power and money themselves, the historical pattern still reigns—that is, exercising power through possessing men. Women, by granting sex and affirmation to the male, attain power over men. D. H. Lawrence's novel *Women in Love*, written in the early 1900s, depicts such a situation in the relationship between the female character Gudrun and the male Gerald, a powerful industrialist:

> she kissed him. . . . Her fingers went over the mold of his face, over his features. She kissed him, putting her fingers over his face, his eyes, his nostrils . . . to know him, to gather him in by touch. . . . Ah, if she could have the precious *knowledge* of him, she would be filled, and nothing could deprive her of this. . . . Her fingers had him under their power.

Wanting to be filled and having the man under the woman's power are only desirable in relationships where the man is strong and potent, that is, has an important position, financial security, or other accouterments of success.

Woman and the Paternal Husband

> Males are not polygamous by nature at all. Nor are females really monogamous. Rather, both genders are sexually strategic by nature.
>
> —Susan Maushart

> *"Do I think that she has a lover? Nope. I don't think so. She isn't interested in sex at all, not just with me. I think she is very loyal in that sense. I would be shocked if I find that she has a lover. In some way I wish she had. Do you know what I mean? Maybe that would make her more sexually alive, just for her own sake."*

Most female mammals are not monogamous, and they don't, by and large, require their males for survival. Their need for impregnation is easily achieved because many fewer males are required for that purpose than half of the species—and males seem to be extremely enthusiastic about impregnating females for their own innate reasons. Nevertheless, whenever a male makes a larger commitment to a female and her offspring, the female tends to grant him sexual exclusivity. This, in return, forges a stronger bond between the two. There is no morality of faithfulness, as there is among humans. This bonding is only explainable at a very primitive level as an innate reproductive strategy. In humans, the same innate strategy may exist on a subliminal level. Thus, a woman, who selects a healthy and attractive man, who is also a vigorous protector, reciprocates by being faithful, especially if the man has an affectionate bond with the children.

Susan Maushart notes that men have needed females, initially to reproduce and then to ensure the survival of those offspring. Females, especially in the past, have required male protection and provision as a consequence of the enormous physical demands of human pregnancy, birth, and lactation. Human infants are far more defenseless for a longer period of time than most other mammals. Essentially, then, Maushart emphasizes that the chief beneficiary of monogamy is the child. Everything beyond the survival of one's offspring is a symptom of monogamy, not a cause, including passion, economic security, companionship, and so forth.

What Does Man Want? Multiple Sex Partners and Maternal Care. Monogamy Is for the Birds.

> Very well; of the delights of this world man cares most for sexual intercourse. He will go to any length for it—risk fortune, character, reputation, life itself.
>
> —Mark Twain

"I am, I am trying to behave. I don't know why, but I am always looking for women. My wife is young and beautiful and very good in bed. I cannot claim to be deprived of sex. Nevertheless, even after a few hours following very satisfactory sex, I find myself eyeing other women. I can't listen to any reasonably good looking woman because I am constantly imagining what she would be like in bed. I love my wife, my family; I don't want to do any harm to them. I would never leave them for another woman. Nevertheless, I tell other women or I sort of imply that I might leave my wife if that is what it takes to get them to sleep with me. I even go as far as lying that my wife is having an affair with my best friend and will soon be leaving me. If anything I am the one who is trying to sleep with the wives of our friends.

I know, I know, this is going to get me in trouble one of these days. Did I tell you we just hired a young associate, who has a pair of legs you wouldn't believe? The other evening I offered her a ride. She jumped at the opportunity. We didn't stop talking all the way. She couldn't understand why my wife would even consider having sex with another man and leave someone like me—intelligent, handsome, witty. When we got to the parking lot of the train station, noticing how unaffected I was with her flattery, she resorted to a more convincing tactic. Oh my, oh my . . ."

Monogamy is not common in the animal kingdom, although it occurs more often in birds than mammals. In particular, monogamy seems to evolve when the young will not survive without the extraordinary efforts of *both* parents. This is clearly the case with most species of birds: most require both male and female parents to tend to building the nest and obtaining food. Interestingly, we used to believe that monogamy was typical of 90 percent of bird species. We now know, however, by special DNA techniques, that this is not so in as many as 40 percent of birds, note David P. Barash and Judith Eve Lipton. In other words, the birds hatched within one nest were not always from the same male.

Men, like women, want to be good partners in marriage. They also want to be taken care of, not unlike what their mothers offered. They yearn for stability at home and emotional attachment to their wives and children, but they may also be genetically programmed to seek sexual excitement elsewhere. From animal research with voles (animals like rats but with heavier bodies and shorter tails), we find there are two hormones, both produced in the hypothalamus, that are involved in pair bonding. These are vasopressin (more important in the male) and oxytocin (more important in the female), though both sexes have both hormones. Interestingly, one species of vole is monogamous and another is not, and not surprisingly there are differences biochemically in the receptors for these hormones in each species, note L. J. Young and colleagues.

Rat research has also shown that with merely one shot of oxytocin to the brain of a virgin female, the female rat will behave like a mother. This is quite remarkable inasmuch as these rats are typically vicious (at least to others' babies): a single shot of hormone changes their behavior to that of nurturing, caretaking, and nest building, says Blum. How animal studies relate to humans is still open to question, but there does seem to be a hormonal basis for behaviors like pair bonding and parental care, and one's decision to be monogamous may be biologically as well as socially driven.

Both men and women's libidos also decline within the context of a monogamous relationship. Says comedian Bill Maher, "Every marriage is same sex marriage. It is the same sex every night." A woman may complain about the boredom, rather than seek a new partner. If a woman bears children, by shifting her focus on them she may at least partially compensate for her lack of sexual excitement. Men, often not being able to get the same degree of compensatory pleasure from their children, may instead seek that rush of excitement in being desired outside of marriage. Helen Fisher, in *Why We Love,* explains that what creates excitement is novelty. Novel experiences increase the level of dopamine in the brain, and elevated levels of dopamine increase our attention and motivation. Using functional magnetic resonance imaging (fMRI), she studied the brains of those in love. Even different parts of the brain, like the caudate nucleus and ventral tegmental area, light up differently when someone is in love! Fisher also hypothesizes that romantic, passionate love does not last because it takes too much time and energy. Adaptively, our bodies seem programmed to get on with the business of everyday life rather than "die of sexual exhaustion" if romantic love were to persist. Fisher compares romantic love to an addiction, with its tolerance, withdrawal, and relapse. After a while, humans are ready to relapse into that state again should the opportunity present itself.

Monogamy, the pairing of one male with one female, is not common in the animal kingdom:

* Monogamy seems to evolve in nature when offspring need the efforts of both parents for survival, such as with many species of birds.
* Both men's and women's libidos decline within a monogamous relationship.
* Monogamy lowers a man's testosterone level.

Monogamy diminishes not only a man's libido; it also lowers his testosterone level. Each new female contact, on the other hand, has the power to produce a new burst of sexual interest and energy. This has become known as "the Coolidge Effect," so-named after an oft-repeated (perhaps apocryphal) tale told about President Calvin Coolidge, as reported by Kalman Glantz and John Pearce:

> The President and the first lady were given separate tours of a model farm. Coolidge's wife, upon observing an active group of chickens in the yard, noted that the rooster was being kept quite occupied. She suggested that her husband might be quite interested in her observation. When Mr. Coolidge arrived at the chicken coop, the guide promptly relayed the following message: "Your wife wanted me to point out how frequently the rooster copulated in a single day." The President, deep in thought, then asked, "Same hen?" "No, Mr. President," replied the guide. "Well," said Coolidge, "tell *that* to the First Lady."[2]

No one seems to know how this story came to be associated with President Coolidge. Even the Calvin Coolidge Memorial Foundation could not provide documentation, though it acknowledged the president was fond of barnyard humor. The term Coolidge Effect, however, became popular by animal researchers in the 1950s.[3] This amusing anecdote needs a little scientific scrutiny. First, sex in males is not one thing; it has two major components: erection and ejaculation. In men and rats, for example, males do want to copulate with each new female and even may have an erection but not always ejaculation. Gordon Bermant's research demonstrated that when a new female is introduced, a male rat experiences sexual arousal but not necessarily ejaculation. Says Bermant, "Put another way—even if the spirit was willing, the flesh was not." Another mammalian male, the ram, is more in line with a human male fantasy. In their research, Bermant and his associates noted that, when rams were given a new ewe, they not only had the same strong erection but also ejaculation each time—"the Coolidge Effect in all its glory, clear and unabashed."

Interestingly enough, the male sex drive is, to a large extent, determined by brain mechanisms that require only a certain threshold of testosterone for full operation. This explains why the sex drive of normal men is not increased by injections of testosterone—men are already above threshold in this respect. The sex drive of women, however, or men who are deficient in testosterone for some reason, can be enhanced by additional testosterone. Women, unlike other animals, are biologically available for sex at any time. They may be most interested in sex, however, at different times during their cycles—at ovulation, when a woman is most fertile (a kind of "pregnancy instinct"), and during menstruation ("safe pleasure instinct"), notes Wilson.

Wilson explains that the enhanced sexual activity at ovulation may be the result of a slight peak in testosterone at that time; high levels of estrogen (though falling by that stage), though, would probably offset such an effect. There is an estrogen peak in the postovulation phase, but it would not have the same effect on receptiveness because of very high levels of progesterone, the hormone that maintains pregnancy and that appears to work against sexual activity. Around menstruation, however, both estrogen and progesterone cease production, perhaps leaving testosterone free to evoke a stronger, male-type sex drive. Sexual variety does seem to enhance interest and performance in both sexes when they engage in sexual behavior outside the marriage. Researchers caution, however, that such behavior does not necessarily strengthen the marriage, acknowledges Wilson.

Relationships outside of marriage may be the only durable aphrodisiac. It is equally true that such relationships may emotionally poison the marital well. Cyril Connolly puts it more poetically: "As bees their sting, so the promiscuous leave behind them in each encounter something of themselves by which they are made to suffer."

Historically, Blum notes, some societies have sanctioned polygamy, where men (usually only the powerful ones) married (or at least had available) multiple women. This acceptance in the early societies is now replaced by "serial monogamy" (i.e., successive marriages in which the first partner is succeeded by a new, and often better, one). Some cultures allow a kind of polygamy whereby there is acceptance of a mistress as a more or less condoned arrangement. A few years back, there appeared a French cartoon depicting a charming tolerance to the adulterous affair: An attractive woman and two young children were looking down from their apartment's window. In front of the building, a man was getting out of a car driven by a young blonde. To the question "Who is that woman with Daddy?" the mother replied, "Oh, she?—she is our mistress!"

Robert Wright explains that long ago, when human society was more primitive, gaining a second wife did not necessarily mean abandoning the first one. He explains that staying near and giving protection to offspring and a mate make genetic sense. As a result, he feels that men may be less programmed for desertion and more for polygamy. In a country like the United States, where monogamy is the law, says Wright, and where mistresses are usually hidden, serial monogamy is as close as men can come to polygamy.

What Does Man Want from a Wife? Submission, Politically Correct or Not, and Tolerance.

> . . . giving men marriage tips is a little like offering Vikings
> a free booklet titled, "How Not to Pillage."
>
> —Robert Wright

Male animals have ways of demonstrating the desirability of their genes to their females. They do so by flaunting what they have. They may also display competitive qualities, such as a particular stance that is threatening and frightening to other males. This type of unprovoked or covert aggression rarely culminates in an actual fight: every animal knows innately that even victors do not emerge from the battle without some injury. And the injured male is not all that desirable. Females not only prefer victorious males, but they also would like them intact and ready to defend their territory again.

Perhaps the simplest expression of similar physical or sexual display in human males is the matter of sheer height, whereby tall men stereotypically are regarded as more attractive by women than shorter ones. Overtly or covertly, this single trait seems to be endowed with positive connotations of strength and success and is thus overly appreciated by society in general. This familiar phenomenon is attributed to the simplistic and concrete, yet enduring, equation between height and power. Observations in the business world, for example, have shown that tall men generally are more likely to be accepted for jobs, climb the corporate ladder faster, and have higher salaries. Blum explains they are both literally and figuratively "looked up to." Bruce Ellis notes a man's sexual attractiveness to women is related to traits that were important in our natural environment thousands of years ago. In other words, back in the time of the hunter-gatherer, "tall" might truly have meant stronger and more able to protect.

Another less obvious physical trait that also serves as a positive signal, especially among males, is symmetry. In fact, plastic surgeon Joseph Rabson notes that the degree of mathematical symmetry in a face is one criterion for assessing beauty.[4] Indeed, all nature, human and nonhuman, seems to share the view of symmetry as synonymous with an ideal of genetic perfection, health, and balance in development, and asymmetry as an expression of imperfection, imbalance, and genetic inferiority, notes Matt Ridley in "Swallows and Scorpionflies Find Symmetry Beautiful." At best, asymmetrical things may be more interesting, but also more flawed. Human infants seem to smile more often at symmetrical faces; in later development, females, both young and old, seem to show preference for an evenly balanced male face. Research has shown the astounding finding that boys with more symmetrical faces and other even more subtle symmetries (such as foot, wrist, ankle breadth, or ear length) start having sexual intercourse earlier and have more partners than their asymmetric counterparts, note Randy Thornhill and Steven W. Gangestad in "Human Fluctuating Asymmetry and Sexual Behavior."

How are we to comprehend these findings? Evolutionarily, beauty and sexual attractiveness in humans, which is based on symmetry, may be reflective of our hormone functioning and our overall biological, that is, hormonal, health, explain Randy Thornhill and Karl Grammer. More specifically, testosterone is responsible for the development of certain accepted characteristics of male attractiveness, such as cheekbones, chin size, and a strong lower jaw, note Thornhill and Gangestad in "Human Facial Beauty." A comparable connection occurs in the relationship between estradiol in females and the occurrence of symmetry—with women who are symmetrical found to be more desirable and fertile (i.e., developmentally and reproductively healthy) than those who are asymmetrical. The implication is that the chance for asymmetry increases when an embryo is exposed to deleterious environmental conditions, such as pollutants, parasites, or extreme temperatures or genetic anomalies.

The universal sex ratio is set equally at approximately 50 percent each for human males and females. Although males slightly outnumber females at birth, the general survival rate of females tends to be higher. This means that, in the final analysis, the overall equal sex ratio remains remarkably constant, emphasizes Blum.

What is not balanced, however, is the desirability of men and women at different phases of the life cycle. Men, irrespective of how old they are, are almost invariably interested in women of child-bearing age. Young women, in turn, are often reciprocally interested in men who can be substantial providers—the contemporary definition of tall and strong—for their offspring. As a consequence, it is the female, in her choice of mate, who frequently determines the shape and design of the desirable male. And the man complies. Yet in his zeal to be desirable to women, man may have evolved at his own expense. The male traits that men have cultivated are not necessarily useful to them, even though these same traits, such as aggressive competitiveness, drive for money and power, and accumulation of material wealth, such as cars and houses, or symbolic wealth and power, such as awards and honors, may be attractive to women. Randolph M. Nesse and George C. Williams, who report research on different species, showed that if females of a particular species start to select males with certain desirable characteristics, such as the large attractive feathers of a peacock or the great antlers of an elk, a process of "runaway selection" results. Males with these select features (what Geoffrey Miller calls "sexual selection's greatest hits") are, therefore, at an advantage simply because females choose them. In turn, these males breed sons whom the next generation of females prefers, thus compounding the particular selection of even greater numbers of the same characteristics. Yet this positive feedback loop may select a trait that ultimately could be detrimental to the everyday functioning of the males of a particular species. There has to be a delicate balance between attractiveness and function. The goal, after all, is survival of the species, not a species' extinction. For example, if a peacock's feathers were to become so large the peacock could not move, mate, or protect and feed itself, its feathers, though attractive, would be the cause of its demise.

In fact, some traits in humans may make males vulnerable to all diseases. This is because most of the male secondary characteristics are testosterone based—and testosterone is known to inhibit the immunologic system even though it is the feel-good hormone! Perhaps, paradoxically, those males who are most preferred by females may also end up being those who are relatively immunosuppressed and vulnerable to all sort of illnesses. The woman who marries such a man may have to prepare herself to be a widow at a young age.

John Gray tells a wonderful tale, "The Knight in Shining Armor," which can be briefly paraphrased as follows, of a knight in shining armor, who comes upon a princess in distress.

> Seeing that she is trapped by a dragon, the knight quickly and
> competently kills the dragon with his sword. He wins the heart of
> the princess, her family, and the town.

Some time later, he again hears the distress cries of the princess. Before he can take out his sword, however, the princess suggests that he use a noose, which will work better. He hesitates and in so doing burns himself. He feels less competent.

The next time the princess again gives a suggestion: use poison rather than the noose or sword. By this point, the knight doubts himself, and he does not know what to do.

When, however, he is out of town, he hears another woman in distress. His confidence renewed, he slays another dragon. What's more, he never returns to his princess. The knight in the story, instead, marries an adoring and submissive commoner from the village and continues to slay dragons.

Fairytale stories are more likely to end with "They lived happily ever after." Marriages, however, are more complicated. The moral of the story is: if you want your knight to stick around, don't undermine his competence with too much advice and input, especially in his own areas of expertise. Otherwise, you run the risk of psychologically castrating him. As one man put it, "I don't want to have sex with my critic and judge."

Nonsexual Intimacy: Verbalize Your Feelings; They Cannot Be Hidden. When They Appear Nonverbally, They Diminish and Irritate Your Spouse.

"What annoys me the most about you? It is that expression that you wear when I am talking with friends at a dinner table or a small party. You cringe as if you bit into a rotten lemon. I don't know what that is. Well, occasionally, I may be telling a story that you have heard, but that is not totally it. You look in pain, whenever I talk. You don't do that when we are alone. So it must be that somehow I embarrass you in front of our friends," he said.

"Are you serious? I swear I have no idea that I am doing anything except attentively focusing on you. Occasionally, you repeat the same story to the same group, and they listen as if it is the first time they are hearing it. Now that embarrasses me. The stories are also so long and elaborate that it looks like you are holding court. Dinner parties aren't a stage for a one-man show. But I had no idea that it shows on my face."

In spite of our highly developed cortical brain or new brain (i.e., our civilized mind), the subcortical brain or old brain, which also contains the emotional brain (the amygdala), still remains our innate biological motivator, notes Joseph LeDoux. Our emotions are, in effect, our energy, comprising the fuel that moves us. Moreover, our emotions amplify and intensify our lives. Insofar as emotions are experienced as subjective feeling states, they may seem to be purely psychological entities. Yet, they have essential biological and hormonal components within the body over which we exert very little control.

The biological and physical components of our emotions precede the psychological ones. By the time we have experienced an emotion, the body has already perceived its impact. Furthermore, by the time we have evaluated that impact, it is already too late, even though the entire biological/psychological/cognitive process may have lasted less than thirty seconds.

Human beings are preprogrammed at birth to react with specific emotions such as joy, pleasure, fear, anger, disgust, and affection. These innate emotions are easily observed in our facial expressions. These are programmed facial muscles, suggesting that all cultures more or less attribute similar meanings to these expressions. This is an especially salient finding, since nonverbal communications sometimes tend to create the greatest impact socially.

Our automatic emotional reactions often reign supreme in controlling our behavior and sometimes preempt our willpower and conscious efforts. In *The Expression of the Emotions in Man and Animals,* Charles Darwin relates that he once bravely tested whether willpower could overcome a strong emotional reaction. He put his face close to the thick plate glass in front of a puff adder in the zoological gardens, with the firm determination of not recoiling if this poisonous snake attempted to strike him. As soon as the snake moved forward toward him, however, his resolution disappeared, and he jumped immediately and suddenly backwards. He regarded his will and reason as powerless against the imagined menace he had never even experienced.

Cultivate emotional trust and intimacy with each other:

- Express your emotions, but don't dump them on your spouse.
- Don't have too high or too low expectations.
- Put negative feelings on hold during eating, sleeping, or love making.
- Make sure that your spouse feels safe in self-expression.
- Flirt, laugh, joke, banter, and be playful with your spouse.

Not only do our emotions preempt our cognition and behavior, they are also our most honest reactions. Attempts to disguise strong emotions in social and work situations are desirable. Not so, however, in intimate relations. Your successful disguise deprives your spouse of your feelings and thus fails in appropriate reciprocation, frustrating both of you. An unsuccessful disguise, such as your face betraying your words, will be perceived as an insult to his or her intelligence or intellect—a patronizing containment of emotion, exposing your duplicity, and undermining the ground of intimacy. Say it as it is, the first time, because sooner or later you are going to say it verbally or nonverbally. It will spare you from the impact of additional negative feelings.

Emotional Predispositions: Woman Is Predisposed to Depression, Man to Anxiety.

Ken: *"What is wrong?"*

Beth: *"Nothing."*

Ken: *"Nothing? You have been sulking the whole evening. So what is it?"*

Beth: *"What is today?"*

Ken: *"Today? Today is Tuesday."*

Beth: *"No, I mean the date?"*

Ken: *"The fifth of August. Why?"*

Beth: *"It doesn't ring any bells?"* she murmured in a pained voice.

Ken: *"The fifth of August? The fifth of August! Gee, I must be losing my mind. No, it doesn't ring any bells. So what is it?"* He was already exhausted.

Beth: *"The first time we went all the way, don't you remember?"* she scolded him.

Ken: *"That was sixteen years ago. By the way, did I remember that last August?"* He was wondering what was for dinner.

Beth: *"No. You didn't remember then either."* She began to cry.

Gender-free behavior is a myth. In addition to our genetic predispositions, we learn to behave either like a man or a woman. As with other social roles, some of these stereotypic attitudes and behaviors may have become less differentiated in recent times, such as who is the breadwinner and who remains at home to raise the children. There are, however, other discernible differences that seem to have remained intact, such as the matter of dealing with special dates (e.g., birthdays, anniversaries). In general, for women, this is a deadly serious business: they give far more importance to anniversaries than most men and are enthusiastic about their recognition and celebration. They become dismayed over missed or belated remembrances. They are also equally attentive to the significant dates of their husbands, children, relatives, and friends. Most men, on the other hand, try to underplay their own birthdays and anniversaries, and they neglect to recognize them properly or, for that matter, can never remember others.

My husband is a callous bore:

- He doesn't remember our anniversary.
- He forgets important dates like the children's birthdays.
- He resents spending money on "retailer-schemed" celebrations, like Valentine's Day.
- He, at times, pretends to be attentive, but mostly he is totally oblivious to important dates and anniversaries.

Your husband is not a callous bore. His genes carry a linear clock. For him, time means deadlines:

- Remind him matter-of-factly of pending dates for celebrations.
- Commemorate sad and unfortunate events as well. He'll understand them better and may be conditioned to the circularity of your calendar.
- Anniversaries should be fun, not an occasion for unfriendly competition. They are not about who is a better person or who is more sensitive, more loving, or buys the better gifts.

This difference appears to be not only metaphorically but literally deadly, according to Dr. David Phillips, Camilla Van Voorhees, and Todd Ruth, who reported a study of over two million people. Their research revealed the startling finding that women are more likely to die in the week following their birthdays than in any other week of the year. In contrast, deaths among men peak just before their birthdays. The author interprets these results as suggesting that one's birthday is a kind of deadline for males, whereas females are more apt to view their birthdays as joyous celebrations. Women consider their birthdays as special and significant times in which relationships with those they cherish are renewed. Men are more inclined to see a birthday as time to take stock of their accomplishments. In short, men view birthdays as "deadlines" by which they are to have achieved certain goals, while women look upon such dates as "lifelines" that connect with others. The study ventures to suggest that, in keeping with these respective gender-specific beliefs, women appear able to prolong life enough to enjoy these occasions, while men seem to succumb, perhaps out of dread of the upcoming deadline, or out of a sense of resignation at finished business. Of course, this doesn't really explain why a woman is more likely actually to die in the week following her birthday. The reason may have a more diagnostic rationale than Phillips, Van Voorhees, and Ruth suggest.

My wife's constant drumming up of romantic expectations is exhausting:

- She remembers when and where the first time we kissed and expects me to remember.
- She plans elaborate celebrations of my birthday which I hate.
- She even remembers her distant cousin's birthday.
- She is too serious and too enthusiastic about dates and anniversaries.

Men tend to be anxiety prone, though they will hide, deny, or bury it with alcohol or other substances; women are more prone to depression, which they more readily accept and for which they seek treatment. Anxiety is related to anticipation of a disaster, real or fantasized, whereas depression is a response to a disaster that has already occurred, again real or imagined. When birthdays are imminent, men may have more anxiety and agitation *before the fact* and women more depression *after the fact*. The anxiety and depression that occur through various physiological and biological pathways—excessive secretion of cortisol being the common one—cause or contribute to the fatalities, especially in individuals with compromised health conditions.

Your wife doesn't drum up romantic expectations. Her genes carry a circular clock. For her, time is a lifeline of dates:

- Put on your calendar every date that your wife considers special.
- Celebrate those days with some recognition (e.g., gifts).
- Be appreciative and grateful in receiving attention (i.e., your birth date).
- Anniversaries are serious, but they are not deadly.

Notes

1. See also John Kord Lagemann, "Why Young Mothers Are Always Tired."

2. Kalman Glantz and John Pearce, *Exiles from Eden,* 132. See also Gordon Bermant and Associates, "Sexual Behavior," 76–77.

3. Letter to the authors, July 2, 2003, Mrs. Cyndy Bittinger, executive director of the Calvin Coolidge Memorial Foundation, Plymouth, VT. The "Coolidge Effect" term became popular with animal researchers in the 1950s: see Glenn Wilson, *The Coolidge Effect,* and Gordon Bermant and Associates, "Sexual Behavior."

4. Letter to authors from Joseph Rabson, M.D. (plastic surgeon), Plymouth Meeting, PA, June 23, 2004.

CHAPTER 2

Sex in Marriage

While sex is a biological imperative, it requires certain psychological conditions for its consummation, maintenance throughout the marriage, and full enjoyment by both spouses.

For Woman, Relationship Is Foreplay; For Man, Foreplay Is "Forework."

Initiating sex ought to be called "forework," not "foreplay."

—Michael Vincent Miller

Men and women sometimes seem to exhibit vastly different sexual needs. Some authors have even suggested that for men, marriage is the price a man pays for sex, whereas for women, sex is the price a woman pays for marriage.[1] Susan Maushart has emphasized that often a woman's interest in recreational (rather than procreational) sex declines after marriage. She says, "Women who spent most of their single lives running after sex often find that they spend a good deal of their married life trying hard to avoid it."

Many men do not appreciate the importance of cuddling for a woman. They see any sign of physical contact, like kissing, cuddling, or hugging, as a prelude to sexual intercourse exclusively. Many women, therefore, feel grossly misunderstood that their husbands do not appreciate their needs. They have even repeatedly expressed the notion to friends and therapists that they might be more amenable to sexual intercourse if their men could just learn to cuddle without a sexual agenda.

29

Women:

- Cuddling and kissing are ends in themselves.
- Follow "lust-at-last sight."
- Tend to be choosy about sexual partners and want sex less.
- Complain about decrease in sexual frequency when a husband has less interest in the relationship.

What we can say is that, in comparison to men who can have sex more casually, most women need to trust the affectionate bond of the man before they can be sexually receptive, that is, a sort of "lust at last sight." This is neither a moral nor a philosophical distinction, but a physiological one. There is no specific hormone from which sexual desire in women is derived—though testosterone is strongly suspected. In fact, as we have noted, testosterone (usually in cream form) is given to women to increase their sexual pleasure and interest. Women's own sex hormones have an entirely different role.

Men:

- Cuddling and kissing are preludes to sex.
- Follow "lust-at-first sight."
- Tend to be indiscriminate about sexual partners and want sex more.
- Always complain about a wife's decrease in sexual interest.

In *Sex on the Brain*, Deborah Blum explains that while testosterone in men can spike any time they are attracted to a potential partner, in women rising estradiol (the main estrogen) does not follow what she calls the dictum of "lust-at-first sight." Instead, estradiol peaks during ovulation. Perhaps as a result, women are less likely to complain about the frequency of sex than men. This doesn't mean that females don't enjoy sex or orgasm, but it does suggest that they need a special form of foreplay, a relationship. In fact, women are more likely to complain about decreased sexual frequency when they fear the decreased frequency reflects less of an interest in the relationship itself on the part of the man. If the man, however, can also bring the woman to orgasm, and for good measure, to the high standard of multiple orgasms, another kind of bond—the pleasure bond—can develop between them, which brings a secret smile on a woman's face.

Robert Wright also explains that biologically women may be programmed to have more "reserve" sexually. More sex for women does not necessarily mean more offspring since women generally cannot have more than one pregnancy a year, no matter how many sexual partners. So women have evolved to be choosy about sexual partners and want sex less, whereas men have not. In other words, maintains Wright, for women having more sex may not be "worth the trouble." Men, on the other hand, "unless on the brink of collapse or on the verge of starvation," will continue to want sex because each new encounter "offers a real chance to get more genes into the next generation."

Enmeshed Friendship Kills Passion.

> Where they love they do not desire and where they desire
> they cannot love.
>
> —Freud

In Donald Barthelme's "Critique de la Vie Quotidienne," the male protagonist reads the "Journal of Sensory Deprivation," which, he explains, is a metaphor for his marriage to Wanda. He notes: "Our evenings lacked promise. The world in the evening seems fraught with the absence of promise." Loss of love, or the prospect of no longer being loved, is one of the most dreaded feelings every lover has. At times, the two will ask each other, "Will you always love me?" and never be totally reassured. They may have vowed to be together "till death us do part" and they meant it then, or at least they wanted to mean it. Irrespective of civil and religious marital vows, however, every couple intensely wishes to secure the permanency of their love.

Frequently, though, the couple develops a way of relating that classically destroys that love: enmeshed friendship—trying to be and to do everything together. Such pairs give up their individual friends to socialize together with other couples and sometimes even give up other couples to be only with each other. Some go even further, not only living but working together. This enmeshment gets displayed in public as couples will speak for each other and behave interchangeably, that is, finishing each other's sentences and even thoughts. While their affectionate love may seem to grow with such involvement, their passion inevitably declines. As the promotional advertisement for the last episodes of *Sex and the City* proclaimed, "Sex this good can't last forever." Such couples fail to understand why this happens. Is it the passing of time, they wonder? All passions decline, after all. Is it getting older? Is it the children or job demands? The answers are "yes," but these answers are only relatively so. Passion may decline with time, but not necessarily totally. Jobs and children-related stresses are obstacles, but only obstacles. And yes, youth is the age of passion, but older people fall in love passionately too. A couple loses passion when the two sacrifice their independence and establish an identity in merger—becoming one with the other so that they disregard their separate selves. Soulmates may like to think of themselves as "one." But passion requires an independent other. Some couples proudly display their oneness with each other. These relations are similar in familiarity to that of a brother and sister, with more powerful affection, concern, and altruism. In contrast, passionate love demands distance, unfamiliarity, and even aggression. Maintaining independence within the marriage is a solitary journey undertaken separately, and also in tandem. As Kahlil Gibran so poignantly depicts it in *The Prophet:* "Love one another, but make not a bond of love: Let it rather be a moving sea between the shores of your souls. Fill each other's cup but drink not from one cup. Give one another of your bread but eat not from the same loaf. Sing and dance together and be joyous, but let each one of you be alone."

Dependency Generates Sexual Disempowerment.

Beth: *"You hired the interior decorator? Isn't that the role of the woman of the house? What am I supposed to do now? How humiliating! She would never listen to me now. You meet with her, the two of you figure out the whole thing. I hate this house anyway."* She was hurt and angry.

Ken: *"Look, I asked you at least ten times; call this woman and get the game rolling. You even liked her and yet wouldn't just pick up the phone and meet with her. You never follow through with anything we decide to do. In the middle of everything I have to do at work, the last thing I need is to be involved with a decorator. We moved in here three months ago; I still don't have a chair to sit on, a lamp for reading. Speaking of follow-through, did you ever return the next-door neighbor's call?"* He was irritated.

Beth: *"No, you do it. They want to socialize with you, anyway."*

Independence is more commonly associated with male traits. Viewed from an evolutionary perspective, however, we know that the basic female mammal is fairly independent herself. As primary caretaker of her children, she is responsible for her own survival as well as that of her young, providing all her own food as well as theirs, until the young are weaned. Moreover, a female protects her children from others of her own and different species, often with a ferocity that is so extreme as to risk her own life for her offspring. Since humans are mammals, human females also have the physical and psychological equipment to carry out these tasks: the motivation, drive, and strength to see that their infant is fed, nurtured, and protected from threat of survival.

As the paternal role increased in importance for the survival of the family, however, the human female entered into an interdependent relationship with her male. Total independence was no longer a viable or preferred social strategy; new emotional behavioral responses were required. Many women, though, went to the other extreme and developed what Colette Dowling calls a "Cinderella Complex," that is, "the deep wish to be taken care of. . . . Like Cinderella, women today are still waiting for something external to change their lives." Other authors, such as Kalman Glantz and John Pearce, disagree. They believe this biological conduct is mediated by a woman's new emotion—anxiety about being independent. Since group hunting/gathering times, this emotion enabled her and her offspring to survive. In modern society, that fundamental effect remains. Women get a feeling of discomfort when faced with being totally on their own. The "price," as Glantz and Pearce call this, that women have to pay for this trait of dependence is a source of their mild chronic unhappiness if they submit to it, or chronic anxiety if they reject it. Either way, this state of mind may be one of the sources of conflict in a woman's marriage. If members of a couple are on different levels of a hierarchy of power or influence, that hierarchy can interfere with their sexual intimacy. A pattern of helping someone else establishes an unequal connection between the two people—no matter how willing the other person is to accept that help.

As Deborah Tannen points out, there is invariably a paradox embedded in offering or providing help. To the extent that it serves the needs of the person who is helped, it is a generous gesture that demonstrates caring and builds rapport. To the degree that it is also unequal, it puts one person in a superior position in relation to the other. Providing help to someone carries a message: "I am more competent than you." In terms of the sexes, men may perpetuate such asymmetry in their relations, by always offering help—not always useful—and women frequently request help—not necessarily needed—to perpetuate an unequal relationship. It is not always men who have the superior position in the hierarchy of the couple. Women are finding that earning more than their husbands has unexpected and unwanted consequences in their relationships. A cover story in *New York Magazine,* by Ralph Gardner Jr. in the fall of 2003, notes that as wives become more powerful, "their husbands seem to diminish in direct proportion." The couple's sexual life is often a casualty of their hierarchical relationship. Said one woman quoted in the article, "When someone seems like a child, it's not that attractive." Once the woman begins to lose respect for her husband, she may find herself emasculating him directly or indirectly. For example, she may become irritable and argumentative. Nothing about him pleases her, and she expresses a general dissatisfaction with the relationship.

Equals Are Passionate, Unequals Affectionate.

"I don't know why I don't feel sexual toward him at all. I mean I love him, but I cringe at the idea of having him lie on me, kissing me on the lips and entering me. It seems so bizarre. It isn't that he is unattractive, but I feel actually nauseated at the idea of sex with him, just the idea. I would do anything for him, including cleaning his dirty laundry. The other day he was trying to vomit but couldn't after he ate something spoiled, I guess. I put my fingers in his throat and had him vomit; meanwhile I got splattered with his vomit all over my face. Believe me, I didn't mind. But seeing that little glitter in his eyes and his saying "how about a little hanky-panky" makes me puke, unassisted. I feel guilty for not being a sexual partner to him, but I am not, I cannot be, and I don't know why. I know he wants that badly and tries all sorts of schemes—flowers a few hours before, dinners in expensive restaurants, little gifts. I feel awful, but I still cannot bring myself to lie under him. I can only pretend so much, and then I feel like jumping out of my skin."

Men and women are expected to get married and have sexual relations throughout their marriage. They are also expected, however, to establish personal intimacy and genuine friendship with each other. While a sexual relationship between men and women occurs naturally, friendship and affection require cultivation. Intimate, personal friendship develops when we resonate with another's mind. We identify with each other's values and goals, share interests, and have a common ground. The more two people are alike, the more likely they will be friends and generate warmth. Lovers are more like two opposite poles, always capable of generating lightning.

Passionate love requires equality between men and women, by which we mean an equality of desirability, and a comparable level of assertion, if not overt aggression. Affectionate love may be less equal and less sexual: interest in each other is not loaded with passion. Equality between men and women is rare; so is, therefore, the passionate love that we witness more in movies and books than in real life. The characteristic man/woman relationship has a gender-specific asymmetry.

Asymmetric relations are patterned on the parent-child relationship. In short, the way we represent our genders to the world (as we endeavor to be women or men) is by appropriating the selves of our parents as we experienced them in our childhood. Later on, these gender-specific identities are socially reinforced by various displays of other adults. Men are essentially defenders: they are the purveyors of certain responsible and caring acts on the female's behalf. As an everyday extension of this, they are the conveyors of chivalry—at least in the past, they were the ones to open doors, offer seats on subways, lift heavy objects, and save damsels in distress. Just as the protections of childhood come at a price, so, too, do the privileges of this asymmetrical relation. Male behavior fosters an erosion of women's rights and, ultimately, depreciates her status as an adult. A classic example is the oppressed and unappreciated Nora in Ibsen's play *A Doll's House*. Being deemed the dominant one endows that person with competence and respect, whereas the recipient of protection becomes subservient and, therefore, incompetent. Such asymmetry desexualizes their relationship. You'll see couples who are totally devoted to each other, without any real sexual interest. Their affectionate love comes with deep-seated personal loyalty, but not necessarily sexual loyalty. Only Nora's rebellion restores her identity as a person.

* Passionate love requires equality of desirability and comparable assertion, if not overt aggression.
* Passionate love is pitiless and ruthless; it brings desire, poetry, exaltation, as well as potential violence, obsession, paranoia, and betrayal.
* Affectionate love is less equal and less sexual.
* Whereas passionate love lifts, in contrast, affectionate love anchors its recipients.

Whereas passionate love lifts the afflicted, affectionate love, in contrast, anchors its recipients. While passionate love is an exclusionary phenomenon, affectionate love can be all-inclusive. One cannot be *in love* with more than one person but can *love* many. Occasionally, we encounter someone who is indecisive between two lovers, but on closer scrutiny, we find two different kinds of love. Most commonly, in fact, that person is caught between a passionate love, typical of an affair, and an affectionate love, typical of an emotionally dulled marriage. Someone may be ambivalent about a passionate love, but rarely, if ever, about an affectionate love. The reason for such exclusivity is in the nature of falling in love. The major ingredient of passionate love is the projection of the self onto another—that is, seeing yourself reflected in your lover's eyes. Since there is only one self to project, once projected, there is no other self. If you ever encounter a person in love with more than one individual, you will discover that person's self is fluid and unformed. Proffered love for two people is a manifestation of the confusion of sense of self. A primarily affectionate relationship leads to mutual empathy and invokes a calm and soft-edge marriage.

In Paul Theroux's *My Secret History,* a man is inwardly smiling as he observes his awakening next to his lover:

> "Good morning, darling." And she kissed me.
>
> I could not help but think that those words and that kiss were for lovers alone. Did married people say *Good morning, darling,* and kiss each other at the crack of dawn? I didn't, and when I tried to picture it the effect was absurd and precious. Most people woke up and muttered *Aw shit.*
>
> "Why are you smiling?"
>
> I could not tell you why.
>
> "I just remembered where we are," I said. "Did you sleep all right?"
>
> That was another lover's question, and so was *Can I get you anything?*"

What would happen to these two lovers, should they get married? Well, we have for example the fate of another couple—two famous lovers from literature. In Leo Tolstoy's novel *Anna Karenin,* the single officer Vronsky falls madly in love with the married Anna:

> Her look and the touch of her hand set him on fire. He kissed the palm of his hand where she had touched it and went home, happy in the knowledge that this evening had brought him nearer to the attainment of his dreams than the past two months. . . .

After their union, initially reticent:

> Anna felt unpardonably happy. The more she got to know Vronsky, the more she loved him. . . . To have him entirely to herself was a continual joy, his presence always a delight.
>
> Vronsky, meanwhile, notwithstanding the complete fulfillment of what he had so long desired, was not entirely happy. He soon began to feel that the realization of his desires brought him no more than a grain of sand out of the mountain of bliss he had expected. It showed him the eternal error men make in imagining that happiness consists in the realization of their desires.

Now Vronsky's prominent emotion was just ennui. Consummation of his passion killed it. Anna's happiness, however, different from Vronsky's, had little to do with passion before and after their union. Vronsky and Anna's outcome is typical of love affairs that deteriorate with marriage. Many couples equate their passionless marriage with dying.

Says Lynn Darling, "Marriage, when it works, is a mystery made up of such a complicated ebb and flow of affection, admiration, fury, ritual, and gradually unfolding understanding that with the right person it's not a bad way to live a life. But if it means giving up fire and first kisses, then it seems like more than a little death." But even if passion dies it need not be the death of the marriage. These other emotions growing between partners are powerful enough to sustain a satisfactory marital relationship: mutual affection and empathy, which are the source of dissatisfaction as well as the satisfaction in marriage. The dulling of passionate emotions may generate boredom but also lowers the level of anxiety. We are equally addicted to both passion and comfort. Frequently, lovers run back to their spouses after a passionate encounter and, after a peaceful interval, venture out again seeking excitement.

The excitement need not be a love affair; a brief flirtation with a stranger generates liveliness. Even at an ordinary party when they are with other people, both spouses tend to feel sexier, wittier, and even more knowledgeable, though temporarily. One of the characters in Peter De Vries's *Reuben, Reuben* speaks of the "matrimonial yoke" that couples slip off when they go out to parties. They can separate for the evening and enjoy themselves individually before they go "back into the cage again."

Romantic love and marriage are not simply difficult to sustain, but virtually impossible. Why? Writes Susan Maushart, "Because, to put it bluntly, the role structures within marriage could not be more inimical to erotic love. Wives are not sexy. Wives are safe, and safe is the opposite of sexy." The same is equally true for husbands. Once a couple begins to get to know each other as people and not just objects, once the two establish empathy for each other, passion typically declines. A character in Edith Wharton's "Souls Belated" explains the source of their decline in passion: "We've been too close together—that has been our sin. We've seen the nakedness of each other's souls."

- Sharing a bathroom or walking around naked desensitizes couples to sexual stimuli and makes them more like roommates than passionate lovers.
- Sharing a double bed or even the same bedroom may be detrimental to maintaining passion in a marriage.
- Don't get too involved with your spouse's grooming and personal hygiene regimens.
- Don't infantilize your spouse with baby talk and pet names.

There was a wonderful episode of *Sex and the City* in which the newly married Charlotte who had had an extraordinarily passionate relationship with her husband-to-be, Harry, finds herself somewhat disgusted by his walking completely naked around their apartment once they are married. Embarrassingly, she was more preoccupied with her husband's naked rear on her white sofa than any possible interest in sex: she enjoyed seeing him—"just not so much of him!"

Emotional intimacy and sexual passion hang in delicate balance. An excess of one interferes with the development of the other. In-depth emotional familiarity, which is crucial in preventing incest, is also the cause of a lack of sexual interest in married couples. Husbands and wives become more like roommates. We thought we were the first to suggest that sharing a bedroom and a double bed may be detrimental to maintaining passion within marriage. Then we found the following statement from Mae West, the worldly-wise actress and self-styled expert on matters of love and marriage, in *Mae West on Sex, Health and ESP*: "I've always believed that separate beds, and even separate bedrooms, can be the secret of a happy marriage." Nor should a bed be a depositing ground for unsorted mail or a library for piles of books. One spouse, who did not feel particularly sexually attracted to her husband, admitted that the bed they shared often had "mountains" of papers and mail on it that actually became a physical barrier between her and her husband.

A couple's affection for each other generated in the marriage is highly desirable. It may have a contaminant feeling, however—a sense of feeling sorry for the other—that shadows all affectionate adult attachments. The affection grows with familiarity. And although familiarity may not necessarily breed contempt, it can invoke pity. A person when seen too closely is pitiable. Thus, when one member of the pair assumes the role of being lovingly caring, pity or self-pity also enters the picture and undoes the desire. So it was in the story of King David, 1 Kings 1: 1–4:

> King David had grown old, and although he was covered in blankets, he couldn't get warm. His officials told him, "Your Majesty, let us search for a young woman who has never been married. She can stay with you and be your servant. She can be in your arms and keep you warm." So they searched throughout Israel for a beautiful young woman. They found Abishag from Shunem and brought her to the King. The woman was very beautiful and she became the King's servant and took care of him, but the King did not make love to her.

Abishag's love for the king was laced with maternal care and pity; the king was full of self-pity. Passionate love, on the other hand, is pitiless and ruthless. It brings desire, poetry, exaltation, as well as violence, obsession, jealousy, paranoia, and betrayal. One of the secrets of maintaining passion for a partner is each individual selfishly attempting to generate excitement for him or herself. The partner will spontaneously respond. Nothing is more erotic than a partner's orgasmic excitement. One can have sexual relations within a marriage or monogamous commitment with the same reverence and intimacy without boredom, guilt, or obsession. Sexual relations can be regular without being routinized; or they can be satisfying to a greater or lesser degree, with successes and failures, without being either exalting or dysfunctional. The key in this is to preserve the equal relationship. This simply requires that neither partner assumes a sibling or parental role.

Resistance to appropriating the role of either a parent, older sibling, or a child requires vigilance by both parties. Simple behavior such as sharing a bathroom or walking around naked (which results in desensitization to sexual stimuli), or innocent behavior such as giving each other pet names, using baby talk, or desexualizing intercourse by making jokes, all work against sustaining passion. Always making decisions (because the other is indecisive), performing the other's work (because it is easier), or behaving with an excessively tolerant or patronizing manner, all generate asymmetric relationships and undo sexual peer relations. Insisting on doing everything together as a couple can be a sexual turnoff to one spouse, except early on in the courting relationship when being together is still a novelty.

For example, a man should not offer to accompany his wife while she gets a manicure or her hair cut, nor should he stand over her while she is getting dressed. Noticing how she looks afterward is all the attention most women want. Anything more can feel oppressive and intrusive. Nor should a man pay too much attention to a woman's period unless she is specifically asking for his attention to her menstrual cycles, because of fertility issues, for example.

In "About His Retirement," from *Suddenly Sixty and Other Shocks of Later Life*, Judith Viorst puts it so well when she writes:

> . . . He's sitting beside me while I'm tweezing my eyebrows.
> He's standing beside me while I'm blow-drying my hair.
> He's sharing those moments when I am clipping my toenails.
> You want my opinion? He's overdoing share. . . .

Peers do not tolerate such treatment; only children do (albeit resentfully), and as we all know too well, they always escape to seek the company of their peers. If the spouse is a stand-in for a parent, or a sibling, she or he will search for a sexual partner outside. More commonly, both will ensconce themselves into a sexless life, occasionally complaining, but not doing anything about it. Leaving the marriage is out of the question, because one doesn't divorce one's sibling or parent. Eventually, hormones will collaborate, by themselves declining, and an asexual marriage ensues.

A Primarily Sexual Marriage Leads to Mutual Objectification and Invokes a Stormy and Hard-Edged Relationship.

Man: *"I called this afternoon; you weren't home; where the fuck were you? This has happened many times before. Is this the female equivalent of 'Chloe in the afternoon?'"* He was serious.

Woman: *"Are you out of your mind? I don't sit around waiting for your calls. I have chores to do. How do you think your favorite dish, grilled tuna over linguine, came about? And why would you think that I am having sex with someone else? I can hardly keep up with you, you Don Juan! It is your own fantasy to have sex with someone else in the afternoon,"* she said.

Man: *"Yeah! Did you not sleep with whatever his name was when you were fourteen, and I am the Don Juan? Did you not sleep with half the football team in high school? Is it really that far out to think that you may still be seeing some of those guys, whenever they are in town?"* He stopped eating.

Woman: *"Sweetheart, why do you do that each time we have a lovely evening planned?"*

Man: *"How could you, I mean, where is your morality, to give me a blow job on our first date? How could I trust you? You could easily do that with anyone else."* He got up, ready to leave.

Woman: *"Do you want to make love?"* she asked.

Man: *"You see what I mean?"* He quickly got undressed.

Relations built on a sensual-sexual foundation tend to be highly charged, without the buffer of accompanying affection. Sensuality, says Nietzsche, often hastens the growth of love, but at a price: the roots remain weak and are easily torn up. Passion usually declines within the first few years of marriage, probably as a result of our brain's chemistry, as Helen Fisher explains in *Why We Love*. Perhaps, as she claims, it is even adaptive. This is actually a relatively benign version of the outcome of sensual love. A more malignant form can generate what Charles Odier refers to as the "neurosis of abandonment" with its corresponding early primitive feelings: panic, dread, and a sense of becoming unglued. A deadly battle will ensue, a battle of mutual "objectification," a fight to make the other an object of desire, to possess totally not only the present and future but also the past of the object of sensual love. The ultimate striving here is for the annihilation of the other person as an independent being. In Noël Coward's play *Private*

Lives, Amanda explains to her lover the source of their ugly battles with each other:

> Amanda: *"Selfishness, cruelty, hatred, possessiveness, petty jealousy. All those qualities came out in us just because we loved each other."*

Later on, as she is becoming a little battle fatigued herself, she raises the same issue in question form and gets rather an undesirable but a time-tested response from her lover, Elyot.

> Amanda: *"Shall we always want to bicker and fight?"*

> Elyot: *"No, that desire will fade, along with our passion."*

Nonetheless, even at its priapic worst, love's pain—a product or by-product of being truly alive—is truly exhilarating.

Ownership of Spouse Is Neither Sexual Nor Affectionate, and It Invokes Rebellion or, Worse, Submission.

> Wife: *"You are stultifying me; you are always in my face; I cannot even go to the bathroom without your shadowing me. If I am on the phone with a girlfriend, you eavesdrop and then quiz me about what I said— what she said. It is woman talk, for God's sake. Do I ask you who you had lunch with today, who called you, and what you talked about? You are so intrusive, worse than my mother was. How do you know the dates of my period, when even I don't? What do you care which books I read? And what is the idea of going over the sentences that I underlined? You don't want a wife with a mind of her own, you just want a concubine. You want me at your beck and call. What happened to your first wife? She ran away, right? Because you oppressed her the same way you oppress me. Yours isn't love, believe me. It's more like possession. I don't know what it is, but it doesn't feel like love."*

There are many people who are incapable of genuinely loving other human beings and, at best, can love only pets or other "things." M. Scott Peck even suggests that this may explain the large numbers of American soldiers who initially had idyllic marriages to foreign war brides with whom they could not verbally communicate, and when their brides learned English, their marriages began to fall apart. Such love, whether of animals or war brides (who are not deemed equals), is the love of "objects"; it is possessive and demands no assertion on the part of the spouse.

Every love is, to some degree, possessive, if not transgressive. The need to merge is innate in us. It is predetermined. This primordial need, from adolescence on, utilizes erotic love as the means of entry to another. The desire to merge, though, is not without ambivalence, even under the most advantageous of circumstances. It becomes emotionally loaded when one member of the merger begins to treat the other as an object and demands complete dissolution of the other person. What seems to be desirable and inevitable, such as the complete merging of an infant with its mother, is no longer acceptable even with a two-year-old. Any determined attempts at possession generate either rebellion or, worse, total submission, often with ever brewing resentment.

The ambivalent feelings between offspring and parents become more explicit as the dependency of the child declines with time. In adolescence, this ambivalent love/hate relation reaches a crescendo. The same process transpires between a young wife and her older husband when the maturing woman begins to assert herself. Attachment and separation themes commonly occur in other situations as, for example, in the teacher-student relationship, mentor-mentee relations, or a father/son business partnership.

The only solution for preventing negative feelings from overtaking the positive ones is enabling the other person to let go, to allow a kind of "separate togetherness" to develop. The individuation phase, which begins in early childhood and continues throughout life, is fraught with powerful emotions and misjudgments. Trying to maintain full control of a relationship, however, is exhausting and counterproductive. Such possession and clinging generate opposition and resentment, if not rebellion. If you let go, the other may not even leave. In this regard, Sogyal Rinpoche tells a wonderful paradoxical story:

> Pick up a coin. Hold it tightly clutched in your fist and extend your arm, with the palm of your hand facing the ground. Now if you let go or relax your grip, you will lose what you are clinging onto. But there is another possibility: With your arm still outstretched, turn your hand over so that it faces the sky. Release your hand and the coin still rests on your open palm. You let go. And the coin is still yours, even with all this space around it.

Just How Important Is Sex in Marriage?

> There is no doubt that the average marriage bed is a highly unerotic space for women and a somewhat less unerotic space for men.
>
> —Susan Maushart

In a study of 102 happily married couples from youth to old age, researchers Margaret Neiswender Reedy, James E. Birren, and K. Warner Schai evaluated six components of love: emotional security, which ranked first for all age groups; respect, which ranked second; communication; help and play behaviors; sexual intimacy; and loyalty. They found that the nature of love in satisfying relationships is different at different ages. Not surprising, passion and sexual intimacy are relatively more important in early adulthood, whereas tender feelings of affection and loyalty are relatively more important in later-life love relationships. The study found that over time satisfying love relationships are less likely to be based on intense companionship and communication and more likely to be based on the history of the relationship, traditions, commitment, and loyalty. From their study, the researchers concluded that there is considerably more to love than sex and that at any age emotional security—the feeling of concern, caring, trust, comfort, and being able to depend on one another—is the most important bond of love. What may be essential, though, for a satisfying sexual relationship is that both spouses have an equal interest in sexual intimacy, whatever their ages or type of marriage. Problems emerge in a relationship when one spouse feels deprived sexually by the other; often, this spouse looks outside of marriage.

- Couples should expect that sexual needs of each or both may change over the course of their marriage.
- There is considerably more to love than sex, and at any age emotional security is the most important bond of love.
- What may be essential for a satisfying sexual relationship is that both spouses have equal interest in sexual intimacy.
- Problems more likely emerge when one spouse feels deprived sexually; that spouse usually then begins to look elsewhere.

Swimming Upstream: Reproduction Is the Ultimate Goal of the Body.

"During her periods she doesn't want to have sex. I cannot do it anyway. The moment I see a little blood oozing out of her vagina, I lose my erection. I don't know how other men do it. A single friend of mine actually likes to go down on women during their periods. I think he is a little perverted. Anyhow, the week around her periods my wife always

*gets depressed. Never mind having sex, she hardly talks to me. She is ac-
tually furious at me. I do nothing, and she is so angry toward me. When
I confront her, she apologizes and says she has no control over it and
that in fact she looks for reasons to attack me. If she can't find any, she
confesses, she gets even angrier.*

*The whole week prior to her periods she is not approachable. This time
she is premenstrual: she is irritable, anxious; she cannot sleep; she gorges
herself with food and cries for hours if you look at her cross-eyed. So I
have a narrow window of opportunity to make love to her. During that
five to seven days, though, we have another kind of problem: she is just
too much. She wants to have sex all the time. You would think that you
are dealing with two different women. She behaves like a hypochondriac,
no, that is not the word, hypomaniac? Not that either. You know, sex
crazy person, someone who's lost her head, composure. Ah . . . nympho-
maniac! I am not eighteen years old.*

*I tried to fake orgasms a few times; she went berserk. I don't know how
she knew because I made the same noises and the same body contractions
like minifits. But she knew. Strangely enough, though, she wouldn't just
turn around and go to sleep or get up and leave the room as she does cus-
tomarily at other times. She stays put; if I lose my erection, she even sucks
me, which is totally out of character for her. She doesn't give up until I
do come inside her. Go figure!"*

Our minds design various goals in life—to be successful, or rich, to get a good
education, to attain a certain profession, to be a good human being, to love
and be loved, to serve God, and so forth. But our sexuality dictates only a single goal—to reproduce. The suggestive term "the whispering within" which
David Barash uses for the title of his book, has usually been used in reference
to women. It is applicable, though, to both sexes with regard to reproductive
urges and has universal priority for both genders. The other biological survival activities, such as eating and sleeping, are subordinate to reproduction.
In terms of species preservation, the only activity that supersedes reproductive
behavior, albeit temporarily, is nursing an infant. Even the natural interval between births is critical with respect to maximizing reproduction. More specifically, if that interval is too brief, the initial baby preempts its successor by still
requiring milk, attention, and care. The succeeding infant will fail to survive.
Alternatively, if the birth interval is too prolonged, a mother wastes her reproductive years. We also know that developmentally, when the young child
is about two years old, there is generally a conflict between the mother's genetic interests to conceive again and the first infant's interests to continue
nursing.

Sex was genetically designed for reproduction:

- A woman is biologically available for sex at any time but sexually most receptive around the time of ovulation and during her menstruation.
- The natural interval between births is designed to maximize reproduction and survival of our species.
- Men are biologically wired to impregnate as many women as possible.
- Since women can reproduce only once a year, from a biological perspective, their having more sex is "not worth the trouble."

Cindy Hazan and Phillip Shaver have studied romantic love as an attachment process, analogous to the stages infants experience when they are separated from their primary caretaker. According to the model, there are three types of attachment: secure, avoidant, and anxious/avoidant. Those with a secure sense of attachment believe in enduring love and find others trustworthy. Avoidant types fall in love frequently but have difficulty finding true love. Significantly, the researchers believe that romantic love is a biological process designed by evolution to facilitate attachment between adult sexual partners; they can then be motivated to remain together to conceive and nurture offspring. This evolutionary process occurred, of course, before the introduction of birth control.

In another study, Hazan and Debra Zeifman show how reciprocal attachment between two people takes approximately two years to develop. Reciprocal attachment, typical of adults, is symmetric—each partner is a provider and recipient of care and a seeker of security, as well as a target of security seeking.

Attachments at any age develop in the context of close physical proximity and intimate contact. In order for an attachment to form, therefore, there must be a strong force promoting closeness. For adults, that is sexual attraction. According to Hazan and Zeifman, sex is what holds adults together long enough for an emotional bond—what they call a "psychological tether"—to form. In the environment in which humans evolved, caring for the young was particularly costly for the female and increased the need for male caregiving. The natural cycle of conception, pregnancy, and weaning in non-Western societies is about four years. Ironically, worldwide census data indicate, as reported in Fisher's *Anatomy of Love*, that more relationships end at the four-year mark than at any other time. Hazan and Zeifman conclude that it is highly adaptive for parents to be psychologically and emotionally bonded to each other because it ensures the survival of their vulnerable young. Sex provides the motivation for the kind of physical contact that fosters the formation and maintenance of affectional bonds between adult lovers.

A woman's body is exquisitely conditioned to facilitate reproduction, even against all odds. For example, because of a separate aperture, that is, the vagina, the female is vulnerable to infection, endangering reproduction. Her organs, however, also have considerable built-in protections, including the normal outward movement of secretions and the antibacterial properties of cervical mucus that make it difficult for viruses or bacteria to enter the woman's body. One means of protection, note David P. Barash and Judith Eve Lipton, is the acidification of the vagina, which reduces the danger of infection. The authors also describe how women can end up using their low vaginal pH as a "sperm-screening device" so that sperm become "acid-resistant, armored, gladiatorial sperm whose voyaging capacity might rival that of Marco Polo." Yet there is a single significant exception to this constant downstream direction—the indisputable fact that sperm cells swim *upstream* (i.e., from the vagina through the uterus to the fallopian tubes). This unusually selective receptivity of the female reproductive system, in conjunction with the sperm's agility and motility, highlights the miraculous process that may culminate in pregnancy.

For both sexes equally, reproduction is a high priority from an evolutionary perspective. Sex now, however, with modern birth control, is often independent of its reproductive purpose and function. Besides the hormonal differences (testosterone, the hormone of sexual desire, being high in men), the accumulation of sperm and prostatic fluids naturally force males into seeking discharge. There are no equivalent physiological needs in women. Here is advice to men: if you want your spouse to be easily accessible, hang around her during her ovulation or around her period. As we have noted, often these are times she is more sexually interested and available. She'll be naturally receptive. If you want sex at other times, you need to work a little—patiently flirting, especially after that initial passion fades.

In their discussion on the reproductive strategy of the male, Glantz and Pearce define the "iron law of maleness"; males must impregnate at least one female or they will not transmit any of their genes to the next generation. This obvious principle occurs across species, including fish and even insects. Some insects plug a female's genital tract by a coagulation of secretions after they deposit their sperm. This mechanism has two functions: it prevents the sperm from leaking out afterward and prevents other males from depositing their own sperm. Other insects use themselves as a genital plug, after depositing their sperm, and thus prevent any other males from entering. Barash and Lipton call this the equivalent of a "chastity belt."

Stephen Jay Gould discusses the male anglerfish, *Ceratias holbolli,* for example, which is at most merely two inches long. Its female counterpart, by contrast, can mature to twenty-six inches long, a discrepancy so striking that when originally observed the males were thought to be babies of the much larger females. Eventually, researchers realized that the male actually had its mouth embedded in the flank of the female, so that it was not possible to tell where one fish began and the other ended. Says Gould, "The male had become a sexual appendage of the female, a kind of incorporated penis."

Even more extreme are the males of certain mantis species that virtually sacrifice their own lives for the transmission of their genes. Female mantises engage in "macabre cannibalism," says Richard Dawkins. They are large carnivorous insects which will attack anything that moves. When the male and female mate, the male cautiously creeps up on the female, mounts her, and copulates. If the female gets the chance, she will eat the male, beginning by biting his head off; amazingly, copulation continues! Dawkins even goes as far as to speculate that since the head is the seat of some inhibiting nerve centers, the female may improve the male's sexual performance by eating its head!

Romanticization of the Don Juan character in various art forms notwithstanding, promiscuity of men is still regarded as psychopathology in civilized societies. For some psychoanalysts, it reflects an avoidance of emotional intimacy; for others, it is a manifestation of latent homosexuality. A man's wish to sleep with as many women as he can may also be a remnant of primitive genetic urges to impregnate (not just have sex with) as many females as possible. If you consider the potential dangers that the promiscuous man is risking—being beaten or even killed by husbands, facing legal and other social complications, catching sexually transmitted diseases—you might agree that such a man's behavior is no less determined than that of male mantises. A man won't listen to advice when he has that inclination. We could say, "Look fellow, don't lose your head; no genes are so fabulous to transmit to the next and many generations." Our advice for women is: carefully check and verify the sexual history of a man before you let him in.

Natural Drive: Don't Let Your Mind Intrude into Your Sex Life.

Husband: *"The doctor said my testosterone level is normal and all other physical parts are okay. He thinks that it is all psychological. He gave me some samples of Viagra to try. If you want, we could try tonight. He said that it works better if I don't eat much food prior to taking the pill and avoid alcohol as well. But apparently I would still need your help. The pill doesn't automatically give an erection. You still need to stimulate— your favorite activity! I told him that if you would suck me, I mean really enthusiastically suck me and have pleasure with that yourself, I wouldn't need Viagra at all."*

Wife: *"You told the doctor that?"*

Husband: *"Yeah, why not? Why go to the doctor and not tell him the whole thing? You sent me to him, may I remind you."*

Wife: *"Yes, but not to be so graphic. How embarrassing! We see him occasionally at some parties; how will I face him now? I mean he is always going to associate me with an image of a reluctant oral sex partner. Oh gee!"*

Husband: *"Ah, don't worry about it. I am sure he isn't getting that much either. Actually, he knows quite a bit about it. He suggested that I should wash my genital and anal area thoroughly and maybe put on some of your favorite perfume. He thinks that most women don't like giving a blow job because of the smell of the crotch."*

Wife: *"What a disgusting conversation! So are you indirectly asking me why I don't do it or the name of my favorite perfume? Here are my answers to both anyway. The mouth is not vagina. The perfume that I like to smell on others is soap."*

Husband: *"So shall I take the Viagra or not?"*

Wife: *"Look, if I wanted an artificial penis, I would use my vibrator. It not only is permanently erect, it moves better and is quite a hunk!"*

Husband: *"Well, bring it along; we'll have a ménage à trois."*

In primitive creatures, the visceral brain, as the highest center for coordinating behavior, takes care of all the instinctual behaviors and basic drives involved in its survival, says Joseph LeDoux, who studies aspects of the emotional brain. Even in man, this visceral brain still controls functions like thirst, hunger, breathing, and procreation. Higher level animals also have ways of processing the emotional meaning of a stimulus even before their perceptual systems have completely processed it. In other words, explains LeDoux, our brain can know "something is good or bad before it knows exactly what it is." One of the coordinators of this system is the amygdala, a tiny almond-shaped part of the brain in the temporal lobe that is involved in "appraisal of emotional meaning." The amygdala is often particularly involved in assessments of danger, and its connections have become far more complex as our brains have grown. LeDoux explains that our "prepackaged responses" occur automatically. What makes humans different from many other animals is that we can go from "emotional autopilot" to a more controlled response. In other words, we can "shift from reaction to action" so that our brains can "buy time."

Humans possess the same repertoire of emotions as other animals but also very complex, sophisticated, and subtle states: exaltation, existential despair, altruism, and the like. In the next step of man's evolution came the cortex and neocortex. With that, the brain had the ability to abstract, create symbols, form language, think, evolve complicated plans, as well as to anticipate, formulate, and execute plans. The brain not only could attribute meaning to something but could now search for meaning and purpose.

The connections between this newest region of the brain and one of its oldest parts generate an entirely unprecedented class of emotional experiences and psychological conditions for humans: guilt, shame, embarrassment, psychological impotence, psychosomatic disorders, hypochondria, eating disorders, and loss of self-esteem. Some animals, such as house pets, in close contacts with humans, are even beginning to demonstrate the rudimentary effects of such connections.

Meanwhile, if you want to have good sex— hormonal and neurological pathways being intact—you need to be more animalistic: that is, not to think and not to talk about sex, but simply do it. And do it when you really want to do it; do it for pleasure, not as a performance; do it spontaneously, without elaborate planning; do it simply, without some technical wizardry. That is, take your cortical brain out of sex and let your visceral—primitive—brain do what comes naturally. The more novelty and excitement you can bring to your sexual life, the more you stimulate the brain and the more chance you have of maintaining passion.

Note

1. See Sally Dallos and Rudi Dallos, *Couples, Sex, and Power: The Politics of Desire* (Buckingham, UK: Open University Press, 1997), 139.

CHAPTER 3

The Power Play in Marriage

Patterns of dominance and submission play out in all relations. In marriage they may either set off a vicious circle of aggression and abuse or help both partners grow together and separately.

Men Claim Power from History.

> Beth chuckled: *"The woman made of man's rib? What a laugh! If you said man's sperm, you may at least have a half-shot at it. Furthermore, you cannot say that for every man's sperm, either."*

In the mythical and biblical past, we were both male and female. In Chinese myth, a person has qualities of both the masculine Yang and the feminine Yin. In ancient Greece, we all began as hermaphrodites, both female and male, according to Plato in "The Symposium."

In the nonmythical and scientific world, we all begin as female; about half of us, then, differentiate into males. That differentiation encompasses a wide spectrum. Not every man is a "man," however, and not every woman is a "woman." In other words, some men are more male than others, and some women are more female than others. Marrying the other sex, therefore, has limited generalizability. A man who married a beautiful woman was disappointed a few years later to discover that she didn't want to have children. His therapist asked him why he had not discussed the issue of having children with her before the marriage. He replied, "Well, it never occurred to me. Don't all women want to have children?"

We are not made out of each other's ribs or any other parts. There is no biological reason for sexual second-classness. The relative dominance-submission pattern is established on a hormonal and psychological path and is highly relative. A dominant member of a couple can become a submissive one in relation to another person and, of course, vice versa. The assumption of a man's superiority over a woman, even without its assertion, pervades every argument, including inconsequential ones. Should a man explicitly exercise his superordinate rights, he may either have chronic fights with an angry wife or a totally repressed and unhappy one.

Women Claim Power from the Family.

> Ken: *"My wife talks with her mother almost everyday. I mean she is a fifty-year-old woman; enough already! And our two daughters, both already with their own families, are constantly calling her or she, them. And what do they talk about? Regular stuff, as if they are all living together: whom they visited; what they had for lunch; what they bought; their new hairdressers; who is constipated. Calls start with "just checking in" and end with "give my love to Dad" or "your husband" and "how is he, by the way?"*
>
> *I am sort of incidental to their lives. I play some role, but it is a role. I know they love me, in a little different way from how they do each other. But none of them ever calls me "to check in." Ha! They may call to ask for a check though. Sex? Forget it. My wife accommodates me when she notices that I am getting angry. She isn't really interested. How do I know? She does things that she never liked to do, like just have me come and get it over with, so that she can go back to her calls or whatever."*

The family is essentially configured among the female relatives of the wife and children; the man is tolerated. In most species of fish, males deposit their sperm on the top of eggs, left earlier by females on the floor of some quiet body of water. This is the extent of their parental investment. Both fish will swim away immediately after completing their respective tasks, and there is no further connection between the two. This reproductive strategy of male and female fish has one bright side to it—both sexes are equally uninvolved and both are equally unfaithful. In their witty book *The Myth of Monogamy*, David P. Barash and Judith Eve Lipton emphasize how it is only in the case of monogamy that male mammals provide *any* paternal care. A monogamous male mammal has more confidence of his paternity than one whose sexual partner is likely to have been inseminated by one or more males. The authors also note that the more paternity is in doubt, the less likely there will be paternal behavior toward the young.

In mammals, females invest more than males in their offspring. Not only do they carry the fetus to maturity and give birth, but they also feed (especially since milk is the only food an infant mammal can eat) and protect the offspring for extensive periods of time. This difference in their reproductive roles generates different capacities in males and females with respect to their relationship with each other as well as their offspring. In fact, in most mammals, the sensitive and intimate connection is primarily between mother and her female relatives and their offspring. Only when the female is sexually receptive is a selected male allowed entry. In fact, he is seductively recruited into this tightly affiliative unit around the time of the female's ovulation. In humans, unlike some primates, ovulation is relatively concealed, with no external marker, so the situation is more complicated. Most women do not even know when they ovulate. Unlike other female mammals, however, they are sexually receptive at any time in their cycle. Barash and Lipton have speculated that concealed ovulation may have contributed to monogamy in that males may have been more likely to affiliate with a specific female if her time of particular fertility is not identified, ensuring at least some chance of inseminating her.

At other times, when the female is not sexually receptive, the male/female relationship has a quality of aggression/compliance rather than that of mutuality. The female monkey presents her rear in a copulation readiness position to placate the powerful male monkey's aggression, note Kalman Glantz and John Pearce. The fact that the same behavior occurs when a strong male attacks a weaker male validates the survival instinct of such compliance in the form of sexuality. However, if the female is not threatened, she is not available for copulation with any male during the off-season. During ovulation she is selectively receptive to the dominant male; she responds to biological cues of choosing the male with the best genes, the one that can promote survival of the species. One interesting outcome of this female selecting the male process is that the female's genes dominate every generation, emphasize Glantz and Pearce.

Men Are Genetically Weaker than Women.

Beth: *"I just came back from visiting my friend Julie. Her husband is in Sloan Kettering again. I think this time he is dying. Poor Julie doesn't know what to do. She is so confused and frightened. The children are still young. They have some money, but she has to go back to work. At the age of fifty she isn't going to be so easily employed. She hasn't worked since she had her first child. Why do you guys marry someone fifteen or more years younger than yourselves, burden the poor innocent woman with children, and then kick the dust and leave them to their own devices?"*

Ken: *"Poor, innocent woman? You pursued me to get married."*

Beth: *"Yeah, but when I met you, you were seventeen years older than I was. I was this bright eyed, idealistic, idealizing girl who was dazzled with your wisdom, maturity, steadiness, patience, and kindness. I didn't know that those traits in men were paternal traits. You were the kind of father I wish I had. And, you bastard, you exploited it. Now you are going to die, of course, after I provide lengthy home care, and I'll be stuck with two children and all the responsibility associated with them. Most likely, we'll be spending every penny that we saved on your around-the-clock nursing. I'll be too old to remarry, too young to die soon after you. It just isn't fair."*

Genetically, human beings possess a total of forty-six chromosomes, or twenty-three matched pairs based on each parent's equal contribution of half. The final pair is of primary importance since it carries the infamously influential X and Y chromosomes. These are the ones that genetically determine the distinction between male and female.

The genetic plot thickens, however, when we attempt to predict the statistical odds of the human male-female ratio. Since mammalian females have two X chromosomes, in contrast to males with one X and one Y, the male determines the biological sex of the child. Beyond this, we still know precious little regarding sex prediction. For all intents and purposes, we see the odds are generally equal, a 50-50 probability of receiving either two Xs, which produce a female, or an X and a Y, which produces a male, explains Deborah Blum in *Sex on the Brain*.

Blum further notes that the genes in the Y chromosome are solely responsible for the initial "male" signal that causes the maturing human embryo to form the testes; the resultant testosterone then serves as a messenger to establish a male body. If testosterone is not introduced into the human embryo, the fetus will evolve into a female. Moreover, if testosterone is blocked, we can even retain the classic male XY chromosome pair and still produce a body that looks female. It is for this very reason that biologists (as well as others) refer to the mammalian structure as fundamentally female, or what Natalie Angier has called the "female-as-default model."

Don't blame your wife for not bearing you a son: it is the absence of your own Y chromosome that is responsible for the outcome. Don't blame your wife for the effeminate body of your son: if anything, your Y chromosome's incapacity to signal testosterone at the appropriate time in fetal development is responsible for it. Furthermore, don't blame yourself either. You are both at the mercy of your genetic makeups. Neither of you has much control over or influence on it. Sex is biologically determined. It cannot be psychologically or socially constructed, though we can, at birth, make sex assignments in the case of those infants with ambiguous external genitalia. Blame, guilt, control, and so forth are psychological concepts and have no relevance over the heterosexuality or homosexuality of your children or their body shapes associated with male or female. On the other hand, you can take some credit or accept blame for your children's masculine and effeminate manners, interests, and behavior because gender, that sense of maleness or femaleness, is influenced by exposure, training, and identification (i.e., culture), as well as genes.

As Blum points out, the *Y* chromosome has males at a disadvantage. She suggests that, like the safeguard of a computer, we need to have a backup. So if we inherit an *X* chromosome with a defective gene, along with another *X* chromosome with a nondefective version of the same gene, the good copy falls into place. If one is *XY,* however, no alternate version is available. The male, who has only one *X,* has no other choice, which is precisely why men are more likely to suffer *X*-linked disorders, such as hemophilia, muscular dystrophy, or color blindness. Indeed, there are over two hundred such disorders that appear more often in males than females. If a female happens to develop one of these disorders, she has had the particular misfortune of inheriting the identical malfunctioning gene on both *X* chromosomes.[1] Furthermore, the *Y* chromosome, notes John Travis in an article by Virginia Morrell, is a "shrunken shadow" of the *X* chromosome, "carrying a paltry complement of active genes." Questions Maureen Dowd, columnist of the *New York Times,* "Why oh *Y* are men so insecure . . . perhaps that's why men are adapting, becoming more passive and turning into 'metrosexuals,' the new term for straight men who are feminized with a taste for facials, grooming products, and home design."

If you marry an older man, prepare for a shorter marriage:

- Man is a relative outsider within his own family. This lack of tight intimacy lowers his immunological system, making him vulnerable to acquired diseases.
- A man doesn't benefit from generational affiliation, that is, father-son intimacy. Thus he is emotionally vulnerable.
- A man suffers from about two hundred genetic diseases—because he is XY, he has no genetic backup copies.
- Even under the best circumstances, a man naturally lives many fewer years than a woman.

A woman who marries an older man may have a quieter, safer, and calmer marriage, but she may also tend either to repress her sexuality or have affairs, interestingly enough frequently with other older men, though slightly younger than her husband. One might think that this woman would at least be yearning to have a romantic relation with someone of her own age. The husband, the older man, tends to be more understanding and forgiving of his wife's extramarital activities and rarely initiates an end to the marriage.

Anyhow, women should think of marrying younger men or at least try to marry men close to their age; women who marry older men better have a backup plan.

Aggression and Passivity in Marriage

> *"Ken, you don't talk to me, you growl at me. Your eyes never smile, even when you are laughing. They are cold and threatening. When you need to pass by me or get me out of your way, you don't gently touch me, you forcefully move me or shoulder me away. We never sit down and have a pleasant, leisurely dinner. You wolf down food before I finish my prayer. I take a sip of wine; you have already bottomed up the first glass and poured the second to the rim. Why do I try to avoid your sexual advances (which is confined to 'let's fuck')? Because afterward I am all black and blue. I feel like I am living in a battle zone."*

Aggression and action are regulated by noradrenaline and testosterone. Comparably, affection and calmness are regulated by serotonin and estradiol, the major estrogen. The two sex hormones and these two neurotransmitters are intertwined and function with exquisite balance in relation to each other.

Blum explains that of the two transmitters, serotonin has a mellowing influence, which produces a calm and rational effect on a person, controls impulses, and suppresses aggression. Our capacity to resist temptation and avoid physical fights or other violent acts results, in part, from the effects of serotonin. In short, serotonin cools the heat of battle. In contrast, noradrenaline promotes action and reaction, adding sparks to the fire. These two neurotransmitters function in complement to each other: they ebb and flow, rise and fall in the brain, such that when we have higher serotonin, we will tend to have lower noradrenaline, and vice versa.

Moreover, there appears to be a gender-related baseline for these two neurotransmitters. In general, women's serotonin is about 30 percent higher than men's. This is in agreement with the stereotypical observation that females are more prone to a conciliatory response than their more contentious males and are less likely to commit violent crimes themselves.

Woman isn't really wimpish. She just has some higher levels of nice hormones and neurotransmitters circulating in her brain:

- Serotonin makes her mellow, less aggressive, and more conciliatory.
- Estradiol, the major estrogen, makes her emotional and affectionate.
- Oxytocin makes her maternal and want emotional connection.

In a 1995 newspaper article, Blum interviewed scientists who study violent offenders, such as those men imprisoned for assaults or U.S. Marines discharged for physically abusive or violent behavior. These researchers found unusually high levels of noradrenaline and testosterone in these men. Blum noted that Bruce Perry, a neurobiologist whom she had interviewed, expressed concern to her "that a hostile environment acts like acid on the brains" of these men, "etching the changes in permanently."

A study of almost seven hundred male prison inmates by James Dabbs and his colleagues in Georgia confirms that inmates who had committed crimes involving sex and violence had higher testosterone levels than inmates who had committed property crimes such as burglary, theft, or drug offenses. Further, inmates with higher testosterone levels (as measured by testosterone in saliva) also violated more rules in prison and had higher incidences of overt confrontation while in prison. The study notes that men with high testosterone are dominant and confrontational, and they often engaged in illicit activity. The men violated rules in an aggressive and violent, as well as intractable and unmanageable, way.

Another study by Alan Booth and James Dabbs examines the relationship of levels of testosterone to marriage and divorce in a large sample (over four thousand) of former servicemen. The subjects were compared with U.S. census population data for men from thirty to forty-four years of age. What they found was that men with higher testosterone production reported they were less likely to marry, and if they did marry, more likely to divorce. Once married, these men were more likely to leave home because they were having trouble getting along with their wives, more likely to have extramarital affairs, and more likely to be violent toward their wives.

Ken, in our clinical example, wasn't a violent or physically abusive man in the commonly understood sense of the word, but his aggressive, hard edges were experienced by his wife as intimidating and threatening. His natural tendency, in verbal and behavioral expression, was to be rough, though he had no conscious

Man isn't really a bad person. He just has some higher levels of nasty hormones and neurotransmitters circulating in his brain:

- Testosterone makes him horny and nonmonogamous.
- Testosterone also makes him aggressive and dominant.
- Noradrenaline makes him active and combative.
- Testosterone/noradrenaline combination makes him nonpaternal.

intention to intimidate. When confronted, he would be surprised, if not offended, as if accused of being a bad person. He could behave softly when he closely and constantly monitored what he said and how he behaved, but he could never be genuinely mellow. Selective serotonin reuptake inhibitors (SSRIs), like Prozac, Zoloft, or Paxil, which increase the brain's serotonin level, might help soften Ken's edges.

Why Don't You Behave Like a Man? Dominance and Aggression Are Context Dependent.

Beth: *"No, no, no! You are aggressive only with me. There is a major difference between being a gentleman and being a wimp with other men. You are a wimp. We were there first, at least ten minutes before that guy came. Plus, the cab stopped in front of us. You let this man take our cab. Meanwhile, we had to wait another fifteen minutes in the freezing cold and almost missed the show."*

Ken: *"What? Did you want me to get into a fist fight with a stranger over a cab?"*

Beth: *Ken, you don't fight with friends either. That man looked sixty-five or seventy years old and half your size. He physically brushed you aside, for God's sake; you didn't even protest."*

Ken: *"Well, you did enough for both of us."*

Beth: *"Damn right. But why should I always be put in that position? The same thing happens in restaurants. They keep us waiting; you don't say a word; the maître d' gave us a table by the kitchen door and not a peep out of you. The waiter ignores us and brings a wrong order, and you quietly accept it by some rationalization: 'baked or mashed potato, steamed*

*or sautéed broccoli, so what is the difference? Let's not make a fuss.' Well,
I ordered baked potato and steamed vegetables. I want what I ordered.
Why should I be saddled with their mistake? But you, you don't like making scenes. Are you aware that when we walk together you take the building side? The man is supposed to walk on the outer side of the sidewalk,
you know, to protect his woman."*

Testosterone increases aggression so that males of all species are more aggressive
than their female counterparts. Males also manufacture estradiol and females,
testosterone. What influences the difference in behavior, however, is *how much*
of the particular hormone circulates in the bloodstream: specifically, Blum reports in *Sex on the Brain* that men have approximately ten times the testosterone
level of women, and women have ten times the distribution of estradiol, the primary form of estrogen.

A man's testosterone declines:

- As he gets older.
- When he gets married.
- When his wife gives birth to a baby.

If a woman has a considerably higher level of testosterone than estradiol,
she may be more aggressive. A husband may ask, "Why are you so aggressive—
can't you be ladylike?" No, she cannot, not really. Years ago, daughters exposed
in utero, particularly during the second trimester of their mothers' pregnancies,
to male hormones, such as DES (to prevent miscarriage), have, as adults, fewer
so-called female characteristics. These women were more apt to have been
tomboys and later had less interest in having children. They were also more apt
to pursue more male-dominated professions. Researchers, like colleagues J.
Richard Udry, Naomi Morris, and Judith Kovenock, further note that the
mechanism through which these fetal androgens work involves influencing actual brain structures and pathways. Equally, a man's ratio of estradiol to testosterone can make him wimpish, that is, not aggressive enough. A wife may ask:
"Why are you not standing up as a man—don't you have 'balls'?" Figuratively,
he does not.

An interesting study by Anne Storey and her colleagues demonstrates that
low levels of testosterone may be associated with men becoming more paternal
after their wives give birth. These researchers found that men with lower

testosterone levels were more responsive to infant cues. Some of these men with lower testosterone levels had also shown their own sympathetic symptoms of pregnancy, such as nausea, weight gain, and fatigue during their wives' pregnancies. Men in the study had testosterone levels that were a third lower in the time after their wives gave birth than in the last weeks of their pregnancies. The study concluded that prolonged contact with a pregnant partner may be important in developing paternal qualities and actually changing levels of hormones, such as testosterone.

Vicious Circle of Aggression— Dominance—Rise of Testosterone

Beth: *"Why don't I want to make love after a dinner party? You interrupt others' stories, anticipating the punch lines of their jokes and wrongly, if I may add. You don't talk with people, you cross-examine them. You are a bully. If you don't respect these guys, why do you socialize with them? I think you get an ego boost in putting them down. Have you noticed each time after such a party you get into the mood for fucking? I won't even glorify it as lovemaking. Furthermore, I would rather you not take your Viagra. What do men take Viagra for? I don't need an artificially inflated penis to rub inside of my vagina. I mean you are either naturally interested or not."*

Ken: *"Why do I take Viagra with you? Because in the last few years you have become a ballbuster. You seem to have forgotten what is feminine and sensual. I feel like I am with another man. You cut me down in front of other people. A woman is supposed to bolster her husband, not diminish him,"* he said.

A man's testosterone declines and he loses his sexual drive and overall sense of well-being when:

- He works for a harsh, exacting boss.
- He is married to a critical and demanding wife.
- He constantly fails in whatever he is involved with, including games.
- This situation is reversible by changing the situation (i.e., leaving the boss, wife, game, etc.)

Beth: *"I do that to save the few friendships we still have left. You bore the hell out of me and, I am sure, them. Don't you yourself always quote Oscar Wilde that there is no greater sin than boring other people? There you go. You are one of the most sinful men I know. And what was that again? You take Viagra with me. That means you don't with someone else."*

Ken: *"What I meant, oh forget it . . . I masturbate alright! I have no problem in having an erection all by myself."*

Beth: *"Okay, then fuck yourself."* She turned her back and pulled the cover over her head.

Evolution favors males who are dominant and possess high levels of testosterone. Allan Mazur and Alan Booth make the point that it is important to distinguish between aggression and dominance. Aggressive behavior implies intent to inflict physical injury; dominant behavior implies intent to achieve or maintain power or influence.

Mazur and Booth note that this distinction between aggression and dominance is particularly important for humans since much interpersonal interaction occurs to establish dominance without aggression, unlike lower animals. Although aggression is not well regarded in civilized society, it is sometimes the raw ingredient of dominance. In lower animals, the distinction between aggression/hostility and dominance is blurred. Sometimes, dominance is established through aggression, or even better, through threats of aggression. Stuart Altman, who has studied primates, notes that a dominant rhesus monkey keeps his head and tail raised constantly and deliberately scrutinizes other monkeys, frequently reaffirming his dominance by a display of aggressive postures. Although such dominance-seeking behavior has negative social consequences—such as provocation—it also has rewards: access to females and new territories. Frans de Waal, in his extensive, classic study of chimpanzees, *Chimpanzee Politics,* notes, "The female usually presents her backside to the dominant ape to be inspected and sniffed." Males are more inclined to fight, to posture, and to dominate in order to ensure the transmission of their genes to the next generation. A diluted version of this behavior occurs in our species.

In an interesting study of monkeys, Michael Raleigh and his colleagues gave some of the monkeys drugs like Prozac that enhanced serotonergic activity and other monkeys drugs that decreased serotonergic activity. These researchers found that giving the monkeys drugs like Prozac made them approach other monkeys more easily and groom them more. They also had much less aggression. All of these behaviors actually resulted in these monkeys' becoming more dominant in the monkey hierarchy. The drugs, on the other hand, that decreased levels of serotonin made the other group of monkeys less likely to be dominant.

This particular study, therefore, observed a difference between dominance and aggression, noting that attaining male dominance may be less dependent on actual fighting ability than on the monkey's ability to recruit allies and approach and groom other monkeys—a kind of "win friends and influence monkeys" type of behavior. We can see parallels to humans in that the SSRI medications that make people less shy and more able to approach others may enable them to rise in a kind of dominance hierarchy among their colleagues.

Even though aggression offers women no strong advantage with regard to carrying genes into the next generation (a single successful pregnancy once a year at most), we are experiencing an increased pattern of dominance-seeking behavior. Regardless of gender, however, dominance elicits certain physiological changes in men and women (i.e., increase of testosterone levels in the blood), which alone promote further aggression and dominance-seeking behaviors. This higher level of testosterone, in return, increases sexual aggression and lowers monogamous loyalty—in both males and females.

Women with higher levels of testosterone are:

- More apt to pursue traditionally male-dominated professions.
- Less interested in having children and less maternal.
- Less interested in wearing makeup and jewelry.

What effect does testosterone have on the lives of individuals and couples? Both sexes with high testosterone tend to be highly competitive and combative. One need not check their blood levels of testosterone to verify that; their looks, postures, assertive language will suffice. They tend to pursue aggressive games and professions, that is, prosecutors, surgeons. Blum summarizes research in this regard: whereas clergy tend to have relatively low levels of testosterone, high levels found in the most aggressive hockey players were not too different from those found in some nonsport professions, like criminal lawyers.

In a different vein was testosterone's effect on motherhood, or at least the desire to be a mother. Here, women with high testosterone levels had less desire to have children, actually had fewer offspring, and were more comfortable with a paternal role than their lower testosterone counterparts. Moreover, lower-testosterone females demonstrated much greater interest in children and in all of the related activities leading up to marriage and child rearing. They were more apt to like prototypical female behaviors, like dressing up, wearing makeup, and adorning themselves with jewelry. They also had professional preferences generally associated with the female gender: teachers, nurses, psychotherapists, interior decorators.

Sneaky Fuckers: Husbands of Domineering Women Have a Penchant for Affairs.

"It isn't only that I have no sexual desire for her. I don't like being with her. Isn't that an awful thing to say about one's wife? But it's true.

She is such a ballbuster. She talks to me as if I am her child or her servant. If I protest her bossy behavior, she gets even nastier and explains impatiently why she has no choice other than to be exact with me, because I always fail in my role as a man and as a husband, that I am irresponsible, inadequate, you name it. Ironically I am, in her presence. Something happens to me when I am around her. I even mumble when I talk to her. No one else in the world, by the way, considers me in anyway physically or psychologically impotent. With Gwen, I am like a superman. She says she never had orgasm through intercourse before she met me, and I have no problem in having an erection with her, nor with anyone else before her. I feel good just being with these women even without sex. What would my wife say if she finds out that I am having an affair with my secretary? Don't even go there! I don't know. But I'll tell you, at first she wouldn't believe it . . . 'Him? He can't even find his way to first base.' I am almost sure she would say something like that. Then, if the facts are overwhelmingly confirming, she might actually cut off my penis."

The least recognized aspect of decreased testosterone hormone is its effect on the psyche of human beings: a loss of a sense of well-being. In the animal kingdom, a dominant male's testes get larger and produce more sperm with increased motility. In contrast, other male testes in the vicinity of the dominant male shrink and the production of sperm declines. This psychological castration, however, is reversible. As soon as the dominant male withdraws from the situation, a replacement male discovers that his testes have begun to enlarge. The hierarchy of dominance in a group is usually well established. Males tend to perceive where they exist in the ranking hierarchy and await an opportunity for injury or aging of the alpha-dominant male to assert themselves. Although the testosterone level of the low-rank male may be diminished, he is not altogether castrated. Occasionally, these males experiment to assess the tolerance of the dominant male or sneak behind him to have intercourse with females. They are "sneaky fuckers," explain Glantz and Pearce, who try extraordinary techniques to access females. Some male seals, for example, will disguise themselves as females by hiding their noses, in order to gain access to females, says Burney Le Boeuf.

This situation in humans isn't that dissimilar, though perhaps subtler and more complicated. Accepting one's status within a group or relationship on the spectrum of dominance/submission may reflect social intelligence; it may be instrumental for the survival of the individual, but it also affects the person's testosterone level and, accordingly, his well-being. In contrast to animals, where it is the male-to-male interaction that determines the dominance-submission pattern, in humans, it is the female-male relationships that determine the outcome. "A silverback woman," so to speak—not unlike a silverback gorilla, the dominant male—could easily lower a man's testosterone and force him into a submissive relationship with her. He may then seek "dominance" outside the marriage.

In addition to these biologically based factors, there are many subtle and not so subtle purely psychological factors. As Ivan Boszormenyi-Nagy and Barbara R. Krasner say, problems of spouses about sex and intimacy, as well as extramarital affairs, may reflect a complicated set of loyalties and disloyalties. For example, an affair can be disloyal to the marriage, or a marriage may be disloyal to the family of origin. The affair may, therefore, appear to be justified because it allows a spouse to be indirectly loyal to that family of origin. The affair then undoes the original disloyalty. There are other factors in affairs, of course. On a peer level, extramarital relations are often an attempt to rebalance the couple's own ledger of fairness. "You've nagged, you've been distant, in essence you've always had things your way. I haven't gotten from you, so now I'm taking my turn."

Note

1. The situation is apparently even more complex, as Carrel and Willard explain in a 2005 article in the journal *Nature*, (see *Nature*, 434: 400–404 [March 17, 2005]). These researchers have found there is considerably more genetic variability involving the female *X* than previously suspected. What this means is a much greater degree of heterogeneity between males and females and even between one female and another than originally thought. For a humorous discussion of these male–female differences, where there may be an "inability-to-remember-birthdays-and-anniversaries gene," see Maureen Dowd, "X-celling Over Men," *New York Times*, March 20, 2005, Sunday, Week in Review (Op-ed), 13.

CHAPTER 4

Communication in Marriage

Unless spouses understand and value differences in the communication patterns of men and women, they will not be able to talk about their problems with each other or about anything else for that matter. Instead, they will only bring the subject to an impasse and hurt their relationship.

Women Have More of an Analogue Brain; Men, a Digital One.

Cultural variations notwithstanding, 65 percent of the population has right-brain dominance, and these people are made to feel inadequate and less smart from the start. Women constitute 75 percent of these right-brained individuals. They disproportionately represent, therefore, the prototypical right-brain characteristics. The two sides of the brain can be *grossly* summarized as follows, as noted by Onno van der Hart:

left side of the brain
grammatical
rigid time
linear
rational
sequential
analytical

right side of the brain
visual
flexible time
multidirectional
spontaneous
simultaneous
intuitive

Though the story is far from complete, researchers believe that the left brain is more focused on detail and the right brain on a broader picture—a kind of trees from the forest approach. In other words, as John McCrone explains in a summary article, one side of the brain thinks and sees in wide-angle and the other side zooms in for details. Evidence seems to lean toward the two halves of the brain differing in their processing styles and often working in complementary ways. Ernest Hilgard, back in the 1970s, analogized the brain to a computer. In other words, we can think of the left hemisphere operating more like a digital computer (i.e., a stimulus-response brain) and the right hemisphere, more like an analogue computer (i.e., a Gestalt brain). A digital computer is one that performs calculations and logical operations; there is less room for error and interpretation. An analogue is one in which numerical data are represented by measurable physical variables, so there is more room for error and being imprecise.

My husband is an emotional dwarf:

- My husband is uncommunicative.
- My husband is too rigid: everything has to be planned ahead of time and executed accordingly.
- My husband is all brain, no heart.
- My husband is intolerant and impatient.
- My husband always tells me to come to the point and demands facts and facts alone.

This may ultimately be too simplistic a way to look at left-right brain functioning. What is more likely is our wrong assumptions. But, as T. S. Eliot says, "If we can never be right, it is better that we should from time to time change our way of being wrong."

Men's Intentional versus Women's Linguistic Medium of Communication

Stanley complained that Phyllis, his wife, who is a writer, can remain on the telephone for hours at a time. When he asked her what she converses about, she reminded him of a cartoon George Orwell remembered seeing in the British humor magazine *Punch,* in the 1920s, of a young man who declares one day that he intends to "write." "And what do you intend to write about, dear?" said his aunt. "My dear aunt," he replied, "one doesn't write about *anything.* One just *writes.*" "Now substitute 'talk' for 'write,'" Phyllis said: "One doesn't talk about anything. One just talks."

Especially for women, conversation is an instrument of social interaction. Women's dialogue proceeds by the exchange of sounds of words as much as by its content (since much of what we say is redundant anyway). Men-to-men or women-to-women's conversations are fairly congruent, but difficulties classically begin to occur when men and women try to communicate with each other. For example, women tend to verbalize their inner lives to any reasonable or available listener (e.g., hairdressers, saleswomen, clients, coworkers, etc.). That quality in women also enables them to be better patients for psychotherapists, especially for female therapists. Deborah Tannen says this women's tendency toward engaging in "troubles talk" is confusing as well as distressing to men. Men mistake such a ritual lament for a request for advice, rather than as just one aspect of an ongoing conversation, often one they are also having with themselves—a kind of internal soliloquy. Here, offering solutions is not only often beside the point, but men often misunderstand and sabotage the underlying intention of engaging in

---

Your husband is not an emotional dwarf; he primarily has a left brain:

- Don't talk to your husband, talk with him; and more so, just listen patiently—tolerate long silences.
- Take charge of your social life; make plans. Set your clock one-half to one hour ahead (symbolically or literally).
- In the long run the surest way of getting to a man's heart is through his brain, not his stomach. Address his brain directly, not his emotion.
- Don't call your husband at work just to chat. During a candlelight dinner with a promising night, he will be more receptive to "rapport talk."

the verbal interchange. Indeed, solving the articulated query aborts the particular discussion at hand: women will then naturally counter with another "grievance" as a means to secure the conversation. Men and women, therefore, feel considerable frustration at the others' manner of response. Whereas women do not necessarily appreciate men's prototypical requirement to take action and provide solutions, men respond negatively to the passivity implied in discussing problems without attempting to act. Author John Gray makes this point cogently in *Men Are from Mars, Women Are from Venus.*

Differences between males and females are detectable even in early childhood. Boys and girls have very different game-playing behaviors as well as very different ways of conversing with their friends. Not only are their favorite games not alike, but their manner of utilizing language in those games is markedly different.

Boys communicate, notes Blum in *Sex on the Brain,* in order to establish a hierarchy within a large group: who tells whom what to do and how to do it, and who resists or complies. Boys' games have winners and losers and elaborate systems of rules that are frequently the subjects of arguments. Success is measured by a relative position in leadership. For boys, conversation is a form of war engagement. Girls, on the other hand, play in small groups or in pairs; the center of a girl's social life is her best friend. Within the group, intimacy is fundamental: success is measured by relative closeness, often manifested by the typical clique of young girls. Girls' conversations are an element of their grooming each other.

Tannen further notes that girls and women frequently use a little "tag" question at the end of their statements. "It is a nice dress, isn't it?" The tag is related to a woman's hesitancy in assertion and a way of engaging the other in conversation. Further, women converse differently; they focus on different details from men.

Barbara Johnstone studied the differences between men and women in their conversational narratives. She found that men's stories are about "contest," whereas women's are about "community." More specifically, men are more likely to present "a world of contest in which individuals act alone to overcome a challenge or a threat." Women related stories about "a world of community in which disturbances in the *status quo* are managed jointly." Johnstone further noticed that men's stories tend to focus on physical (e.g., fighting) and social (e.g., intellectual skill to defend honor) contests, as well as contests with nature. As might be expected, men rarely tell stories where women are the protagonist. The men in these stories act alone and are successful.

In contrast, women frequently relate stories of joint actions by groups of people, about assisting others in distress, or in other words, about the importance of working together as a community. Furthermore, in women's stories, the people have names whereas people in the men's stories are usually nameless. The women's stories are about social power, that is, disturbing or dangerous events that require the power of interdependence and community. The women present themselves in their stories as powerless, such that things happen to them. Johnstone's study had a sample of less than fifty people (about half men, half women), so her conclusions must be taken in that context, though Tannen's own informal comparison studies demonstrated similar results.

Cognitive Map for Men versus Affective Map for Women

> Aristotle could have avoided the mistake of thinking that women have fewer teeth than men by the simple device of asking Mrs. Aristotle to open her mouth.
>
> —Bertrand Russell

Men have made many assumptions about women over the centuries because men use themselves as a point of reference for normality. Now women are beginning to do the same. There are three problems associated with this: (1) there is no such thing as psychological normality, unless one is talking statistically; (2) most men and women are actually different in the makeup of their brains, as we have said, thus different in their minds, and these changes begin in utero, as men and women are exposed to different hormones; and (3) rejecting differences causes perpetual conflict between the two sexes. A truthful, but not derogatory statement, would recognize that most women converse more than most men. Blum notes that most men would assert that. Most women have brains designed to further hearing and talking. Most men listen with the right ear (thus the asymmetrical substantial utilization of the left brain). Women, however, tend to listen with both ears (thus the symmetrical use of both sides of the brain). Men and women, therefore, differ in the way they listen and talk.

My wife is a soft-headed hysteric:

- My wife is always changing her mind.
- My wife always repeats herself.
- My wife has no sense of direction.
- My wife never follows my advice.

Another assumption men make about women is that they cannot utilize maps and have considerable difficulty following directions. "My wife gets lost in our house," said Stanley. Women simply process the information differently from men. Mental mapmaking in men is numerical and mathematical; in women, it is narrative and relational. Simple observation seems to support this type of contrast, such as the stereotypical manner in which women tend to provide directions versus the way men are inclined to do it (and even how men typically won't even request directions from others). Women more often give directions by delineating landmarks, such as "turn left at the grocery store," whereas men will give exact distances and specific street names, such as "go down Oak Street for one mile."

For Women, Life Is Material for Conversation, and for Men, a Problem to Be Solved.

Phyllis complained that anytime she begins to tell Stanley, her husband, something, anything, he says, "get to the point."

> *"The other day I was telling him about my day (mind you, first I asked him about his day, and he replied with his dismissive attitude: 'Same old, same old'). So I began telling him what a frustrating day I had—the housekeeper didn't show up; she didn't even call; she usually does; she is a very responsible woman; my hairdresser cut my hair too short. I told her dozens of times, just trim at the edges. Damn it—the telephone guy couldn't find the cause of the static on the phone; I can't stand that background noise, it just drives me crazy. And to top it off, the dry cleaners lost a favorite skirt of mine. Anyhow, Stanley looks at me and says: 'So, what do you want me to do?' The man has not a single empathic bone in his body.*
>
> *I said 'Forget it.' Now noticing that I am hurt, he kept asking: 'But what am I supposed to do? Just tell me, and I'll do it! We can sue the cleaner, hire a new housekeeper, rewire the in-house telephone system, or change to Verizon; maybe it is a central problem. As for your hair, at least your hair will grow out of a crew cut.'*
>
> *I couldn't help laughing. He just doesn't get it."*

Phyllis and Stanley are getting ready for an unpleasant evening. Most men view conversation as a means to discover a solution. Talk is not only practical, but it has a function as a means to maintain status in a hierarchical social order. Language, for men, is also a concrete matter of exchange. Men appear to prefer public speaking to private conversation, during which, James Hillman conjectures, they seem to be seeking "sanity and sensible speech." They may end up sanitizing their speech, on the other hand, when they require accuracy, but the *intent* still can be feigned. In her analysis of men and women in conversation, Tannen refers to this type of male interchange as "report talk."

Your wife is not a soft-headed hysteric; she has advanced software—her mind.

- Be aware of the fact that she'll change her mind.
- If you listen the first time and have had some interchange about it, she'll less likely repeat herself.
- Don't expect her to be the guide for your next trip: her sense of direction is different from yours.
- Offer alternative ideas if solicited, but don't advise your wife—she is not your child.

In contrast, most women converse in "rapport talk." Tannen explains this is a way of establishing interpersonal connections and negotiating relationships, in which the primary function is to compare experiences with others. Here, the *content* can be feigned, and eloquence is preferred to accuracy. The narrative itself is less important than its emotional role. Moreover, for women, there seems to be greater linguistic free play, whereby a woman-to-woman conversation is like two enthusiastic monologues, often delivered simultaneously.

My wife is stupid:

- My wife is too flexible about time and talks incessantly with anyone who will listen.
- My wife has no idea of the value of money.
- My wife is not seriously interested in world affairs.
- My wife's emotional reactions are too intense and even irrational.
- My wife improvises her life as she goes along.

In Order to Understand Someone Else's Mind, Loosen Your Own Mind's Grip on Your Brain.

Some arguments between spouses result in one spouse inquiring of the other, overtly or covertly: "Are you out of your mind?" This question expresses the astonishment derived from the discordant experience of a nonmeeting of minds. Furthermore, this lack of synergy between minds is compounded by the way our brains process sounds and meanings of words. First, men and women don't always assume or attribute the same particular sound to convey a particular idea. Second, they may have their own idiosyncratic expressions, a personal or familial way of pairing sounds and their meanings. Ideally, when people talk they should have fairly similar respective mental dictionaries. Between men and women, this is not necessarily so.

> Stanley: *"The managing partner called me into his office today and put me on pro . . ."*
>
> Phyllis: *(cutting him short) "Wow, congratulations. I told you, didn't I? Oh, I am so happy for you. God, you worked so hard, you fully deserve it, after all you have done for the firm. So, do I get the earrings then? We've got to celebrate. Let's do something special."*
>
> Stanley: *"Phyllis! Phyllis, please, I didn't get promoted. He put me on probation!"*

Men and women steadily perform an "oral form of back-seat driving" on each other says a character in De Vries's *Reuben, Reuben.*

Women's brains have an extraordinary speed by which they recognize, process, and accumulate words. It generally takes an average person's brain about

---

Your wife is not stupid; she primarily has a right brain:

- Make allowance for her lateness. You want her to be ready at 6:00; think of it as if you had said 6:30 or 7:00.
- Let her have her own account, and let her be responsible for it.
- Your wife need not share similar interests with you.
- You are not the point of reference for what is emotionally appropriate or rational.
- She may be improvising her life because you have overstructured it for her. If you loosen a bit, she will take better control of it.

one-quarter of a second to find a word that names an object, and another one-quarter of a second to pronounce that word. It takes approximately one-fifth of a second for the listener's brain to assess the meaning of a spoken word. Most women may do so even before the speaker has finished pronouncing the word! The downside of this, of course, is that women may very quickly jump to the *wrong* conclusion.

As if all that were not enough, we don't listen to each other for totally subjective reasons. In our self-focused world, we sometimes believe that listening to someone else is a waste of time. What we don't recognize is that listening is a more effective tool to serve our self-interest and to obtain desirable results than is speaking, no matter how convincing the speaker may be. Even in love relationships, it has been said that the ear is the most seductive organ.

Deborah Tannen remembers hearing an interview given by Alice Walker. Walker describes how a woman in her novel *The Temple of My Familiar* falls in love with a particular man because she sees in him "a giant ear." The metaphor expresses Walker's view that although people may believe they fall in love because of sexual attraction or some other physical force or feature, what they are looking for is someone to listen to them. Beneath it all, both men and women desire fervently to be heard—to be heard not only for what they seem to affirm, but for what they really mean. Men, even if they don't talk, still want to be heard. Their silence is a wish to be understood—without speaking.

The Mind, as Software, Is Too Flexible, and Even More So in Women.

Sometimes, in contrast to not wanting to listen, we cannot listen. *Qualitatively,* here, an inability to listen is related, in computer terminology, to the software system: the mind. Tibetans call this "*sem,*" the ordinary mind. *Sem* can only function in relation to internal and external reference points; it is always shifting. The masters have compared *sem* to a candle flame, vulnerable to all the winds of circumstance, in an open doorway. As such, seen from a single stance, *sem* is "irregularly flickering and unstable."

Women's minds are sometimes too flexible. That makes them more accommodative, adaptive, and agreeable but also sometimes more suggestible. Their being more influenced by external factors makes them change their positions frequently enough to verify the old self-justification. "I am a woman and entitled to change my mind." Men have difficulties adjusting to such flickering; they get anxious, feel irritated, and try to force women to a position, unsuccessfully.

My husband is a hard-headed brute:

- My husband never concedes to being wrong.
- My husband doesn't listen.
- My husband won't ask for directions.
- My husband always gives advice—unsolicited.

The Brain, as Hardware, Is Too Rigid, and Even More So in Men.

Quantitatively, an inability to listen is related to the hardware system: the brain. The brain has a genius for inaccuracy. It is not a precise organ with standardized internal corrections for "reality." As extraordinary as it may seem, our brain is predisposed to generate three common and related mistakes:

First, the brain mistakes its perceptions for reality. What we see, hear, smell, and touch are merely a fractional, if not misleading, representation of the real world. These perceptions are, at best, an approximation. The brain interprets events through these perceptions and frequently finds itself perplexed when external reality doesn't correspond to them. Probably no two people experience or perceive the world in exactly the same way. Albert Einstein and Leopold Infeld said that in our endeavor to understand reality, we are somewhat like a person trying to understand the mechanism of a closed watch. We see the outside of the watch, its face and moving hands; we even hear the ticking, but the watch is sealed. We don't see its mechanism, though we may guess at it. We can never be certain if we are correct, that is, if our assumption about its workings is accurate. In short, man not only will never be able to compare his picture of the watch with its actual mechanism, he cannot even imagine the possibility of the meaning of such a comparison. On the basis of such shortcomings, the brain (which has difficulty with not knowing or not understanding) formulates knowledge and then accepts it. The brain once thought that the world was flat. Now it believes in some version of the Big Bang. It once believed in genies, and now it believes in genes. The brain's need for closure and its ability to generalize what it perceives is striking.

In fact, Nobel-prize-winning scientist Gerald Edelman believes that the brain's extraordinary capacity for construction, closure, and generalization make it able to respond to our environments automatically and with considerable novelty. In this way, says Edelman, the brain is not like a computer at all, which requires explicit and unambiguous instructions.

Your husband is not a hard-headed brute; he has advanced hardware—a brain:

- He may not concede to being wrong because he may be insecure.
- Don't talk. Converse.
- If he doesn't take direction, let him get lost a few times. Even the hardened brain eventually learns.
- Don't ask for advice subtly or indirectly; don't behave helplessly, unless you really need help; don't present problems just for the sake of talking.

The second "mistake" that the brain makes is in distinguishing things. It perceives independent entities or categories when such discrimination may be inaccurate and misleading. Eviatar Zerubavel suggests that in order to endow things with meaning, we manufacture such distinctions ("islands of meaning") in everyday life so as to establish order out of chaos. We will often bend our best thinking in order to force some perception into a comfortable, recognizable niche. This may also be a function of the brain's need for closure and avoidance of gaps. For example, the brain perceives a circle drawn sloppily and incompletely and closes it, as if it were closed in our perception. In other words, it recognizes a complete circle. This is an inadequate process of classifying the various entities we perceive into categories. We also have a complementary process of distinguishing these entities from other things. This latter process frequently requires that these mental entities be isolated from their context and regarded as if they were totally isolated from their surroundings. This type of discontinuity of our "experience of reality presupposes a basic distinction between a figure and

Women, don't count on your mind too much; it is deceptive:

- For the mind, words are reality. Thus it easily distorts.
- The mind first tunes into the sounds of words, then their content. Thus, it can easily miss the message.
- Words are just signals. They have no impact on the essence of the matter.
- Better communication doesn't necessarily lead to better relationships, nor does it resolve conflicts.
- The mind listens self-referentially. It resists any independent point of reference.

the ground within which it is perceptually embedded," says Zerubavel. This is a kind of deconstructive approach the brain has in order to comprehend and organize the world around it. By breaking down mental entities to their fundamental components, the brain tries to absorb and comprehend smaller pictures within the more substantial frame, often at the expense of this larger frame.

The third "mistake" that the brain makes is to contrast, that is, to accept an uncompromising black-and-white predisposition. In our brain, opposites are mutually exclusive: all things are either present or absent. Such either/or logic presupposes a digital mode of thinking, which, in direct contrast to its analogue counterpart, as noted earlier, is unable to tolerate any shadings among different mental fields. In this regard, digital thinking of the brain has been likened to the on/off feature of the conventional light switch, whereas analogue thinking of the mind is applicable to the function of a dimmer, according to Zerubavel.

Men, don't count on your brain too much—it is fallible:

- The brain, when it cannot make sense of something, makes it up.
- The brain, in its need for closure, believes what it makes up to be true and real.
- The brain breaks down subjects into their smallest components in order to understand them, meanwhile missing the overall context.
- For the brain everything is either/or, black or white (like an off-on switch). It doesn't tolerate shadings well. It has no dimmer, so to speak.

These three common mistakes of the brain—creating explanations for phenomena that it can't comprehend; creating order or closure out of chaos, as by isolating a thing from its context; and rigidly polarizing between phenomena—exist in both sexes. Men seem to make more of these three mistakes than women. Consequently, women have difficulties in adjusting to such rigidity; they get frustrated, feel oppressed, and try to manipulate men to soften their position, again unsuccessfully.

Just Because You Say Something Doesn't Make It So.

The more rigid the brain, the harder is its product—the mind. The interface between the mind and brain is extraordinarily complicated, for the mind, in return, reshapes the brain through the brain's own mechanism. The mind has no cells of its own but is able to communicate with thousands of other nerve cells in the brain. These cells are making trillions of connections simultaneously. They, however, do not directly deliver these messages; rather, they depend upon a type of chemical messenger known as a neurotransmitter. Neurotransmitters, of which there are many, occur at special junctures, the synapses. In the complex operation of the brain, every sensation or affect we experience and every action, however small, derives from these multitrillion physical encounters among axons and dendrites (both nerve cells) and neurotransmitters. Moreover, this physiological system is exquisite: these events occur, unrelentingly, every fraction of a second, within which information within the brain is processed, sent forth, and received.

The brain and its product, the mind, together, compound each other's limitations when it comes to verbalization—the final pathway of communication. There stands the ultimate source of misunderstanding between men and women when they negotiate "reality." Besides belonging to a different gender, each person differs in this brain-mind verbalization pathway. The fact that there is no actual essence in words increasingly facilitates the ambiguities in reality. At best these words are our own reflection of the essence, whether we are discussing the weather, a movie, or our feelings. Each person thus creates his or her own system of language—a derivative of the communal one—and superimposes it upon presumed universal meanings. This is somewhat like the denotation (dictionary meaning) of a word differentiated from its connotation (what it means specifically to a specific person). Some people take this presumption to an extreme so that, to them, what they articulate becomes what that something actually is. By having uttered a word, they think the occurrence or circumstance is real.

Don't Let Your Language Interfere with What You Are Saying.

> *"Didn't the counselor say, Stanley, we should honestly confront each other about whatever is bothering us? That is what I am doing. I don't like the way you interrupt me in front of our friends, like tonight at the dinner table. I was just explaining part of the thesis of that new book* Fat Land, *how our government conspired with Malaysian businessmen and Japanese scientists to overproduce and underwrite corn production in our Midwestern states and then used its high fructose distillation inexpensively to enlarge the size and calories of food products: hamburgers, french fries, candy bars. And you shot me down with a sarcastic, 'Don't eat.'"*

> *"Because you were boring intelligent people out of their wits. Everyone knows that there is too much food. Were you trying to exonerate your own*

overeating by blaming some Malaysian businessman? Come on! And as if that is not enough you spend another half hour lecturing about weight lifting as the only necessary and sufficient way of losing weight. Don't you see the ridiculousness of your position? My goodness, you are an educator; you've got to practice what you preach. Stop talking about food and exercise; do something about your weight, and if you can't do something about it, just shut up."

There is a universal belief that we can solve our difficulties by discussing them, as if we inhabit a reality based entirely on language. Therapists, writers, philosophers, and ministers tend to overendow language with the significance of reality. This point of view, taken to its extreme, even posits that if a distinction cannot be made in language, it follows that it cannot be made conceptually. In depicting the power of language in our lives, Russell Smith has said that since the concepts people live by are derived only from perceptions and from language we come "pretty close to living in the house that language built."

When, for example, spouses talk about a lack of communication, they are actually complaining not about their verbalization of the issues and feelings, but about their differences in the essence of their respective realities. Obviously, the more the couple is forced to communicate in such situations, the sharper the differences become. Many divorces occur in those who have had joint counseling or marital therapy, presumably with the concerted "assistance" of a therapist, who inadvertently misunderstands the role of language in relationships. In fact, improving communication between men and women has limited usefulness, as language has its limitations.

Although language can help translate entities into abstract, transmittable signals, they are still just signals. No matter how much we can alter a signal and rearrange its presentation, it will have no impact on the essence of the matter. To the extent that words are used narratively and exceed their signal role, they become more distant from reality. Our conversations are no longer an exchange of signals between sender and receiver; instead, they require a complex set of process and content interpretations. Reality becomes not even what is *signaled,* but what is *interpreted.* Sometimes it is this perversion of reality that is the source of considerable unhappiness in marriages.

When spouses complain about each other's communication, they may be caught in this language dilemma: language becomes gesture, whereby speakers charge their words with *meaning.* Nevertheless, language is fundamentally unstable and, therefore, unstabilizing. Ludwig Wittgenstein says that language is, rather, a game where the competitors, by mutual agreement, that is, social convention, establish the rules. Men and women have no agreement on these rules. Language has neither a fixed meaning nor a hidden, independent essence. Instead, meaning is relative and thoroughly context based. Men and women share no durable context.

Communication, even at its best, isn't sufficient to resolve conflicts about the essence of matters. Language as an instrument of the mind is limiting. It is not an instrument of reality. Our overvalued, if not perverted, role of communication comes from our logocentric paradigm, as if words reflect reality, and if they are uttered in a certain fashion, they generate a new reality. "Truth" and "word" don't always coincide. Consultants spend considerable time "wording" a situation in order to convey a meaning that may or may not reflect the personal reality of a particular situation. Words and their representations, in fact, belong to two separate worlds. Disappointments arise when expectations from specific communications don't prompt the expected results. Marriage counselors are too frequently dismissed by one or both spouses.

Don't Confuse "What Is" with "What Ought to Be."

> "Well, I am a very affectionate, very caring person, Stanley. I am always in a good mood in contrast to your ever present irritability; I always ask about your job, your health, and you never do, as if I have no job and no body; I am the one who makes all our social arrangements; you grudgingly show up; I open conversations and you, you stall them; I tell stories, you give legal briefs; I always say 'I love you;' occasionally you reply with a cold 'me too.' I never know by 'me too' whether you mean you love me or you love yourself too."

> "Boy, you can twist words around! All those things that you just said. First of all, the fact that you say them, doesn't make them true. For example you aren't always in a good mood; if anything, you are moodier than I am. I am at least consistently irritable. Secondly, you have a strange sense of normality. You think that stimulating conversation is everything, especially with your determined attitude of 'let's talk.' Have you ever thought that some quiet presence may be more desirable than gibberish conversation?"

> "Do I talk gibberish? Stanley? Try hearing yourself."

This kind of "wounding quarrel" is what Michael Vincent Miller calls "intimate terrorism." It is the mutually intimidating terror of a loss of control and a disintegrating sense of reality, while the couple clings to each other out of fear of freedom. The interpretation of events or the wording of things changes their essence sufficiently enough to be recognized as an alternative reality. Furthermore, some realities have no independent existence by themselves except in their relevance to us, so communication can be multiply distorted.

Peter L. Berger has distinguished between two different types of reality: "Cognitive reality" tells us what the world is like, whereas "normative reality" tells us how to act. These distinctions are integrally related, however, in that all normative definitions derive from and depend upon specific cognitive definitions. Berger offers the incest taboo as an example of one of the most ancient moral principles. This taboo is a cross-cultural norm that stipulates that we should not marry a close relative. In order to follow this norm, however, we must recognize and define who are our close relatives. In other words, the concept or norm that incest is wrong depends on a definition of "kinship." More aptly, the perceptual language of cognition, which informs us about reality (i.e., *what is*), must be unmistakable before we can examine the normative language of normality (i.e., *what ought to be*).

Men and women differ primarily in cognitive reality and much less so in normative reality. Their cognitive perceptions (e.g., the scope of the kinship) may vary but not their normative perceptions, (e.g., wrongness of incest). Sometimes, though, the difference in the normative reality of men and women may sharpen. Conflicts related to "what is" sometimes become "what ought to be." Irreconcilability between them, then, becomes obvious.

If You Always Feel Misunderstood by Your Spouse, You Both Need to Talk and Listen Differently.

"Stanley, you are the only person I have difficulty conversing with. With all my friends, we talk about many things, some important, some silly. I never get bored with them, nor do I sense that they are bored. With you, I am always cautious regarding how long I can stay on the phone before you want to hang up and what subject I can talk about. It takes all the spontaneity out of our relationship. I am not your client. I am your wife, for God's sake. Why can't you listen to me the way that my friends do? The two of us are supposed to be the most intimate with each other," Phyllis complained.

"Your girl friends and your gay friends don't listen to each other. If you don't believe me, tape one of your conversations with any one of them and play it to see whether what you say has any relevance to how they reply or vice versa. Yours is a dialogue of one. You all just need to talk. With whom you talk is less relevant and highly interchangeable. You like to hear your own voices bouncing back from another, the nature of what you say is just a convenience and usually has nothing to do with what you started to discuss. Yesterday, you called to say that you are not feeling well. You ended the conversation with an assignment: make a restaurant reser-

vation because 'a man is more likely to get one.' What happened to your
illness? Did you call the doctor or get to the emergency room? Not a word
about it then, and not a word since. That was just a signal: let's talk and
I have a chore for you. I wish you would call and just say, 'Stanley, make
a reservation for six at such and such a place' and hang up."

"*You know, you are not a nice person, I mean, not a person, period. When*
you pass away I'll put on your obituary a simple announcement: 'Stanley
died.'"

We all expect that people will hear us, listen, and then understand what we have just said. We proceed even further in the hope that the other person—the receiver—not only understood what we said but also what we *meant*. This process is rarely, if ever, a linear, one-directional one. The crux of the problem lies at the very heart of language: language is a system of signs, consisting of the sounds of words and the content of words. The problem is that often we tend to pay more attention to the sound of words than to their content. Listening to sound is one-directional, and it requires less interpersonal effort than attending to content. Listening to the content is multidirectional and demands the attention of all involved. We need an apprenticeship for such listening.

In *The Story of My Life*, Helen Keller writes, "I cannot make notes during lectures because my hands are busy listening." Her degree of absorbed listening is perhaps poetically feasible. For an accurate understanding, verbal communication demands readerly attention. Even then, communication is more than an interpersonal event.

Assuming a person actually has listened to what was said, she will immediately interpret what was heard, primarily in a self-referential way. The listener's interpretive egocentricity, based on her own disposition, pattern, or background, enters the picture. Indeed, there is a whole science of such interpretative phenomena, called hermeneutics. Contrary to common sense, which operates on the assumption that understanding arises naturally and that misunderstanding is an aberration to be overcome, hermeneutics suggests the reverse. It proceeds on the assumption that *misunderstanding* arises naturally and, therefore, that understanding must always be actively sought.

The Bible provides us with one such example of misunderstanding. Most likely it is neither intended to be such an example, nor to be humorous. "The total absence of humor from the Bible," said Alfred North Whitehead, "is one of the most singular things in the literature."

Witness Nebuchandnezzar's dream about a statue made of four metals, as recorded in Daniel 2:1–9. Nebuchandnezzar, the king of Babylon during the second year of his reign of Jerusalem, experienced some troubling dreams. Although he slept, he was distressed and decided to send for his wizards—magicians, psychics, sorcerers, and astrologers—so that they could tell him about what he had dreamt. When they came to the king, he said he had had a dream and was troubled by it. He wanted to know what the dream meant.

> They answered the King, "Your Majesty, may you live forever! Tell us the dream, and we'll interpret it for you."
>
> The King answered, "I mean what I said! If you don't tell me the dream and its meaning, you'll be torn limb from limb, and your houses will be turned into piles of rubble. But if you tell me the dream and its meaning, I will give you gifts, awards, and high honors. Now tell me the dream and its meaning." Once more they said to him, "Your Majesty, tell us the dream, and we'll tell you its meaning."
>
> The King, even more insistent, again replied, "I'm sure you're trying to buy some time because you know that I meant what I said. If you don't tell me the dream, you'll all receive the same punishment. You have agreed among yourselves to make up a phony explanation to give me, hoping that things will change. So tell me the dream. Then I'll know that you can explain its meaning."

Of course, they all felt misunderstood. But they were not alone. To some extent all of us feel misunderstood in life, especially by our spouses.

The Truth Is Sometimes What Your Spouse Doesn't Want to Hear.

> *"Well, do you think it is publishable? I am not exactly Virginia Woolf, but did you like it? I mean, you've read enough novels. If you were a publisher, would you buy it?" she said.*
>
> *"I knew Virginia Woolf, I am not a friend of . . . just kidding. I liked it, very interesting."*
>
> *"Very interesting? Stanley, who are you talking to? Is there any greater insult than calling a work simply 'interesting' to an author's face? Why is it interesting? Tell me."*
>
> *"Look, I am not a publisher, and I am not a book reviewer. What do you want? The main character is interesting. Women are not usually portrayed as murderers without remorse."*
>
> *"What else? Is there other unusual stuff that may not just be interesting but worse?"*
>
> *"Phyllis, I read the book, I . . ."*

"Stanley, tell me, did you really read it? Come on, I am a big girl; if you didn't read it, that's fine. If you read it and did not like it, that is also fine. But what is not fine is your squeamishness."

"I read it, I swear. It just needs your going over it one more time. I think there are some holes in the plot, but only you could figure that out for sure. That is it."

"That isn't it, Stanley. I can tell from your eyes. What is it, out with it!"

"Well, I'm not an expert obviously, but I think writing a murder story in the murderer's voice is a difficult task. The same person cannot speak for herself, as well as for the other characters."

"You are definitely not an expert; if anything you are totally unfamiliar with that style of narration. The best selling book The Lovely Bones *is narrated in the first person and by the murdered young woman, you ignoramus. So, 'I knew Virginia Woolf,' wasn't just a bad joke. Why didn't you tell me that you didn't like it, period? I wasn't going to be offended. As you said, you are not a publisher or a member of the intelligentsia or an author. Your opinion doesn't carry any weight; I was just asking your reaction as a potential reader."*

"Now, you are being ridiculous," he said.

"If you like I could write in third person singular. 'Phyllis skillfully exposed the duplicity of her husband, Stanley, who unashamedly tried to counter by ridiculing her sincerity.' You are right, Stanley, in third person narration I would be more truthful."

Does your spouse or friend ever want to hear the truth? Some people claim they do. Haven't you heard others say—or haven't you said it yourself?—"Please tell me the truth; I won't be offended; I can take it," or "If you are really my friend, you will tell me the truth." As you may know from your experiences, the moment you do attempt to tell the truth, a cold and heavy atmosphere sets in between you and the other person. Immediately, you may try to backtrack in order to recover from your mistake of honesty, only making it worse by losing whatever is left of your credibility. The next in line is the loss of the friendship. What others want is not honesty, but validation, even if it means confirmation of their foolish ideas, praise for their thoughts or actions, an alliance against other friends, or a dishonest loyalty.

Nevertheless, we must risk the potential dangers and be reasonably truthful with our spouse, if the marriage is to flourish. Of course, there are some realities in life so horrific that you may hesitate alarming someone with your naked truth. Some reticence, if not total silence, may be justified on such occasions. For example: a mother insisted on knowing the details of the car accident where her only son had been run over by many oncoming cars after he was thrown from his car over the divider. Her grief-stricken husband had their son's body pieces collected and sown together and then had him laid out in one of his own outfits before allowing her to see him. The husband simply explained that he died quickly by hitting the windshield.

Viktor Frankl recounts another such situation from his Nazi concentration camp experience:

> I shall never forget how I was roused one night by the groans of a fellow prisoner, who threw himself about in his sleep, obviously having a horrible nightmare. Since I had always been especially sorry for people who suffered from fearful dreams or deliria, I wanted to wake the poor man. Suddenly I drew back the hand which was ready to shake him, frightened at the thing I was about to do. At that moment I became intensely conscious of the fact that no dream, no matter how horrible, could be as bad as the reality of the camp which surrounded us, and to which I was about to recall him.

Kierkegaard spoke of "truth-as-relationship." Within this philosophy, he considered that pure objectivity is not only impossible to achieve, but undesirable, and worse, immoral—because we can never view the truth dispassionately. Indeed the need for objectivity is based on an erroneous assumption, that the less we are involved in a given situation, the more clearly we can observe the truth. The point is, whether involved in a situation or not, we can never be completely objective.

When we have a relationship with a given person, we realize that the truth depends for its meaning on the connection between that person and us. Even ordinary life situations, whether one is right in an argument, or did something wrong to another, are totally dependent on the nature of the relationship between the people involved. When the connection is not an intimate one but a situational one (e.g., job, social, recreational), objective truth may become dangerous as it easily fuels anger and resentment. We may be accused of bad motives and bad feelings, of jealousy, betrayal, or ungratefulness. Ironically enough, there may even be some truth to these perceptions.

Such lack of appreciation for the truth was recorded in 1 Kings 22:1–19 at the time of King Zedekiah, when two kings:

> King Ahab of Israel and King Jehoshaphat of Judah, were dressed in royal robes and seated on thrones. . . . All the prophets were prophesying in front of them. Zedekiah, son of Chenaanah, made iron horns, and spoke: "This is what the Lord says—with these horns you will push the Arameans to their destruction." All of the other

prophets made the same prophecy. They said, "Attack Ramoth in Gilead, and you will win. The Lord will hand it over to you."

Then Micaiah, a renegade prophet, was summoned for his prophecy. The messenger who went to find Micaiah told him:

> "The Prophets have all told the King the same good message. Make your message agree with their message. Say something good." To this order, Micaiah answered, "I solemnly swear, as the Lord lives, I will tell him whatever my God says to me." When he came to the King and was asked, "Micaiah, should we go to war against Ramoth in Gilead or not?" Micaiah replied, "Attack, and you will win. They will be handed over to you." The King then asked him, "How many times must I make you take an oath in the Lord's name to tell me nothing but the truth?" At this Micaiah responded, "I saw Israel's troops scattered in the hills, like sheep without a shepherd." At this, the King of Israel turned to Jehoshaphat, "Didn't I tell you he wouldn't prophesy anything good about me?"

The Truth Is Best Received by Your Spouse in a Single Installment.

A half truth is a whole lie

—Yiddish proverb

"Where were you? I tried to reach you in the car half an hour after you left. I got your voice mail. You left early saying that you had an out-of-town client to meet at nine o'clock sharp. I called your office at nine, five minutes past nine, and again. You were not there."

"I didn't say the meeting was in my office. We had a breakfast meeting at a restaurant."

"But your secretary had no client scheduled this morning."

"Well, the client called after my secretary was gone."

"What is her name, your client?"

"Why? Is this a cross-examination? Are you a writer or a prosecutor? He is a man."

"Does he have a name?"

"All right. She. Mrs. Chu from Los Angeles."

"Stanley, why do you lie?"

"Because if I tell you the client was a woman you'll immediately suspect that I am having an affair with her."

"With Mrs. Chu? Come on, is she a shriveled arthritic old Chinese woman with false teeth? Is that why the breakfast lasted four hours? Don't try to deny it. You didn't get to the office until one o'clock."

"Are you spying on me? She wanted to see Ground Zero, so I took her there."

"I presume your office would know where she could be reached. You may also know at which hotel she is staying." Phyllis pinned him down.

"Look, it was Ariel, okay? I didn't want to tell you, because you are unnecessarily jealous and suspicious of her motivation. She wanted me to help her get a good divorce lawyer. That is it. So, now you know everything."

"Ariel, ha? And the Ground Zero business? Is that a metaphor for how deep your relationship is, or how dangerous? Why do you need to escort her to Ground Zero? She knows the place better than you do. She used to live across from the Twin Towers in that Battery Park complex. What kind of stupid lie is that?"

"What I meant is we went to see those five models of the rebuilding of the area; they were on public display."

"Now, just a minute Stanley. Ariel is the one who is the architect. So she took you to the place!"

"Yeah. That is what I meant."

"Oh yeah? And why such a civic or artistic interest all of a sudden when you couldn't tell a postmodernist building from King Tut's tomb? Stanley, don't insult my intelligence, on top of insulting me as your wife."

"Phyllis, I swear, there is nothing between Ariel and me. Believe me, please."

In intimate relations, sometimes the issue is not whether to tell the truth, but *how* to tell it. Sometimes people, to a greater or lesser degree, must learn to "live within a lie," says Vaclav Havel. That may be a political compromise spoken by a poet. In intimate relations, living a lie with someone else violates both people. Such violation of trust brings even the most desired, most passionate, or most affectionate relations to an impasse. Genuine trust is not maintained by love, generosity, passion, protectiveness, or goodness, but simply and only by truthfulness. When confronted with a discrepancy uncovered within the lie, some adamantly reject the accusation, become indignant, and never confess; others will blatantly clarify the situation with further lies. These prevarications all have their consequences and result in considerable damage. One serious repercussion is that gradual revelation generates doubt, in which, says Baltasar Gracián, "the liar suffers twice; he neither believes, nor is believed." The major damage of falsehoods, however, is the disruption of intimacy between two people—even if the lie is never detected. This is because the liar can no longer be totally genuine, sincere, unguarded, and authentic in that relationship. Duplicity and intimacy are mutually exclusive. Further, one lie inevitably leads to other lies.

Truth telling in marriage and the ethics of relationships:

- Pure truthfulness is impossible and even undesirable in marriage. Love, subjectivity, and compassion must also enter your judgment to be truthful.
- Uncomplimentary truths are negative stimuli. Spouses tend to react with depression and anger, especially when these truths are unsolicited.
- The degree of emotional intimacy and the strength of their relationship determine the degree of truthfulness between spouses.
- How you tell the truth to your spouse is as important as what you tell.

In her study of infidelity, Shirley Glass makes the point that the betrayed spouse's need to know should be the determining factor in how much information and detail are warranted. How couples talk about the infidelity afterward is even more important than what they talk about, she feels. Inevitably, though, most spouses need to know something once the infidelity comes to light. Only through directness and honesty can a couple move forward and heal.

Damage becomes irreparable when the truth emerges incompletely and is then given piecemeal, only when confronted. These partial revelations, meted out under pressure, undermine the relationship between spouses and generate enormous mistrust. Even after revelation of the entire truth, the liar will never be believed. To answer only the questions asked, as practiced by the judicial system, is also an unsound model to follow in personal situations. In fact, even in court, holding back a full revelation usually makes the jury end up doubting *both* parties, even though one of them presumably is telling the truth.

The rationalization for gradual revelation goes back to biblical times. Even then, the assertion by the prophets that complete revelations weaken the faith was quite unconvincing to nonbelievers. In "Al Furqan," the nonbelievers asked, "Why was the Koran not revealed to him [the Prophet] entire in a single revelation?" The reply was, "We have revealed it thus so that We may strengthen your faith. We have imparted it to you by gradual revelation. No sooner will they come to you with an argument than We shall reveal to you the truth and properly explain it." Because of the incompleteness of the revelations, however, people kept asking new questions each time, endlessly. This occurred despite the fact that religion requires believing, by definition, and not reasoning. In relationships, such blind faith will more likely be infrequent and temporary. Even the most naive spouse sooner or later demands a convincing explanation. And nothing is more convincing, especially when solicited by one spouse, than a full revelation, no matter how bad it is. And you had better tell it all at once. The cover-up is usually worse than the betrayal.

If You Mean Yes, Say "Yes"; If You Mean No, Say "No."—James 5:12

"Hi Phyllis, it's me," said Stanley. "Do you want to go out to eat?"

"Hmm, if you want."

"Would you like Italian or our seafood place?"

"Either one is fine."

"No small preference?"

"I don't know."

"Then let me see what is available. Seven or eight?"

"I don't care."

"Okay, I'll call you later about both. If it is going to be seven, you'll have to meet me there; if it's eight, I'll come and pick you up."

"Stanley, you are making too big a deal of this. Whatever, wherever, whenever is fine with me. I am late for my therapist."

"Tell her how exhausting I find negotiating with you about a simple evening out. You never make a decision about anything, so that you can complain about mine, not that you are an indecisive person. You are always contentious, as if you are looking for an excuse to irritate me."

"I am the one contentious? Stanley, look what you just did! I said 'fine' to every option you presented about this bloody dinner and you ended up

creating a fight. Why don't you come to my therapist with me, and let's just present her with this conversation? Bye now!" Phyllis hung-up the phone.

"It is a very inconvenient habit of kittens," said Alice in Lewis Carroll's *Through the Looking-Glass,* "that whatever you say to them, they *always* purr. If they would only purr for 'yes,' and mew for 'no,' or any rule of that sort . . . so that one could keep up a conversation! But how *can* you talk with a person if they always say the same thing?" Alice's minimum requirement for conversation remains unflappable. Furthermore, the "yes" or "no" simplicity of condoning something can prevent many misunderstandings, false expectations, and ambiguous manipulations. Language is a tool of communication. In its highly elaborate forms, it tends to become the source of miscommunication.

The first principle of communication is to respond to the other person's questions. Do not be self-referential. The Japanese proverb says, "You must send the message whether received or not." There is, however, another saying: "It is not enough to aim; you must also hit the target." The burden is clearly on the spouse with the truth to tell.

CHAPTER 5

Pregnancy and Infants in Marriage

A pregnancy changes a woman's body and mind and her relationship with her husband. An infant enters the exclusive world of husband and wife and converts the marriage into a family. Spouses can help or hinder this transition.

We Are Convinced That the First Baby Is Like a "Grenade" Thrown into the Marriage.

> Seeds of new parents' individual and marital problems are sown long before their first baby arrives.
>
> —Caroline Pape Cowan and Philip A. Cowan

Two characters in Anne Tyler's novel *Breathing Lessons* are discussing preparation for giving birth:

> *"Breathing lessons—really," she said . . . "Don't they reckon I must know how to breathe by now?"*
>
> *"Oh, honey, you're just lucky they offer such things. . . . My first pregnancy, there wasn't a course to be found, and I was scared to death. I'd have loved to take lessons! And afterward: I remember leaving the hospital with Jesse and thinking, 'Wait. Are they going to let me just walk off with him?' I mean you're given all these lessons in how to balance*

equations, which Lord knows you will never have to do in normal life.
But how about parenthood? Or marriage, either, come to think
of it. Before you drive a car you need a state-approved course of in-
struction, but driving a car is nothing, nothing, compared to living
day in and day out with a husband and raising up a new human
being."

In *Heartburn,* Nora Ephron says, "I realize something no one tells you: that a child is a grenade. When you have a baby, you set off an explosion in your marriage, and when the dust settles, your marriage is different from what it was. Not better, necessarily; not worse, necessarily; but different." She adds, "all the power struggles of the marriage have a new playing field."

In general, the birth of a baby occurs in the context of an already established relationship between spouses. The Cowans emphasize that much of what occurs once a baby arrives is shaped by what has happened earlier in the couple's life together before the baby's birth.

Even the most loving marriages are not immune from the difficulties that occur after the birth of children, especially the first one. For a sizable minority, conflicts that arise will stretch the marriage to its breaking point. In the United States, one-quarter of all divorces, say Caroline and Philip Cowan, take place before a child is old enough to remember living with both biological parents. Approximately 40 percent have taken place by the end of the child's kindergarten year. These researchers further note that 25 percent of couples report their marriages are suffering before their child is eighteen months old. One major risk for a couple, incidentally, is going ahead with a pregnancy when a husband does not feel ready to become a parent and voices his objections.

You should not have children:

- If you are trying to save your marriage by having them.
- If your marital life is unsatisfactory.
- If one of you has a lover on the side.
- If one of you is depressed or drinking excessively or taking addictive drugs.
- If you are in a financial impasse.
- If you are constantly bickering and fighting.

Have children when you are both ready and yearning for them:

- Don't have children to please the other spouse.
- Don't expect mutuality from your children. Parenthood is not about reciprocation.
- You may get divorced from your spouse, if things don't work out, but children are for life. When you have children, divorce is for life, too.

Actually, even before the birth of a baby, changes occur. With pregnancy, the pelvis gets engorged with increased blood flow, making women feel either uncomfortable or in a constant state of arousal, says gynecologist Hilda Hutcherson, whose book *What Your Mother Never Told You about Sex* is well written and comprehensive. Hutcherson notes there is a further increase in blood flow to a woman's genital and pelvic area during the second trimester. Sometimes, Hutcherson notes, this may make it easier to achieve orgasm, such that orgasms may be more intense, and some women even have first or multiple orgasms during their second trimesters. But as the pregnancy advances, in general, there tends to be a loss of sexual interest in both spouses, but more often in the wife, possibly related to her rising progesterone and estrogen levels. To some extent, this anticipates subsequent conflicts between them. The Cowans cite several reasons as reported by couples, such as a woman's general physical discomfort and fatigue, as well as pain and feelings of physical awkwardness. Some men and women express concern they will hurt the baby or stimulate contractions and the onset of labor. Sometimes men feel psychological inhibitions about sex with their pregnant

A baby adds to a family and subtracts from a marriage. Expect changes in your relation with your spouse with the birth of an infant:

- Temporarily, a wife may become a mother, only tolerating wifehood.
- Temporarily, a husband may become another child demanding attention.
- Expect changes in your sexual appetites during pregnancy and after the birth of a baby.
- Make extra efforts to recover your roles as husband and wife as quickly as possible.

wives; they say they "just don't feel like it," or sex seems awkward with someone who is going to be a mother. In the last trimester some physical complications may compound the psychological turnoff, such as breast leakage, varicose veins, and hemorrhoids. After labor and delivery a woman may experience considerable pain and discomfort, and sex is the last thing on her mind. Further rising levels of the hormone prolactin may also suppress any desire.

After many months of avoidance, many couples never get back to their previous sexual relationship. When a child is born, a mother naturally shifts her attention to her baby.

The famous English pediatrician D. W. Winnicott, who gave us concepts like the "good-enough mother" and "transitional objects" (like "security blanket"), called this the state of "primary maternal preoccupation." The husband is tolerated if he can become a member of their affectionate unit. A husband's sexual advances may be received as intrusions. In *The Good Marriage,* Judith Wallerstein and Sandra Blakeslee tell of a woman from their study who confessed that she wanted exclusivity in her relationship with her baby. She felt that her breasts belonged to the baby—as if her husband were "poaching." In Perri Klass's short story "Intimacy," spouses have a new joke: they refer to making love as "waking the baby:"

> *"The last three times we tried, each attempt already a victory over fatigue and the lure of a dark, happy sleep, the baby has woken, loud and frantic in the next room. So last night when he muttered to me, raising his eyebrows and leering, 'If we go to bed early, we might have time to wake the baby,' of course I knew just what he meant, and we both laughed, but by the time I had taken my shower he was sound asleep, and three seconds later so was I."*

Not atypical!

Eventually, hostilities inherent in such jokes may contaminate every aspect of care for the infant: who gets up when the child cries, whose turn to wake up and play with the baby, change, feed, and so forth. There soon may develop an escalating war of passive wills. Even years later, couples may resent each other's role or have distorted memories of what really occurred. One woman, for example, recalls that her husband always claimed that he had gotten up routinely each night to feed the baby. It was at the time she was breastfeeding exclusively!

When new mothers sacrifice lovemaking, among other wifely roles or interests, they may incur the wrath and resentment of their husbands. In other words, some husbands may want to throw the baby out with the proverbial bath water! The following lullaby could have been written only by a man, say Wallerstein and Blakeslee:

Rock-a-bye-baby, on the treetop,
When the wind blows, the cradle will rock.
When the bough breaks, the cradle will fall,
And down will come baby, cradle and all.

The Catch-22 of Mothers:
Women with Infants Can Do No Right.

I have seen repeatedly how the birth of child can trigger the failure of a marriage . . . and [it] forever changes the dynamic between husband and wife."

—Judith S. Wallerstein and Sandra Blakeslee,
The Good Marriage

Since the baby, my wife has become only a mother:

* She hardly pays attention to me.
* She never wants to make love.
* She smells of milk and puke.
* I think she is totally enamored with the kid.

Harold: *"I called you five times today. You were not home. You never are. Each time Ana tries to explain where you might be: 'Missus went to gymnasium'; 'She went to Korean girls (I guess to have your nails done)'; 'She went to the market' (She meant, of course, shopping in Bloomingdale's; you don't go to market to buy food); 'She is eating with friends' (I know you don't eat, you lunch). Today Ana said, 'Missus go to the cinema.' You went to the movies in the afternoon after having left the baby with the housekeeper the whole morning? He is fourteen months old, speaks only a few words and all in Spanish. I mean, what sort of a mother are you?" He was furious.*

Judy: *"Well, what about you? You leave the house at eight o'clock in the morning every day and return twelve hours later. At least twice a week you get home after midnight; you are away a few days each month. You never see your own child!"*

Harold: *"You must be kidding! Is that out of choice? I've got to work. Otherwise, who is going to pay the rent, the food, the maid, doctor bills, not to mention your plastic surgeon and analyst's bills? Incidentally, are we part-owner of Chanel yet?"*

Judy: *"Not funny" she retorted. "You have no idea how much money other women spend. And their husbands always buy them jewelry. When was the last time you bought me a gift?"*

Harold: *"Why bother? You buy them yourself on a regular basis! You know, you're talking to the person who writes the checks. As to other women, I think you should all be ashamed of yourselves. While you are adorning yourselves all day long, the children are left to the mercy of nannies and housekeepers. Doesn't it bother you to see young and old immigrant women pushing babies in their carriages? Why do you all have children? To provide job opportunities for poor minorities?"*

Judy: *"Harold, keep your cynicism for your socialist friends. I think you married the wrong woman. I told you while dating that I don't know what to do with infants and young children. Both of my nephews had to wait until they were five or six years old before I could relate to them. I didn't mislead you. You should have married Carol. She likes the bubbly white puke and the soft yellow shit. I don't. She gushes over every utterance of her son. 'Oh, he said, "apple."' No he didn't, he just burped. When the child begins to talk in full sentences, then we are in business."*

Harold: *"I guess motherhood is a business for you. Carol is one thing, but how many women do you know who would be reluctant to get pregnant to preserve their figure and how rare is it for a woman to demand an unnecessary Caesarian to protect her pelvis from excessive stretching during the birthing, then spend tens of thousands of dollars to remove the scar of the operation? For you, it wasn't delivery of your child. It was sort of removal of a tumor from your precious body."*

In contrast to Harold's attitude in the previous vignette, other husbands are equally critical if their wives' are fully engaged with their babies. If a woman makes her infant her priority, a man often gets angry and feels rejected. If a woman doesn't make her infant her main preoccupation, a man may also get angry. Maybe Freud should have asked: "What does man want?" Most of the time, the answer is simple: man wants to be the sole priority and only preoccupation of his woman. No wonder that women are less happy in marriage than men. Andrew Hacker quotes statistics from the Department of Health and Human Services that indicate more divorces are initiated by wives than husbands. The numbers would have been much larger if more women were financially independent.

Since the baby, my husband has become just another child:

- He constantly needs attention.
- He is hornier than ever.
- He smells of cigarettes and alcohol.
- I think he resents the kid, and maybe me.

Being man or woman, being married, being a husband or a wife, and even being a good husband and a good wife do not qualify you to have children. We commonly associate marriage with having children. In fact, the qualifications for being a spouse (described in the first chapter) have little to do with being a parent. In some ways being a lover-husband or a lover-wife may conflict with being a loving father and loving mother.

For some men and women, being a parent comes naturally. Especially, women tend to be innately inclined to be maternal. But not every woman. Some men and women who do not hear "the whisper within" to have children have them anyway ("the right thing to do"; society and the family "expect us to do it"; "it just happens," etc.). They would fare better in their marriage if they were to understand what children are all about (from infancy all the way to late adolescence) and how most effectively to serve their growth and development.

Bonding and Attachment at Birth Emotionally Stabilize the Infant and, in Return, Help Calm the Marriage: What's the Vagina Got to Do with It?

A human being evolves from a creature floating about in its mother's womb. The fetus is part of another being, a real attachment—literally. Original attachment is as much physiological as it is psychological. Carrying a baby in the uterus for nine months, the mother experiencing its movements in her own body, and in return the infant's biological impact on the mother's body are forerunners of bonding. Childbirth through the vagina without general anesthesia may further consolidate that bonding.

Years ago, E. B. Keverne, P. Poindron, and D. R. Lindsay reported on experiments done with female sheep. They could get maternal behavior to occur in nonpregnant female sheep by stimulating their vaginas and cervixes and giving

Bonded babies help to stabilize the marriage:

- Have vaginal delivery if you can. Vaginal birth releases bonding hormones.
- Don't accept general anesthesia, unless absolutely necessary. Local anesthetics are fine. The pain of delivery is real; so is the experience of delivery in full awareness.
- Let the baby quickly find your nipples. It promotes attachment.

them the hormones progesterone and estrogen. Hormones alone, though, were not sufficient. These stimulated ewes developed the full complement of maternal behavior, such as licking and low-pitched bleats. The unstimulated ewes behaved aggressively toward lambs not their own. The authors conclude that there is something about stimulating the vagina and cervix that induces maternal behavior in these animals.

K. M. Kendrick, F. Levy, and E. B. Keverne note that we now know more about the role of hormones in bonding behavior. The vaginal birth process stimulates the release of oxytocin, which leads to maternal behavior. The role of smell and the olfactory bulb in the brain are also apparently important, explain C. M. Dwyer, W. S. Dingwall, and A. B. Lawrence. Clearly, mothers bond with babies born by Caesarian section, but there may be something about the normal vaginal birth process that facilitates bonding.

The issue may be worth considering in light of recent discussions in the medical literature by H. Minkoff and F. A. Chervenak, for example, as well as among pregnant women, about elective (scheduled) Caesarian sections.[1] Some physicians have supported this idea of elective Caesarians. They cite reasons for electing this procedure, such as reducing the incidence of later developing bladder and bowel problems in the mother after a vaginal delivery, as well as the avoidance of an emergency Caesarian, which clearly puts both mother and infant at greater risk. They also cite infection risks more likely with vaginal births, especially mother-to-child transmission of diseases like hepatitis, herpes, or HIV. Further, they note that vaginal birth can be especially detrimental to the infant when labor does not progress. Birth injuries, such as fractures, cerebral palsy, and nerve damage can result.

Caesarian sections, whether elective (scheduled) or emergency, carry their own risks, of course, including risks of surgery itself. Caesarian sections can lead to later development of scarring—or adhesions—in the mother that may require subsequent abdominal surgery. Other authors have cited the importance of vaginal delivery for the development of the infant's lungs and the transition breathing from in utero to external air.

Most obstetricians would not suggest an elective Caesarian unless there are medical reasons to do so, but some are willing to entertain a woman's request. Some women, especially those fearful of the pain of labor and those who want to exert more control over the birth process, are considering the idea and raising it with their obstetricians. We do not support elective Caesarians unless there is a medical indication, either for the mother or for the infant.

The transition from woman to mother is a complicated one, as is the process of bonding with this new individual who has been a part of the mother's body for nine months. The bonding process is the emotional tie from parent to infant and is distinguished from attachment, which is the tie from infant to parent. Researchers Marshall H. Klaus and John H. Kennell believe that there is a sensitive period within the first few hours after birth that is critical to the bonding process. They do not support anything that would interfere with that process, such as elective Caesarian section. They even encourage breast-feeding immediately after birth and skin-to-skin contact between mother and infant. They have seen this practice lead to a lower incidence of child abuse and abandonment in at-risk populations. They are disheartened by the process whereby newborns are whisked away for routine cleaning and evaluation by the attending staff before the mother is even able to touch her newborn. The researchers also cite the importance for fathers to be in the delivery room and to have immediate contact with their newborns and to look at them "en face" in the first few hours of life.[2] Anecdotally, some mothers have expressed mixed feelings about their husbands' presence during labor and delivery. Witnessing the entire birth process desexualizes a woman's genitals. In fact, perhaps as a result, some couples feel less sexual toward each other after the birth of the baby.

However, many new couples, especially mothers, are so worn out by labor that they welcome the hospital staff's assistance in caring for their babies well beyond the first few moments after birth. One mother even confessed temporary feelings of anger with her newborn for the pain he had caused her during the labor process. The point is that the bonding and attachment process is just that—a process over time. Parents should not be made to feel guilty because they cannot or do not conform to some standard. In most situations, there will be plenty of time for the parents to feel comfortable with and evolve into their new role of parents.

Integrating Father into the Mother-Infant Unit

Harold: *"I wish you would desire me. Since the baby was born, you don't kiss me; you don't let me caress your breasts; occasionally you turn your back and grudgingly allow me to get in; I am not supposed to even breathe hard with the fear that 'his highness' may be disturbed. How many years will this go on like that?"* Harold complained.

Judy: *"Don't exaggerate, Harold, my breasts are very sensitive. Every breast-feeding mother is that way. They hurt with touch; and you don't just gently caress them. You grab them,"* she replied. *"Furthermore, you seemed to be disgusted with my smell anyway."*

Harold: *"I grab them?! You don't complain when the baby is literally hanging on your breasts, biting your nipples. And you always smell of powder."*

The rationale of dual sexes goes beyond procreation—to parenthood. A similar dynamic occurs even among same-sex couples, often with one partner of the couple assuming a more maternal role, and the other, a more paternal one. Said Rosie O'Donnell, after marrying her partner, Kelli, in San Francisco, in protest of a proposed constitutional amendment banning same-sex marriage, "This is my brand-new wife." She added there would be no honeymoon what with four children under the age of ten!

A father socializes children and tames their narcissism:

- A father teaches self-protection by being playfully aggressive.
- A father teaches self-sufficiency by being somewhat depriving and disappointing, compared to mother.
- A father teaches competition by nonsympathy.
- A father teaches reality by somewhat frustrating the child; he enables separation from mother.

It is true that children in our contemporary world can—and *do*—survive with only one parent. There is always the haunting question, however, whether they are able to thrive as well. This is not a matter of simple arithmetic, that is, "If one is good, then two are better." Nor is it an indictment of single parenthood, which occurs for a host of reasons and under a variety of (often unavoidable) circumstances. It takes considerable strength to undertake parenthood alone, for whatever practical or psychological reasons. It can also require enormous psychological resources and commitment to reconstruct a life without a spouse. No one usually questions the importance of the mother; a father, however, provides a separate and different dimension.

Research studies of infant-caregiver bonds, as reported by Deborah Blum in *Sex on the Brain*, have demonstrated that infant-mother and infant-father bonds are qualitatively distinct and independent; the former are centrally concerned with attachment needs, and the latter with socialization needs. The relationship between mother and infant is biologically grounded, as in the case of other animal species. The instinctive response to the need for mother's milk, as well as the calming sound of the mother's heartbeat, implicate genetic functions essential for the baby's well-being at the very commencement of life.

On the other hand, the relationship between father and infant is often more socially grounded. The male role in rearing offspring is much more variable, both biologically and culturally. Beyond the contribution of sperm, the father has the roles of protection and providing. Current evidence increasingly reveals that the interaction between father and child facilitates special strengths. Blum reviews literature in which she notes fathers interact with their children differently from mothers; they tend to play harder, tease them more, and are more apt to emphasize physical tasks, athleticism, and tangible accomplishments. At least by outward appearance, they are prone to comfort them less than the maternal figure and, in general, to be less likely to mollify life's disappointments with demonstrable affection. In short, in contrast to the mother, fathers are not as likely to cushion a child against the slings and arrows of their environment.

Men's less sympathetic handling of their children, such as in being resolute, is constructive. Propelling a child beyond his apparent capacity is not necessarily detrimental. Children need to learn how to manage frustration with its subsequent emotional upheavals and unpredictability. Blum further notes that fathers enable children to accomplish that, by keeping them more off balance than mothers. In addition, perhaps ironically, because fathers may be less emotionally accessible than mothers, time spent with fathers can also better teach children about interpreting covert interpersonal cues. Interestingly, fathers apparently invest more in their families when at least one child is a boy. According to studies reported in the *New York Times,* by David Leonhardt, fathers are more active in the care of a child if it is a boy; they are more apt to feed and diaper a boy and more apt to play for a longer time with a boy.

Fathers should be encouraged to play with their children in a way they feel comfortable. One father admitted he was "green with envy" when he saw another father playing so naturally and with so much enjoyment with his young children. He, on the other hand, was "bored to tears" with the drawing and playdough of a four-year-old. He admitted that his own wife was also critical of him for not wanting to sit and play this way with their children. Instead, though, this wife failed to appreciate how her husband, who was more comfortable with Plato than playdough, made up original silly lyrics and his own music with the names of the philosophers. His own children roared with laughter when he would elongate a name like "Nietzsche" in a sing-song way. What this wife did not realize was that this play counts also. Of course, children use play according to their own developmental level, so they were not necessarily learning the names of the philosophers. They were, however, experiencing the warmth and creativity of this father in a way far more important. The point is that parents need to appreciate each other's strengths and not impose some notion of conformity on what they expect from each other.

Of course, the question is, "Is it only fathers who can provide this other kind of relationship for a child?" Andrew Hacker, in *Mismatch,* questions whether a second parental figure must be a man. "After all, Leo Tolstoy was raised by two aunts." The answer is we don't know. Nevertheless, it does make sense, when there are two parents, that each provides a different kind of relationship for the child. What we know is that a paternal influence is particularly successful in the presence of a mother, who continues to supply a child's need for the more obvious forms of affection.

A mother emotionally grounds her children and promotes healthy narcissism:

- A mother builds a child's self-esteem through love and acceptance.
- A mother cushions the child from the slings and arrows of the world.
- A mother spoils a child with excessive empathy.
- A mother offers assurance with her succoring role.
- A mother offers an exclusive attachment.

Generally, we have been dealing with issues of heterosexual couples in marriage. The issues inherent in same-sex couples who live together warrant another book. This is even more so when it comes to same-sex couples who live together with children.

There is a growing literature on coparenting and adoption by same-sex couples. The American Academy of Pediatrics addressed this issue and noted that there are not even accurate statistics on how many children have gay parents. The estimate ranged from one to nine million children in the United States. Statistics are even less accurate on how many children are actually raised by same-sex parents. Studies are also complicated inasmuch as, at least in the past, parents may have presented themselves as straight, had children, and then divorced. Studying this group of children must take into account they are from divorced homes as well.

Of course, there are other means by which same-sex couples have children, including by adoption and sperm or egg donation. These means contribute their own complications when studying parenting. In providing its technical report, the American Academy of Pediatrics focused on the importance of providing a sense of stability for a child and providing legal rights for same-sex parents who are raising children. This report, which reviewed the literature over the past several decades, concluded that there were no systematic differences between gay and nongay parents in emotional health, parenting skills, and attitudes toward parenting. In fact, the discussion noted that since many same-sex couples have to go through hoops to become parents, they are often unusually dedicated and committed to parenting. They also noted that a child's development seems more a function of the nature of the relationships and interactions within a particular family than with its structural form. For example, it seems more important for a child's development whether the same-sex parents are satisfied with their own relationship and whether each parent shares in the responsibility of caring for the children.

Since same-sex marriages have not been legally recognized in the United States, we have no way of knowing how the institution of marriage will affect same-sex parents and their children. Clearly, children raised by same-sex parents, until recently perhaps, have sometimes likely experienced certain social stigma that have placed different burdens on them as they have grown.

The point is that there are many variables in raising children, even in so-called traditional families. Further long-term studies will emerge as same-sex parenting becomes more common.[3]

The Child Needs a Maternal Woman to Become a Healthy Narcissist.

Arno Gruen describes a scene from the film *International Hotel,* in which the comedian W. C. Fields, flying cheerfully through the clouds, suddenly notices that his supply of beer is getting perilously low. He lands on the roof of the International Hotel somewhere in China, where the country's elite are drinking afternoon tea. With a booming but at the same time slightly shaky voice, Fields asks where he is. When the unexpected reply is "Wu Hu," he immediately cries out in concern, "But I'm looking for Kansas City, Kansas." Upon being told in no uncertain terms that he is hopelessly lost, Fields fends off the imminent threat by mimicking the self-centered certainty of those fragile narcissists without a real center. He thus draws himself up to his full height, throws out his falsely inflated chest, and cries out to anyone in doubt, "Kansas City is lost; I am here!" In adults this is a colorful example of full-scale, unrecovered infantile narcissism.

Narcissism—that self-centeredness—is a natural protective state of the infant. During the first year of life, the child is relatively undifferentiated from her mother. The infant uses the mother in an absolute way with utter ruthlessness. Yet there is an attractive quality in children's self-centeredness. The infant's self is first recognized by mother. The infant eventually understands two important overlapping meanings in mother's statement "I love you." They are "You *are loved*" and *"You* are." In a developmentally relevant way, all children need to see themselves as the center of the family, which by extrapolation invariably also means the center of their universe. Commonly, this healthy narcissism is playfully tolerated by both parents. Siblings, on the other hand, usually have very little tolerance for such spoiled brat behavior—as if they were never once there themselves. The disillusionment of the child from such self-overvaluation commences either with the birth of a sibling or with involvement with preschool groups, when the child begins to associate with peers—other centers of the universe.

To some extent, we all require emotional sustenance, which often derives from being the focus of someone else's attention, throughout our lives. From the normal developmental perspective, we are all recovering narcissists. In fact, we first need to experience, and then to outgrow, this infantile narcissism for salutary adult relationships. Simultaneously, remnants of infantile narcissism become a hothouse for pathological narcissism. These remnants are tolerated only by those who are dependent on the adult narcissist, whether emotionally or financially.

Every child is theoretically born virtually perfect. The infant is an unflawed specimen unto itself upon arrival: earnest, without guile, playful, imaginative, loving and affectionate, accepting and trustworthy. This majestic wholesomeness and specialness will not remain unless the child receives validation from his parents. Children are naive believers: if told they are beautiful and intelligent, they will believe those things and behave beautifully and intelligently. *If they are loved, they will believe they are lovable.* When such validity is not forthcoming consistently, the child comes to accept the natural interpretation: "I am not lovable." The child cannot take objective distance and view herself independently of the parents. The child is unable to express, "I know who I am and I am good, but my parents aren't capable of loving me." Only much later, in retrospect, can an adult, who now possesses abstract thinking, reflect on her parents and make that distinction.

If the mother cannot provide sufficient narcissistic supplies to her infant, that child remains famished for love for the remainder of her life. No matter how positive her later experiences, a child still yearns for the love she has never received.

Besides love, the mother must also convey a sense of safety and, therefore, trust. She must present the world as a hospitable place where reality is trustworthy. The child who doesn't experience such love or security blames himself, and he feels innately there is something fundamentally wrong with himself: "It is all my fault and I deserve what I receive." Such a person alternates between malignant self-centeredness and self-effacement (and lack of confidence) wherein no amount of love and trust in the present life is ever completely reassuring.

On the other hand, self-love represents a healthy mind. Such benign self-centeredness is an adult manifestation of a sense of entitlement of the once loved child. It is not to be confused with infantile narcissism or malignant selfishness. This self-love reflects self-esteem, fosters optimism and generosity of mood, and is the fountain of love for others. In Matthew 26:10–12, the story is told of Jesus in Bethany, visiting the home of a man suffering from a skin disease. While sitting there, a woman unexpectedly comes toward Jesus with a bottle of expensive perfume and pours it on his head. His disciples are distressed when they recognize what she had done: they are concerned that having wasted fine perfume she can no longer sell it and donate the money to the unfortunate. Jesus, however, who knows of their concern, turns to them and asks, "Why are you bothering this woman, who has done a beautiful thing for me?" In his infinite wisdom he allays their anger by telling them, "You will always have the poor with you, but you will not always have *me* with you."

Even Jesus wasn't immune from a healthy sense of self-worth, at least expressed at the recognition of his impending death. We, as mortals, need not wait till the termination of our lives to permit ourselves a reasonable feeling of entitlement, whether given or acquired. A healthy dose of narcissism is beneficial. If we don't treat ourselves well, others will be inclined to follow suit. So, if you never experience someone's pouring expensive perfume on your head, buy some yourself and lavish the fragrance all over your own body and, certainly, at least, on your infant's head. There is even a book called *Pamper Yourself: Wear More Cashmere, 151 Luxurious Ways to Pamper Your Inner Princess,* by Jennifer 'Gin' Sander.

Father Helps the Child Separate from the Mother and Recover from Infantile Narcissism.

As the infant matures, he begins to realize mother's otherness, and he loses this sense of oneness with the mother by an insidious process of gradual disappointment. It is the father, however, who substantially threatens the mother-child matrix and thereby generates the initial tension between mother and child. In fact, the classic little boy's Oedipus complex sometimes has more to do with the father's interference with the mother-child relationship than with the child's overt sexual interest in the mother (though it might manifest that way). A father's relationship with the mother constitutes a powerful threat to the child. Once a little boy begins to sense that threat, he reacts to his exclusion not only in terms of the oedipal wish to destroy the rivalrous father but with a desire and need to reinstate his exclusive attachment with his mother. The father, who innately plays the facilitator for separation, sets the stage for boys and girls to experience separation anxiety and to discover peer attachments, as well, before any oedipal phase. Before adolescence, such comforting peer attachments are commonly directed to the same sex, whereas during and after adolescence they apply to both sexes. All our later attachments are accompanied with some anxiety as they rekindle our original threatened attachments.

Are There Only Poor Substitutes for Maternal Care?

Many professionals frequently advise young mothers against their natural instincts. More specifically, such inexperienced mothers are often asked to deprive their children of needed comfort—under the guiding principle of benign neglect, which, in reality, is a kind of maternal malpractice. On the basis of this contemporary theoretical model, mothers sometimes wean infants prematurely and feel they shouldn't pick them up and coddle them no matter how much they cry, for fear of spoiling them. To raise healthy children, parents need only to attune themselves to a child's developmental stage and respond to a child's specific requirements. There are no generalizable principles, except curbing the excessive needs of parents themselves. Parents are often plagued with guilt when they invite total strangers, sometimes under the fancy titles of nannies, governesses, nurses, or au pairs, to care for their infants and children. These caretakers, either privately at home or more commonly in daycare, help shape a child.

The issue of nonmaternal care for infants and young children cannot be ignored or discounted as more and more mothers continue to join the workforce in the United States, as well as worldwide. Nonmaternal care is one of the so-called hot issues for discussion today, and it affects millions of children daily. According to the 2002 U.S. Census Bureau figures, there were seventy-two million children under the age of eighteen living in the United States. Of those, fifty million (69 percent) lived with two parents, and sixteen and a half million (23 percent) lived only with their mothers. Over sixty-three million children (88 percent) lived in families where one or both parents were in the workforce. About thirty-one million children (43 percent) were living in families where two parents were in the workforce! Among children who lived only with their mothers, thirteen million (79 percent) lived in families where the mother was in the workforce.

What is nonmaternal care? It is care provided to a child within a child's home (e.g., another relative or nanny) or outside a child's home (e.g., daycare center with multiple children or private nonmaternal home with one or several children). Studying the effects of nonmaternal care on children is particularly complicated inasmuch as so many other factors contribute to a child's welfare and development.

Most important, of course, is the quality of the nonmaternal care itself. There are many issues to consider, such as the length of time each week a child spends in this care; the amount of total time spent over the course of the first five years of life; and the age an infant or child enters a nonmaternal care setting. For example, infants may be more vulnerable to separation from a mother *after* the first six months, once the attachment process has gotten well underway, rather than earlier in those first few months. An infant normally develops stranger anxiety—anxiety in the presence of someone unfamiliar—around seven or eight months. The particular temperament of a child is also a factor, as there is some suggestion that shy and withdrawn children may have a harder time in some care settings. All of these factors may contribute their effects in unpredictable and complicated ways.

Maternal care: what is best for the child is also what is best for your marriage:

- Breast-feed an infant, if you can, ideally for a year or more.
- Care for your infant yourself, as much as possible, during those first two years of life.
- Keep an infant in close proximity, but brief separations are good for both mother and infant—especially when it means time for husband and wife together.
- Make child care a priority but not your only priority: your husband counts too.

The National Institute of Child Health and Human Development (NICHHD) has conducted a long-term study for the past five years with over thirteen hundred families. While data are not conclusive, there are several trends noted. There is some indication that it is the cumulative quantity of nonmaternal care that is more predictive of social and emotional adjustment and behavior problems rather than the amount of time spent at any one age. In the 1980s, Belsky and Rovine studied attachment and nonparental care. The researchers found some evidence that extensive nonparental care is a risk factor for insecure attachment in infants.

Additional studies by Susan C. Crokenberg have noted that boys tend to be more vulnerable to nonmaternal care and more likely to show behavior problems by kindergarten. Other studies by Sarah E. Watamura and colleagues have shown that some children in nonmaternal care experience higher levels of cortisol, the hormone that rises when we are stressed.[4] Some studies have shown that other children, in general, become more aggressive and less compliant in the nonmaternal care setting. The statistics, however, are not overwhelming. Not surprisingly, children did better long-term when they grew up with mothers who were not depressed; who were more highly educated, more sensitive in general to their child's needs, more supported by their husbands, and less conflicted about their return to work; and who had greater economic resources at their disposal for their children.

In summary, one has to consider the choices parents have available and the particular sex and temperament of a child in making a decision about nonmaternal care. Obviously, the more stable the environment and caretaker, the better for the child. There is no absolute or correct decision about choosing to use nonmaternal care. Like any other decision, there is a context for the decision and, obviously, like all decisions, there are trade-offs. What is essential, however, is that your decision not reflect your own needs exclusively but rather primarily focus on the best interest of your child.

For example, some mothers may, for their own reasons, avoid any separation from their children, particularly in the first year of life. Their decision to be with their children for twenty-four hours a day may have less to do with the needs of their newborns than their own conflicts about separation and excessive, irrational fears that some harm will befall their children if they are not present all the time. These are the mothers who are constantly running in to check that their infant is breathing. They develop the preoccupation that no one else can care for their children at all. These mothers are so child-focused they run the risk of creating a child-centered marriage if this behavior continues.[5] These child-centered marriages are some that are most vulnerable to affairs, according to Shirley Glass, in her studies on infidelity. Laura Schlessinger, in her aptly titled book *The Proper Care and Feeding of Husbands,* believes it is "life-or-death" to the marriage to make certain a husband feels he is part of his wife's fulfillment—not just her children. She notes she has received hundreds of letters from husbands who feel "marginalized" after their children are born.

Breast-Feeding Makes Both Mother and Infant Healthy and Content, but It May Make the Father Feel Like an Intruder.

Harold: *"Why do you think that when Billy gets hurt or needs something he goes to Ana? Then you get upset. The kid isn't attached to you.*

You keep saying, 'Billy, I am your mother.' It doesn't do, wouldn't do, any good. Yes, you are his mother, but on paper. You gave him up for adoption to Ana. Now you want to fire her because she stole your child? Thank God we have Ana. And so what if she doesn't follow the exact directions for bottle feeding? Furthermore, Billy's colic is not due to her incompetence as you believe, but is, in fact, very common, the doctor said, with cow's milk. You have no right to complain about this, for you didn't even breast-feed the kid for a few weeks, because you were worried that your breasts would sag."

Judy: *"No, not just that. I don't want someone to suck milk out of my breasts. Breast-feeding is a primitive behavior. I am not a cow!" she protested.*

A common need of parents is to view bottle feeding as the norm and see it as preferable and even superior to breast-feeding. Some parents view breast-feeding as purely nutritional and more of a bother than a necessity. They may think of the breasts as sexual organs and feel uncomfortable with the idea of an infant—let alone a one- or two-year-old suckling at the breast. Says Natalie Angier, "Think of your own feelings about a full glass of human milk in the refrigerator . . . the idea is disturbing and almost 'cannibalistic.'"

Part of this "Culture of Misinformation," as Katherine Dettwyler calls it, stems from the multibillion-dollar infant formula industry. The industry, after all, has a vested interest in wanting mothers to switch to formula, as soon as possible and, certainly, at least eventually. Dettwyler compares the infant formula industry to the tobacco industry and wonders if someday cans of infant formula will have to carry a warning label from the surgeon general stating "use of formula may be dangerous to your infant's health."

Of course, before the advent of infant formulas and the availability of clean water, almost all women breast-fed or employed a wet nurse for their babies. In the past one hundred years, breast-feeding has enjoyed intermittent popularity. More recently, as Cynthia Zembo reports, in a review article, breast-feeding is more common among women who are older, college educated, white, married, and of middle or higher income levels. The American Academy of Pediatrics recommends breast-feeding for twelve months or longer, and the World Health Organization recommends it for two years. In the United States today, however, most infants are weaned well before their first birthday—often by two or three months when many mothers return to work.

The advantages to breast-feeding are staggering. Breast-feeding leads to a release of both oxytocin and prolactin in the mother, both of which help the mother to relax and experience a sense of well-being. Breast milk is perfect nutritionally for the first six months, after which iron-rich foods are recommended

Breast-feeding: what is best for the child is also best for the mother:

- Breast-feeding relaxes a mother and gives her a sense of well being.
- Breast-feeding lowers the frequency of colic and other high-pitched distress signs in the infant and is thus less stressful on the mother.
- Breast-feeding lowers the risk of premenopausal breast cancer.
- Breast-feeding keeps a new mother's weight down. It is a superb calorie burner.
- Breast-feeding is a good contraceptive: it tends to prevent pregnancy too soon after the first.

as a supplement. It has over two hundred components, says Zembo, many of which act directly to destroy or inactivate pathogens and protect the infant. It has been called a "gold standard" by Ruth Lawrence and a "broad-spectrum medication" by Doren Frederickson, as well as a "biological soup" by Yitzhak Koch, in a 1996 interview by Deborah Blum. Breast-feeding infants have a decreased incidence of infections (e.g., gastrointestinal or ear), sudden infant death syndrome, and childhood obesity, according to some studies. Their immunity, says Allan Cunningham, in general, is better than bottle-fed infants, and this lasts not just for six months, but for years. There are even studies such as those by P. J. Quinn and colleagues, as well as A. Jain, J. Concatto, and J. M. Levanthal, that conclude breast-feeding promotes intelligence and cognitive development, although these conclusions are more suspect. Further, mothers who breast-feed their children at young ages and for long duration seem, in some studies, to have a lower risk of premenopausal breast cancer, notes Marc Micozzi. And breast-feeding is a superb calorie burner—a woman can consume *at least* five hundred more calories a day and still lose her pregnancy weight, reports Steven Gabbe and colleagues.[6]

Says Angier, "The more we look at breast milk . . . the more we are driven to marvel that anybody can survive, much less thrive, on its wretched artificial substitute. Yet many have." The point is that, in the best of all worlds, breast-feeding is ideal for both mother and infant—from a nutritional, immunological, and emotional view—and we strongly encourage mothers to breast-feed as long as possible, at least for a year. The reality is that for most mothers breast-feeding in our current American culture is not encouraged. Workplaces and public places are not "breast-feeding-friendly establishments," as Dettwyler suggests. Further, work schedules, with fairly inflexible hours, are often not conducive to a breast-feeding schedule for women. And breasts, at least in American culture, are clearly seen as sexual. Millions of women yearly undergo surgery for breast enlargement to make themselves more sexually desirable. Breast-feeding is seen as something like sex, to be done in private. Perhaps, someday, that attitude will change more dramatically than it has so far—the way Americans have changed their attitude toward smoking.

Furthermore, there are women who have pain and discomfort during breast-feeding, such as painful, infected nipples or clogged milk ducts. And some women cannot breast-feed because they take medications that pass directly into breast milk. These women should not be made to feel inadequate by their spouses or friends. Again, the important point is that the decision to breast-feed and the length of time for it should not reflect exclusively the needs of the mother. Interestingly, a father's support is often crucial in a woman's determination to breast-feed, emphasize Heide Littman, Sharon vanderBrug Medendorp, and Johanna Goldfarb.

Colicky Infants Make Spouses Scream at Each Other.

There is another issue concerning the care of an infant that may contribute to stress on and conflict between new parents. This is the issue of colic, or crying that is excessive and prolonged, during which an infant is less able to be comforted. Some sources have used the "rule of threes"—crying for three or more hours at a time on three or more days a week for more than three weeks in defining colic, say Sijmen Reijneveld, Emily Brugman, and Remy Hirasing. Obviously, the prevalence of colic depends on the definition, from less than 2 percent when criteria are most stringent to about 12 percent when criteria are less stringent. Sometimes, colic is in the ear of the beholder.

Ronald Barr, a researcher who has studied colic for the past fifteen years, and his associate, Megan Gunnar, believe that colic remains puzzling and mostly unexplained. He also notes that sometimes this excessive crying may be indicative of disease, but in about 95 percent of cases colic is self-limiting and not related to either medical disease or severely pathological caretaking conditions. In one study of five hundred infants, more than 85 percent of colic cases had remitted by three months, report Tammy Clifford and colleagues. Most parents cope with reassurance that the behavior will remit and is rarely related to disease or their parenting errors. Those, usually the mothers, who require professional assistance are concerned with the infant's consolability, the presence of gastrointestinal symptoms, and the presence of a particularly disturbing, painful cry.

Some have suggested colic is an early manifestation of difficult temperament, but Barr does not accept that hypothesis. He studied the caregiving of the

!Kung San hunter-gatherers in Africa. These mothers hold their infants constantly, in a sling, in an upright position; breast-feed continually (many times an hour for a few minutes a feed); and respond immediately to an infant's crying. Barr found that duration of crying and fretting was half as much with the !Kung San as with American infants, even though the crying frequency was the same. He believes that caregiving strategies may not affect whether an infant cries but could modify how long the crying persists.

The !Kung San style of caregiving demands considerably more than most new mothers in America can offer, and clearly, Barr believes, there is more to the syndrome of colic than frequent feedings and constant holding. Many mothers, however, feel considerable guilt that their behavior contributes to the distress of their infants. In turn, many fathers may blame their wives for their inconsolable infants. The high-pitched scream of an infant is probably one of the worst sounds imaginable. Parents feel so helpless and incompetent. This environment is hardly conducive to intimacy between spouses.

The point is that the more educated the parents are, the less likely they are to blame each other for their infant's distress. Knowing that the behavior is transient may enable parents to work together, rather than as adversaries.

Who's Been Sleeping in My Bed? Only Your Spouse Belongs There.

Consoling a crying child may lead to a rift developing between parents. Often one parent, usually the wife, wants to bring the child into the parental bed. This may occur at any age in a child—from infancy on—and may have serious consequences on the relationship between the parents.

When parents allow a baby to sleep with them, they may themselves have separation issues. For example, a mother or father may fear something will happen to the baby in the parent's absence, for example, sudden infant death syndrome (SIDS). Initially, parents may bring a crying baby into the parental bed for comfort. Sometimes, the baby may actually be ill. Later, out of their anxieties, they may develop a pattern of bringing the baby into bed and finding reasons to repeat this behavior nightly, regardless of the infant's needs.

Sometimes, a mother, in particular, may use a baby as a wedge between her and her husband, sometimes as a means of avoiding sex. Older children are often used this way. An older child may complain of a scary dream and wish to get into bed with the parents. Parents, then, to avoid intimacy with each other, may allow a child to stay night after night. Sometimes, parents have even admitted they will bring a child into their bed and have the other spouse sleep in the child's room—or else one parent will go to the child's room and sleep with the child—leaving the other spouse alone in the parental bedroom.

Clearly, children sometimes need to be comforted, especially at night. When parents, however, are using their children for their own needs and creating a wedge between each other as a consequence, their marriage will undoubtedly suffer.

Mother's Voice Feeds the Infant's Brain: Let Intelligent Children Strengthen Your Marriage.

Judy: *"Harold, I bet your mother never breast-fed you, sang lullabies, played and talked with you all day long. You are an obsessive, hypercritical, stingy, and overbearing person. Since I got pregnant, you have been on my case. I can do nothing right. As if you are always looking for an excuse to criticize me. Since the middle of my pregnancy you wouldn't even make love to me."*

Harold: *"Because your attitude toward Billy turns me off. No, my mother didn't do all these things either; she was a sick woman. But what is wrong with you? Here is our son who is trying to engage you with his smiles and touch, and you are holding him as if he is a doll. You are going to make him a neurotic person."*

Judy: *"It makes no difference who feeds him as long as someone does. Let Ana sing the lullaby; she has a better voice than I or you do. No, on second thought, please don't sing. You cannot even carry a simple tune and your voice is like, like aah . . . , as if it is coming not from your lungs but from your bowels. Have you noticed that the kid cries the most when you sing to him?"*

Women, especially mother herself, communicate with an infant in a special way during feedings, even if it is a bottle feeding. Infants are particularly sensitive to their mother's voices. The higher scale of a woman's vocalizations for infants is not only emotionally soothing but also stimulating to the brain for verbal and emotional receptivity. Mothers use a particularly high, sing-song voice when talking to their infants. Ann Fernald has found that mothers, to elicit an infant's attention, use wide-range contours but often end with a rising pitch. Fathers, as well as other adults, also speak more slowly and with higher pitch to an infant. This same maternal voice pattern of high pitch and exaggerated intonation occurs cross-culturally, including among American, European, Asian, and African cultures. Fernald notes that initially this pattern of speech serves to engage the infant's attention and to communicate affective meaning. Only later, by the end of the first year, does this intonation serve more linguistic functions. Fernald further notes that it is surprising how recent research on infants' perceptions of emotional signals has focused on the face almost exclusively (recognition of which actually develops slowly) rather than the voice, which is more powerful than the face as a social signal to the infant. The voice, then, becomes an important tool for the infant to experience what Fernald calls an "emotional communion," not unlike child researcher Daniel N. Stern's "emotional attunement" between mother and infant. It is, in fact, the mother's voice, even more than her heartbeat, that is preferred by infants. Mothers, though, instinctively seem to cradle their infants on the left, where the heart is.

The psychological birth of an infant helps cement the relationship between spouses:

- Keep the baby on your left side to tune into your heartbeat. The baby will be calmer and may gain more weight (low anxiety and low basal metabolism).
- Talk to your infant with a sing-song, high-pitched voice in his left ear; it stimulates the right brain's verbal and especially emotional receptivity.
- Look into your baby's eyes long and patiently: it establishes an emotional communion.
- Frequently touch, caress, and later on tickle and tease your child. It fosters the child's psychological birth.

Hold the Infant Close to Your Heart (Literally); It Helps in Language and Affect Acquisition.

In the early 1970s, pediatrician Lee Salk noted this finding and concluded that babies preferred the left because the sound of the mother's heartbeat had a soothing and comforting effect on infants. Of over 250 right-handed mothers, 83 percent held their babies on their left side during the first days after birth. Even left-handed mothers overwhelmingly (78 percent) held their babies instinctively on the left. Salk also noted that in almost five hundred works of art (paintings and sculptures), 80 percent of these works depicted the infant being held on the mother's left side. Salk went so far as to say that babies exposed to the sound of a maternal heartbeat (when this sound was presented day and night experimentally in the newborn nursery) gained more weight and had less crying in the nursery.

Salk, further, studied over one hundred mothers who had separation from their newborns within the first twenty-four hours after birth—usually as a result of premature birth. He compared these mothers with over two hundred others who had no separation within the first twenty-four hours. The mothers who had been separated from their infants did not show a side preference (53 percent). Salk concluded that this early separation (but not necessarily the length of the separation) affected the mothers' preferential holding response. He likened this response to a kind of "imprinting" response similar to that seen in birds.

More recent studies question some of Salk's conclusions. Nevertheless, the observation that mothers do prefer left-sided cradling does stand. J. S. Sieratzki and B. Woll focus instead on the role of communication of affect between mother and infant and believe protection and facilitation of this interchange is at the core of left-sided cradling. They focus on the role of the right hemisphere of the brain. These authors note that language is produced by the interaction of both hemispheres. The left hemisphere controls word, content, grammar, and syntax, whereas the right hemisphere controls intonation and affective intent. In left cradling, the mother communicates affective signals to the infant's left ear, which in turn are processed by the infant's right hemisphere. There is a kind of feedback system between mother and infant. The authors suggest that these neurolinguistic mechanisms may be important in the early course of language development for the infant.

Look into the Infant's Eyes Lovingly. The Baby's Self Is Formed in the Maternal Gaze. In Return, an Infant's Strong Sense of Self Will Help Your Marriage.

> Thus wondrously within your eyes I saw myself unfold.
>
> —Friedrich Hebbel

We begin by being loved. The mother-infant gaze-to-gaze mirroring attunes both of them to each other, inducing attachment, establishing mutual validation. The mother as the first "other" is an absolute necessity to the very constitution of the child's self. Her love for her baby initiates a self-organizing process for the infant. This love in mutual gazing is what distinguishes ordinary personal relations from a self-forming relationship.

In this animate dialogue with the mother, the infant experiences the mother's love. This early experience is the elementary basis of all knowing. That is why it is said that the root of knowledge is love, not reason. Ultimately, coming into our own being requires the knowledge of being loved, hopefully, by both parents. From such a child emanates an all loving attitude that heals many wounds in a marriage.

But if we are not loved in those formative years, our self never crystallizes. Such a person will engage only in the craving for love and not for its fulfillment. Parents will experience frustration and will not know how to meet the child's needs. In exasperation they tend to reject the child or attack each other for causing it. Such children seem interested in the repetition of this initial rejection, not in its contemporary reparation. When they grow up, these individuals love others excessively, if not fantastically (i.e., based on fantasy). Those who are deprived of parental love seem to yearn for it in life and find themselves only reassured in its absence. This seeming masochism may be temporarily interrupted by being loved, but not for too long. The search for love from the unloving isn't primarily masochistic—it is a search for self-invalidation. As paradoxical as it might sound, for such persons, their identity is in not being loved. Even at its most excruciating moments, this profound yearning for love can provide a deep emotional high, unsurpassed by any other experience in life—including that of being loved.

Children's genetic illnesses (physical and psychological) are lifelong stresses on the marriage:

- Don't marry even distant relatives.
- Don't marry within your tribe.
- If you must marry within your tribe, get genetic testing.
- Don't decide to marry someone while on birth control pills. You may be attracted to the wrong genetic male.
- Don't smoke, drink, or use recreational or over-the-counter drugs, and be advised about prescription drugs from the beginning of insemination until birth. Women should continue these cautions through breast-feeding.

Affectionately Teased and Tickled Infants Learn to Be Playful and, in Return, Bring Joy to the Marriage.

Tickling and grooming of the infant are the earliest expressions of affection and intimate playfulness. By the fourth month of the child's development, tickling becomes an important form of communication. Interestingly enough, L.

Weiskrantz, J. Elliott, and C. Darlington note that infants younger than four months old cannot be tickled! Never mind the prospect of delighting in it; tickling during those early months seems to disturb them. Relating to someone requires differentiation from that person. The psychological birth of the child as well as development of proprioceptive senses takes over two years to develop.

As unusual as it seems, we can inflict suffering on ourselves, but we cannot provide affection. Although we can give ourselves a solo tactile sensation, such as the excitation of masturbation or other self-stimulation, we cannot tickle ourselves, emphasize Weiskrantz and colleagues. The reason for this is that tickling is an *interactive* tactile response. It is a prototype of affectionate engagement with another, a pleasurable losing of our own boundaries. The tickling sensation declines with age, and verbal teasing replaces it. In addition, it sometimes becomes removed from the privacy of two people and later requires an audience. For example, in some cultures, verbal teasing assumes the quality of friendly argument. Deborah Tannen notes that Eastern Jewish couples' bickering and argumentative positions in social situations are sometimes forms of bonding and grooming in public and not necessarily reflective of their disagreements or dislike of each other. Such sparring continues for hours as long as there is an audience. This bickering becomes stabilized into a family routine and reflects signs of a bond and genuine friendship. Deborah Schiffrin makes the point that arguments, particularly, are designed to show just how close the relationship is. In other words, it is close enough to withstand what would be considered verbal assaults by outsiders.

Robin Dunbar's exploration of grooming, gossip, and the evolution of language describes how apes and monkeys, for example, spend much time stroking, scratching, and picking at each other's fur. However, they are apparently not performing these behaviors for the assumed purpose of hygiene. This is based on the observation that even after having removed all signs of ticks or fleas from a coat of a fellow ape, these animals will still show various forms of seemingly nonutilitarian grooming behavior, like petting and pinching. Moreover, they will continue until the recipient of their attention and affection is rapt in apparent pleasure. The time and devotion given to grooming, which at least theoretically would be better spent in more life-preserving behaviors, such as foraging, suggests that these interactive, communicative behaviors also have priority in these animals' lives.

God Is the Busiest Abortionist: Don't Get Upset with Miscarriages; In Fact, Be Grateful That Your Body Is Doing You and Your Family a Great Favor.

A substantial proportion of all fertilized eggs are never implanted or are aborted spontaneously very early in pregnancy. Most of the latter show chromosomal abnormalities. It thus appears that the human female body has a remarkable mechanism for detecting abnormal embryos and aborting them naturally. In fact, this special prenatal phenomenon serves as a significant adaptive function: it prevents an unnecessary investment—psychological and physical—in a growing fetus marked for dire consequences, that is, a newborn who invariably will die young or be greatly handicapped should it survive beyond infancy.

In her article "The First Week," Deborah Blum interviews the anatomist Allen Enders, who notes that the average miscarriage rate, usually due to severe genetic errors in the developing fetus, is approximately 50 percent for a one-week-old human embryo. Blum notes that Enders used to attend antiabortion rallies to argue that nature is far more efficient and ruthless than any abortionist and that, in fact, we can consider God the world's greatest abortionist!

Diversify Your Portfolio of Genes: The Best Gift You Can Give Your Children is the Genes from Another Tribe.

"I was too young and uninformed when I got married. We lived in a very small town. So I had no idea that Eastern European Jews have all those genetic illnesses. The only thing that everyone was concerned about was whether I was Jewish enough to be accepted into his family and his congregation. But now that our daughter is born blind and not growing at all, I realize what a serious situation I am in. I had no idea we were both carriers for Tay-Sachs disease—no one suggested we get genetic testing.

She is going to die, the doctor says. I want to have children. But do I dare to get pregnant again? Benjamin says I must not lose my faith. Which faith? Don't you think he should have at least mentioned that his sister had a miscarriage. What am I going to do? I was beginning to like being Orthodox; now, whenever I am in the synagogue, I watch other women around me with a mysterious smile pasted on their faces. I hate them. There is another victim with reddish hair, a little older than I. She glances at me occasionally with the conspiratorial look of a prisoner."

Through our dominant genes, we inherit our physical characteristics and personality traits, and also our predispositions to physical and even psychological disorders. To possess a dominant gene means that if you have even one copy of it, you will acquire all of its characteristics. This can become a serious matter as it relates to genetic illnesses. Fortunately, most genetic disorders are transmitted through recessive genes. Unless we receive two copies of the same genes from our parents—which is more likely to happen in the marriages of close relatives—we are immune from that genetic disorder.

Randolph M. Nesse and George C. Williams discuss some of the diseases that can be inherited genetically. For example, Tay-Sachs disease, which kills its victims 100 percent of the time by early childhood, is found in 3 to 11 percent of Ashkenazi (Eastern European) Jews. When two Ashkenazi Jews marry, they, of course, should be encouraged to have genetic testing prior to conceiving to see if they are both carriers.

If the couple in the above vignette had discussed their genetic disposition and if they had had genetic testing initially, they would not have found themselves in that particular medical nightmare. Their condition was definitely a rare one, but more common genetic inheritances can be prevented with genetic counseling. Does this sound like a business transaction? Yes, it is. Marriage, at times, is as much a business transaction as are many others.

Interestingly, almost all religions prohibit sexual relations between blood relatives. These taboos become stronger as the family circle narrows. The further away we are from our own extended family, and even from our own town and tribe, the less likely we will replicate our genes, including the ones leading to disorders.

A dictum against incest has transcended the boundaries of time, culture, and class—as well as reason. William Mueller notes that early Christianity was among the most extreme, calling it "incest" even if you married your thirty-second cousin. He tells of seeing an ancient manuscript, the "Table of Affinity and Kindred," in St. Mary's parish, Yorkshire, England. In this document, the church delineated forty-eight degrees of forbidden marriages, including warnings against men and women cohabiting with their opposite-sexed grandparents. Blair and Rita Justice note that traditionally Chinese men were forbidden to marry any woman who merely happened to possess the identical surname. They also describe how a host of societies and cultures has viewed incest as so inherently evil and deserving of God's wrath that these cultures have blamed incest for major global natural disasters and epidemics, such as the sterility of cattle in ancient Egypt and the failure of the potato harvest in Ireland.

Recalling Marriages Consummated While on the Pill: Don't Pick a Husband While on the Pill; You May Choose the Genetically Wrong Father for Your Child.

"I never, never thought I would marry the guy next door. I disliked everything about Scarsdale: my family, all our nouveau riche neighbors, the goyish Rabbi and his equally phony and pretentious clients, and I

mean clients. I don't know what happened. I ended up marrying literally the guy-next-door.

When we were in high school, I wouldn't even talk to Michael. He was a sort of nerdy kid, a kind of relative that you are embarrassed by. I dated a number of guys whom I thought of as potential husbands. During the college years, I saw him occasionally during the holidays and never exchanged more than a few words. Three years ago when we met at a party, he seemed totally transformed. He was a budding lawyer, tall and self-confident. I slept with him that night; he was fine. God, in those days thanks to the pill everyone slept with everyone. Except him; obviously he was a virgin. Can you believe that? So, he was so thrown off with his experience with me that he proposed the following week, and I actually liked the idea and accepted his proposal of marriage. He wanted children quickly, so I stopped the birth control pills. Bingo! Nine months later we had Laura. Since the beginning of my pregnancy we had no sex, I mean I didn't want to. I couldn't stand his even touching me. I am ashamed to say that I despise him. And the man has done nothing wrong. He is a good man. But all my high school feelings toward him came back with full vengeance. What have I done? What am I going to do?"

There are other natural selections that prevent the formation of incestuous gene pools. Research by Claus Wedekind and his colleagues suggest that women are most attracted to the scent of men with genes different from their own. One implication is that our biology predisposes us toward a mate who will provide a presumably healthy mixture of genes. These researchers studied MHC, or major histocompatibility complex—a group of genes that are a key marker for distinguishing self from others immunologically that influence body odors and body odor preferences. They found that women's preferences depended on their hormone status, that is, in this situation, whether they were taking oral contraceptives.

In a study using odor from men's T-shirts, the researchers found that the pleasantness of men's body odor, as scored by women students in their twenties, depended on MHC. Women who were not taking oral contraceptives perceived men who had different MHC as more pleasant than those men with similar MHC. The reverse happened when the women were on oral contraceptive pills.

Here again, we have managed to interfere with a healthy natural phenomenon. The scientific progress that devised the pill to prevent pregnancy also resulted in disrupting a woman's hormonal specificity that enabled her to be attracted to the right genetic male, that is, a man with an immunological system opposite to herself. Unfortunately, women who take oral contraceptives found themselves most attracted to men with similar immunological systems. Thus, the contraceptive pill seemed to interfere with finding one's natural mate, that is, one with an appropriately different immunological system. Wedekind and colleagues explain that perfumes and deodorants, as well as the pill, may also disturb normal hormonal and olfactory mechanisms in mate selection. In *Sex on the Brain,* Blum thus poses a highly charged question, "whether the pill has influenced a whole generation of women toward the 'wrong' men."

Wedekind and colleagues also note that MHC may influence a woman's ability to conceive with a particular man. These authors found that couples who suffer from recurrent spontaneous abortions often share with each other a higher portion of their MHC than control couples who don't share as many. The researchers conclude that in inbred populations, these effects could be adaptive: avoid inbreeding by using MHC as a marker for kinship.

Avoid Toxic Substances: Even Minor Mutations in Your Genes Can Generate Various Illnesses and Behavioral Problems in Your Children.

"I cannot believe our child, our own little Al, whom we love dearly, and taught our life values, is drowning kittens in the bathtub. We've emphasized good manners, how to be a compassionate human being, care about other people, and fear of the law. We are God-loving, decent people. No one in my family or my wife's family ever had any problem with the law. Both of my brothers had learning disabilities, and I think they were a little unruly in school and got suspended a few times, but that is it. Al has a minor version of it, according to the psychologist who tested him in second grade. Anyway, my brothers wouldn't hurt an ant. We don't have guns in the house; we don't watch violent shows; my wife and I never fight, at least never in front of the children, or say nasty things about someone else. I am a mild-mannered person, as you know. I never hit him or scolded him very harshly. And we thought he was an equally gentle kid; he was, until his sister was born a year and a half ago. Since then we've noticed some aggressive behavior toward his mother but nothing to be alarmed about. We thought he was just a little jealous of his sister's coming to displace him from being the only focus of our attention for over six years.

About two months ago, when our cat, which he loved, had a litter of four kittens, he was very happy. Of course, we were thinking of giving away all but one to friends or whoever wanted them. A month ago, one of the kittens disappeared. While we kept searching the house, Al was watching television, totally indifferent to the whole thing. It was so uncharacteristic of him that I had to take him aside and ask him whether he knew where the kitten was. I thought maybe he was playing a sort of hide-and-seek game with us at the expense of the animal. He had a strange smile on his face that I had never seen before. Have you seen Jack Nicholson's movie The Shining? *That expression: 'I found the kitten dead, so I put it into the garbage bag.' I told him that he should have alerted us of the kitten's death and not simply disposed of it. I let it go, though with unease. A few days later my wife found another one of the kittens dead in the toilet bowl. Of course she was petrified. This time Al looked upset himself. So we all concluded the kitten tried to drink water from the bowl, fell into it, and couldn't get out and drowned. Case closed! Wait, it gets worse! The following morning the other two kittens were floating dead in the bathtub. This time, Al couldn't even deny it because his hands were full of scratches and bites. The poor kittens must have fought hard to save themselves.*

Well, here we are. Al doesn't explain why he did it, except 'there were too many.' No signs of guilt or remorse. Is the boy crazy? Can he hurt the baby? We are coming to the end of our rope!"

We enter the world with inborn wiring that provides us with the necessary hardware—about ten trillion cells—for living our normal lives. Our bodies, brains included, are the consequence of the multiplication of the two original cells that are differentiating and replicating simultaneously. The considerable precision by which this process occurs is highly resilient as well as sensitive and vulnerable. For example, say Nesse and Williams, it requires only a single error in the DNA of a sperm or an egg to cause a fatal genetic disease. Such mistakes emerge from many sources, including chemical damage, copying errors, or ionizing radiation. Surprisingly, given the many sources of error and their disastrous impact, these mistakes do not occur more frequently. The likelihood of any genetic alteration has been estimated as one per million per generation. This translates to approximately 5 percent of the population beginning life with at least one original mutation from either parent. Amazingly, in most cases, these mutations have no discernible effects except in the brain; in others they may cause only minor physical effects. Just a few are fatal.

Minor errors in chromosomes, however, can have considerable impact on an individual's psyche, and even seemingly insignificant mutations may alter dramatically one's psychological makeup. Unusual patterns of thinking, feeling, and behaving are manifestations of genetic brain conditions, some of which are obvious and predictable, such as the tangential speech of schizophrenics and the circumstantiality of manics. These are the results of major alterations. A minor mutation may tend to reveal itself under the umbrella rubric of minimum brain disorders, such as attention deficit, hyperactivity, and learning disabilities.

Some undetectable mutations in genes can generate certain behaviors. These are *not* manifestations of disease, but rather aberrations nevertheless, in a person who otherwise behaves quite normally. For example, parents are often shocked to learn that their otherwise gentle son tortures animals or that their well-bred daughter shoplifts. Others in the community can barely believe that an honorable judge makes obscene phone calls, a respected teacher joins a cult, a minister steals money from his congregation, a priest molests altar boys, or a presumed devoted mother kills her children to be available for her boyfriend. Society usually attaches a diagnostic label to such behavior, such as "psychotic" or "sociopathic." In spite of all these classification attempts, these individuals are sometimes unclassifiable as they remain widely different. For most of these aberrations, we have not as yet mapped their locations on the genome. Aberrations of these sorts will increase multifold with each generation. Nesse and Williams note that only about 7 percent of human genes differ from person to person; a count of potential variations and combinations, however, is in the millions. Furthermore, our brain is very malleable and fluctuates constantly based on our life experiences. We are all born with a basic set of instructions. How we conjure up the experiences and images of our life, explains Benson, depends on a pattern of brain activity called a "neurosignature." Each of us has a unique neurosignature, depending on these experiences and the emotions we call upon as well. The human brain, however, constantly acquires additional nerve cell activation patterns. In the final analysis, there is no "normal" human genetic makeup, and there is no genetic standard. We all have our own, highly individual genetic flaws, which constitute ourselves.

Short of genetically manufacturing babies (even that wouldn't necessarily prevent mutation), the only thing parents can do is to minimize the potential for aberrations. This would mean that both spouses avoid toxic substances at the time of conception and, in fact, preferably long before that. It would also entail protecting the child from harmful substances during growth and development, as well.

These toxic substances can be legal and recreational, such as cigarettes and alcohol, or illegal and recreational, such as marijuana and cocaine; they can be prescription medications, such as commonly used sleeping pills, tranquilizers, antidepressants, or uncommonly used ones. They can also be teratogens, such as foods with certain preservatives, or they can be environmental, such as pesticides, high voltage electricity, polluted water, toxic dumps, and car fumes.

Notes

1. H. Minkoff and F. A. Chervenak, "Elective Primary Cesarean Delivery," *New England Journal of Medicine* 348 (10) (March 6, 2003): 946–50. See also letter to editor in

reply, "Elective Primary Cesarean Delivery," *New England Journal of Medicine* 348 (23) (June 5, 2003): 2364–65.

2. Marshall H. Klaus and John H. Kennell, *Bonding: The Beginnings of Parent-Infant Attachment,* ed. Antonia W. Hamilton, rev. ed. (New York: New American Library, 1983, 1–2); Marshall H. Klaus and John H. Kennell, "Routines in Maternity Units: Are They Still Appropriate for 2002?" *Birth* 28 (4) (December 2001): 274–76; John H. Kennell and Marshall H. Klaus, "Bonding: Recent Observations That Alter Perinatal Care," *Pediatrics in Review* 19 (1) (January 1998): 4–12.

3. American Academy of Pediatrics: Committee on Psychosocial Aspects of Child and Family Health, "Coparent or Second-Parent Adoption by Same-Sex Parents," *Pediatrics* 109 (2) (February 2002): 339–40. See also Letters to the Editor: "Adoption by Same-Sex Parents," *Pediatrics* 110 (2) (August 2002): 419–20; "What's Best for the Child?" *Pediatrics* 110 (2) (August 2002): 420; and Ellen C. Perrin and the Committee on Psychosocial Aspects of Child and Family Health (American Academy of Pediatrics), "Technical Report: Coparent or Second-Parent Adoption by Same-Sex Parents," *Pediatrics* 102 (2) (February 2002): 341–44.

4. For an extensive discussion of nonparental care, see *Child Development* 74 (July/August 2003).

5. For a complete discussion on the politics of motherhood in America today, please refer to Judith Warmer's *Perfect Madness: Motherhood in the Age of Anxiety* (New York: Riverhead Books, 2005, 239–57).

6. See also Liz Galst, "Babies Aren't the Only Beneficiaries of Breastfeeding," *New York Times,* June 22, 2003, 4.

CHAPTER 6

Children and Adolescents in Marriage

Children, especially adolescents, can help either to solidify or to destabilize a marriage. Raising psychologically healthy children helps to preserve a marriage.

Parents Are Coteachers Helping a Child to Become a Person.

Judy: *"You used to bug me for not being a maternal mother to Billy when he was younger. The implication was that as a man you couldn't play mother to a young child but when the time comes you will be a good father—a paternal father. You still never see him. You leave before he gets up and after you come home, he is in bed. On weekends, you bring home a truckload of work or play golf with your buddies. Billy wants to play ball, roughhouse. I can't throw a ball, never mind catch it or roughhouse! A pregnant woman isn't supposed to get physical with a child,"* she complained.

Harold: *"Come on, the kid is only five years old. How much of a physical threat is he? Actually, I tried to throw ball with him and even wrestle a few times. He shies away from me. He only wants to play with you."*

Judy: *"Now, you are going to turn this into my failing again? Oh bullshit, Harold. I sort of agreed with you when you attacked me for not being maternal enough when Billy was younger. But now, you have no right to be critical. You damned well know that I am the one who reads to him, drives him back and forth to school, takes him for a haircut or to the pediatrician, and arranges play dates with his little friends. Harold, be honest. Why do you insist on having children when you really have no interest in them? Now in eight weeks we are going to have a daughter. And I am sure you'll be even less involved. And I'll be stuck with the chores of two children. Have you also noticed that you again lost your sexual desire for me? Why are we in this marriage, Harold? Do you keep getting me pregnant so that I'll be tied down? But why? We at least used to love each other as woman and man. Now by not liking each other as parents, we end up not loving each other at all."*

In their studies of couples, Caroline and Philip Cowan found that the "parent role" is a central part of a couple's identity. Conflicts between spouses about their children generated more turmoil than other discussions. Most parents believe that how their child turns out reflects on them, so of course there are high stakes involved in any disagreement.

We are genetically the products of our parents. However, it is our actual reciprocal relationship with them and others in our environment that ultimately seals our fate. The perennial controversy over whether it is nature or nurture that determines our destiny never gets resolved. Our nature aspect is vaguely defined as our biological inheritance and our nurture aspect as our parents and the environment. It is also erroneously believed that our biological inheritance is defined by very specific genes, and our nurture is nonspecifically defined as parental love and attention. In reality, neither the genes are so specific nor the environment so unspecific. They interact with and modify each other, as we have said. Furthermore, the environment influences and changes itself, and so do the genes. In fact, one set of genes (there are about thirty thousand of them) can behave as an environment for another set, notes Matt Ridley in *Nature via Nurture.*

Many innate behaviors in humans and animals are only potentials, requiring exposure to the environment and learning for their full expression. For example, we all take it for granted that cats will chase mice or, for that matter, any moving object. In fact, the cat's chasing potential is only activated by a moving object at a developmentally relevant time. Researcher Herbert Birch, in the mid-1940s, showed that cats having no experience with moving stimuli were unable to develop into normal chasing felines. Equally, rats whose ability to lick themselves was decreased by means of a special constraining collar did not demonstrate normal maternal behavior at the birth of their litters.[1]

The interaction of genes with the environment, as well as our internal chemistry, can be quite subtle and often a matter of specific timing. The sheer power of genes, for example the particular chirp of birds, is seen in the characteristic sound a species makes. The song of the lark, the sparrow, or the yellow canary, explains Deborah Blum in *Sex on the Brain,* can be sharply contrasted to the wakening crow of a rooster or the fierce war cry of a hawk. Yet genetic expression also depends upon environmental input. Often a young bird must hear the sounds of its own species at a very specific or critical time. If it listens to the song of a different species (e.g., a canary hearing the song of a lark) or at a maturationally improper time, it cannot reproduce the required species-specific melody. The effects can be devastating to its own species, for it has lost its window of opportunity to learn the song it requires to secure a mate. In fact, if some types of sparrow fail to be exposed to their own song at the correct developmental time, they may never be able to sing at all. Comparably, some kittens that are not exposed to light at the proper time may never be competent to develop vision, as Blum explains.

While components of our behavior are genetically preprogrammed and inherited from our ancestors and are species specific, others are shaped during our formative years by our own environment and are thus individual specific. John Watson, the founder of behaviorism, compared shaping the emotional lives of children to a blacksmith's fabrication of metal: he takes his heated mass, places it upon the anvil, and begins to shape it according to patterns of his own. Sometimes he uses a heavy hammer, sometimes a light one, sometimes he strikes the yielding mass a mighty blow, sometimes he gives it just a touch. Similarly, shaping the emotional life of children begins at birth. Of course, the blacksmith has a distinct advantage. If his strokes have been heavy and awkward and he has spoiled his work, he is able to return the metal to the fire and begin the process over again. There is no way, however, of starting all over again with a child.

The most effective strokes are branded on the infant emotionally, as a mother's emotional center in her brain conditions that of the child through affective conditioning. Daniel N. Stern's concept of maternal attunement suggests that a mother who is able to synchronize with her infant's affects also enables the infant to process its own affects. In physical terms, the mother enables her infant to "digest" or absorb anxiety because she "contains" and metabolizes that affect for the child. She then exposes it to the child in a less detrimental form (analogized to a mother bird who will predigest her baby bird's food). If this containing process is successful, the developing child learns to acknowledge that "these are my feelings, and they are ok."

The one requirement is the presence of an emotionally available, sensitive maternal mother: physically and emotionally. Children who are deprived of parental exposure (i.e., maternal gaze and voice, affective attunement, physical touch such as tickling, being breast-fed by mother, and socialization and engaging in roughhousing with father) may be more likely to develop anxiety and depression that manifest in behavioral problems. Behavioral problems of children, in return, may have significant contribution to marital conflicts.

You Can Teach Feminine or Masculine Behavior to Children, but You Cannot Make Them Hetero- or Homosexual.

Judy: *"When we were dating, my friends used to pester me with the question 'Has he tried yet?' Whenever I replied that you were a gentleman and weren't going to just sexually exploit me if you didn't have serious intentions, they all snickered. Billy is gay; he has your genes."*

Harold: *"Billy is not gay; he behaves like a girl because you made him a mama's boy. He slept on your side of the bed or you slept in his bed until he was eight years old. You took him to ballet classes, got piano lessons, and sold him as a child model. He has been using lipstick since then. My genes! My ass!"*

Terri Apter explains that "sex" is a biological definition, referring to the biological features (e.g., penis, vagina) that determine whether one is male or female. "Gender," on the other hand, has less of a biological basis. Instead, it refers to behavior, feelings, thoughts, and fantasies that are related to being male or female. Gender identity, therefore, is primarily a culturally determined phenomenon. In other words, gender is one's *sense* of maleness or femaleness, regardless of whether one is biologically male or female.

Harold: *"What is going on here? Why is Billy bottle-feeding Rebecca?"* Harold tore the bottle and the child from Billy's hand and forced them on his wife. *"Are you trying to make the kid homosexual? I never heard of such a thing: a six-year-old boy plays mother to a sister, while the mother is reading a book!"*

Judy: *"He wanted to do it. That isn't going to make him a girl or even gay. Every man should learn a little about caring for an infant. Why should all that be a woman's job? You never help out, because your mother never taught you how."*

Harold: *"Billy, go upstairs" he said. "Listen, woman, I've had it with your crazy ideas disguised as feminist philosophy. Why do you buy dolls for him to play with? He is the only six-year-old in the neighborhood who still rides his tricycle and also wears a helmet in our yard. He doesn't want to learn to ski. Don't you think there is something wrong here?"*

Judy: *"First of all, I don't believe in buying toy guns. There is no reason to promote aggression in children. What do you think happens when they grow up? They buy real guns, shoot their classmates and teachers; they send bombs in the mail and blow up government property. Dolls tame boys a little, teach them affectionate relations which you men lack. As far as I am concerned, parents who let those kids ride up and down the hill are irresponsible people. It is scary, for God's sake. Billy himself doesn't want to anyway. He is a smart kid and sees other kids fall off their bicycles and go home limping with their bloodied knees and elbows," she said.*

Harold: *"He doesn't want it? You frighten him out of his wits about everything. He cries if I start the car before he puts on his safety belt! Have you ever heard of such a thing? Most kids require lots of cajoling, if not scolding, before they buckle up. This is how you are with a boy; God knows how you'll be with our daughter. She most likely will never leave the house."*

As noted, the expression of genes requires external stimuli for their reinforcement or eradication. On the other hand, the environment by itself, by repetition, may at times generate behavior that is completely alien to the genes. Such associative learning, however, has genetic limitations. The best learning occurs in the context of exposure to what we are innately predisposed to.

Certain environmental (external) cues—such as the appearance of a snake or spider, or looking down from an elevation—generally evoke an immediate fear reaction in humans as well as other primates. Thus, we instinctively avoid certain situations that we have classically associated with particular dangers, like being poisoned by a venomous reptile or plummeting to our destruction or death from a great height. These are automatic, anticipatory responses, and we likewise learn to avoid injury to ourselves. Most of the fears and phobias—rational and irrational—of children, however, develop in the course of their observation of their parents' behavior.

This is what we call "rational fear induction." Randolph M. Nesse and George C. Williams give the example of a newborn fawn: it will stand and stare at an approaching wolf until it sees its mother flee, whereupon the fawn follows her example. This flight pattern is thereby established for the remainder of its

---

Don't complain, and don't blame. Work on the problems of your marriage:

- You don't like your spouse's personality? Don't victimize the victim. He or she is a recipient of a certain genetic fate.
- Don't blame your wife for not bearing you a son. The absence of your own *Y* chromosomes is the cause.
- Don't blame your wife for the effeminate body of your son. The absence of your testosterone signal is the cause.
- You can hold each other responsible for the effeminate behavior of your son or masculine behavior of your daughter: gender behavior is socially determined.

life, transmitted to the next generation by imitation. Nonetheless, these fears are not totally hardwired; they can be conditioned, at least partially—and therefore also unlearned.

Similarly, researchers Anne Ohman and Susan Mineka note that evolution has required the development of a way to cope with dangers that threaten to disrupt the transfer of genes from one generation to another. Viewed from an evolutionary perspective, fear is central to our survival. The authors suggest that humans are innately more likely to fear events and situations that were threatening to the survival of our ancestors, such as deadly predators, heights, and wide open spaces, than to fear deadly objects in our present civilization, such as weapons or motorcycles. The authors conducted a series of experiments where monkeys raised in the laboratory watched wild-reared monkeys behaving fearfully with snakes. These lab-raised monkeys rapidly acquired a fear of snakes by viewing a single video, simply by seeing another monkey's frightened reaction to the appearance of a snake. Even three months later, with no further snake exposure, these lab-reared monkeys continued to exhibit this new fear! It is the amygdala in the front part of our hippocampus at the tip of our temporal lobe that appears to be a central automatic (not conscious) regulator of our fear response. On the other hand, a phobia, learned by imitation, is restricted to a certain extent by our innate disposition. For example, we are less likely to develop phobias to flowers. The researchers concluded that monkeys easily learned the fear of snakes, yet under comparable conditions failed to develop any fear of flowers. We too are innately afraid of snakes, but not innately of flowers. We can also learn *not* to be afraid of snakes—but would have a more difficult time learning to fear flowers. That must frustrate some parents and comfort others. For example, parents can teach children to love or fear water or animals, to be friendly or afraid of strangers; they can even teach them some feminine or masculine behavior, but they cannot teach them to be heterosexual or homosexual.

Don't Blame Your Spouse for Your Child's Personality: We Are Random Cards in Some Divine Shuffling.

> *"The kids have your family genes: they are obese like your mother, stubborn like your father, and, honestly, not so smart like you. Whatever I brought to the table must have been lost in the shuffle," he said.*

Genes interact among themselves and with the environment in determining our outcome. Nonetheless, the sheer number of interacting genetic variables is so enormous that no two children of the same parents are ever exactly indistin-guishable. Even so-called identical twins, who result from a process of natural cloning (albeit a genetic accident), differ from each other because the environment acting on their genetic constitution inevitably varies from one to the other. Thus, through some unknown—perhaps unknowable—divine shuffling, we inherit our genes, and through some stroke of chance or fate are born into a determinant physical and psychological environment. Yet our interactions with this environment are never linear in these early learning stages. We shape our genes as they shape us, in cumulatively spiraling reciprocities.

There is no point, no productive point, therefore, to attack your spouse's personality traits for he or she is equally a victim—at least a recipient—of genetics and biology. There is no malignant intent, and there is nothing personal. Don't feel specifically targeted; you happen to be in his or her shooting gallery—by marriage.

If you marry a younger woman, have children to live longer:

- Young children promote a will to live longer to see them grow.
- Young children are rejuvenating by their joy, laughter, innocence, play, and physical engagement.
- Young children deactivate your cortical brain, your civilized mind, responsible for inhibitions, psychosomatic problems, obsessive ruminations, nihilistic preoccupations, and so forth.
- Young children tap your visceral brain, your primitive mind, so you live naturally: you sleep when you are sleepy, you eat when you are hungry, you have sex when you are horny.

Grow-Up: Have Children with an Adult Spouse.

> They asked me if I had any advice for the young and I said,
> "Sure, grow up."
>
> —Mae West, to Robert Jennings

In their study of marriage, Cowan and Cowan found a couple's decision to have children was related to the meaning of parenthood for them and its impact on their sense of themselves—in other words, being a grownup. They also found that a couple's relationships with their friends, their jobs, and the larger communities in which they live were major contributors. Sometimes, a couple's decision about having children or even when to have children was heavily influenced by whether their friends were also having children. This may be especially so in the timing of a second or third child. If anything, the process should be the reverse: adulthood first, parenthood next. It is true that a child can make a woman a mother, or a man a father. Only adults with a parental disposition, however, can meet children's demands without destabilizing their marriage.

In a provocative article featured in the women's magazine *Redbook* in the mid-1960s, anthropologist Margaret Mead spoke of how, in the past, men and especially women might have gotten married in order to have a child. Now, she said, it seemed that having a child was a way of validating a couple's marriage. Mead was, of course, quite critical of the way the breakdown of some marriages affect parenting. She argued for a style of parenting that would survive any marital breakup. According to Mead, there had to be a mutual recognition that "co-parenthood is a permanent relationship," regardless of the state of a couple's marriage.

Cowan and Cowan highlight signals that forebode difficulties later on in a couple's relationship, such as a spouse's negative views of the other; conflict about the division of labor in the family; discontent with their arrangements for childcare; inability to make family decisions that meet both spouses' needs; vocalized dissatisfaction generally with the marriage.

In Donald Barthelme's "Critique de la Vie Quotidienne," the male protagonist tells a story of a more insidious animosity, namely how his child (here older in the example) intrudes into his territory with his wife, compounding his frustration in his marital life:

> *"I remember once we were sleeping in a narrow bed, Wanda and I, in a hotel, on a holiday, and the child crept into bed with us.*
>
> *"If you insist on overburdening the bed," we said, "you must sleep at the bottom, with the feet." "But I don't want to sleep with the feet," the child said. "Sleep with the feet," we said. "Take your choice." "Why can't I sleep with heads," the child asked, "like everybody else?" "Because you are a child," we said, and the child subsided. . . . But in truth the child was not without recourse; it urinated in the bed, in the vicinity of the feet. "God damn it, . . . Holy hell," I said. "Is there to be no end to this family life?"*

Our adult self is established from our imprinted sense of self garnered from our childhood. Marion Solomon illustrates this with Russian nesting dolls. In this analogy, she suggests that each doll, which is identical to the others but is repeated in progressively smaller sizes, is situated inside a larger doll. Comparably, inside each of us is the newborn, the toddler, the adolescent, and the adult, recreated in larger and larger versions but basically molded from the same template.

Such initial configurations become imprints that remain indelible psychological and emotional influences throughout our lives. They cement our first years with our final ones, providing a "cord of continuity," according to Solomon, that is remarkable in its endurance. The evolution of this initial basic pattern is natural for everyone. What is problematic is our failure to evolve to a mature stage such that we remain fixated on one of the earlier phases of attachment, separation, or preadolescence.

The individual who remains transfixed at the phase of attachment needs desperately to be understood. He requires acceptance, confirmation, and more emotional connections, to be held and touched, and to be shown repeated demonstrations of a proof of love. Such individuals feel depressed and empty when alone and passively try to control others' reactions and behaviors.

Those who are immobilized in the separation phase always seem to suggest, "Don't come too close—but don't go away either." Nor do they themselves depart. In relationships with these people, we feel confused, subjected to a yo-yo experience from which we can neither engage nor disengage. It is a form of bonding from which it is difficult to extricate ourselves.

By comparison, those who are transfixed at the preadolescent stage can relate only through other people and external entities. These range from positive connections, such as games or businesses, to negative ones, such as smoking, alcohol, and drugs. Without such intermediaries, this kind of person has considerable difficulty in relating to someone else. We may see such couples, quite comfortable together when they are with other people, playing golf or participating in some other activities or hobbies. They frequently travel with other couples. But when only one of the couple requires intermediary interests, the spouse may complain about the other person's requirements for ever present objects, games, interests, or friends that interfere with intimacy between the two of them. Either partial fixation or arrest at any one of these stages interferes with the person's ability to parent.

In marriage, love means never blaming the other spouse even when justified:

- Neither of you is responsible for the sexual orientation of your child.
- Neither of you is primarily responsible for the general dependency of your children. It is essentially in our human genes.
- Share with your spouse your negative feelings about your children, such as, resentment and anger.
- Don't scapegoat each other. It makes the situation worse.

You need not be a psychiatrist to figure out at what level of motivation is your spouse, as long as you can tame your subjective enthusiasm and allow some objectivity. Observe the person's relations with parents and siblings and long-term friends. Your spouse's relation with you is more likely to be a variation on the same theme but adjusted to the marital context. The fundamental behavior patterns of our contemporary relationships have roots in our imprinted past. Those patterns also determine how we function in all other life circumstances. The enduring significance of our predispositions vis-à-vis relationships is expressed by the Zen Master Shunryu Susuki. When evaluating the conduct of his students, he said, "I don't pay attention to whether you're following the precepts or not. I just notice how you are with one another."

Nonadult Parents Raise Immature and Dependent Children.

Harold: *"How is it, Judy, that both of our kids are too short for their age and so chubby?"*

Judy: *"So, that is my fault too, somehow?"*

Harold: *"No, I don't know. We are both tall. When I was Billy's age, I was two inches taller. I discussed this with Dr. Newman. She says both kids are physically normal. They have no growth hormone deficiency, they take the right amount of vitamins, their diet is well balanced. Her conclusion is that both have delayed maturity based on some psychological factor. I also told her that they always come to our bed either before they go to their own or come back in the early morning and sneak in with us, both on your side. Billy still wets his bed. I explained to her that we are both out of the house most of the day and that bedtime may be the only time the children have with us. She didn't understand why going half-time to social work school makes you absent all day and asked who takes the children to school and who picks them up. When I said, 'the nanny,' she looked puzzled."*

Judy: *"I knew it, I knew it. You are blaming me for the kids' heights, bed-wetting, not sleeping in their own beds. And you are ratting on me to their pediatrician? Wasn't it you who suggested that Ana take them to school and pick them up?"*

Harold: *"Yes, I did, after you failed on three occasions to arrive on time. The kids had to wait more than an hour, in front of the school."*

Judy: *"Don't exaggerate! It was no more than half an hour, and they weren't upset at all. They had their friends with them. They were having a good time."*

The human infant has the longest physical dependency on its mother compared to other animal species. Under the circumstances, it is amazing that the human species survived so many centuries before it invented instruments to defend itself. Even the human brain, Blum emphasizes specifically, is more immature at birth than that of all other mammalians. In fact, at least in terms of sheer size, the newborn human possesses a brain only one-fourth as large as that of an adult's; by comparison, a monkey's brain is almost two-thirds complete at birth. Any other animal, or every other primate for that matter, would no doubt be regarded as defective if it had merely the degree of development that a human infant has just after birth. For a simple developmental comparison, at approximately the same stage, that baby chimpanzee is already able to walk and play with its companions, while a human infant is barely beginning to roll over.

Never mind living in the wilderness, even in a civilized world, the human infant cannot survive without full maternal attention. This long physical dependency of the human infant has contributed to its even more prolonged psychological dependency.

In parenthood, love means mutual help, support, and learning:

- Help each other to stay reliable for and dependable to your children.
- Watch each other's boundary infringement and potential abuse of your children.
- Take care not to prefer a child to your spouse, especially the opposite-sex child.
- Agree and reinforce the principles to be obeyed by your children and discuss the subsequent consequences, if not obeyed.

If the individual is deprived of a stable and dependable relationship in his early years, that is to say if the parents are psychologically young or just immature, that individual will develop a more extensive and greater dependency later on. Enabling such dependency may seem reflective of affection and love and wishes to protect a child. If anything, however, it is often reflective of substantial (often unconscious) negative feelings on the part of both parents toward the child. Dependence sooner or later turns into resentment, if not hatred, because of the inevitability of disappointment on both sides.

Some other individuals do not allow themselves to be naturally dependent on anyone. This second group may not only have been deprived of dependable parental relations in their early upbringing but may have been physically or psychologically abused. They, in return, manipulate others to obtain their needs and repeat this early mistreatment on others. They contaminate all their relationships. Says John Bradshaw, "Had our childhood needs been met, we would not have become 'adult children.'"

Children Need External Boundaries to Develop Their Own Internal Ones. Children Who Fail to Form Internal Boundaries Act Out and Fragment Families.

Judy: *"You as the father are supposed to set some rules in the house and stick to them. What I mean is, you always give the kids mixed messages: you ridicule them for their weight and then bring boxes of chocolate, you criticize them for being spoiled and then always give them 'pocket money,' 'in case.' In case what? Why would kids that age, especially Rebecca who is never by herself, need pocket money? You take their TV time away for not doing their homework then buy them a cell phone; so instead of watching TV they chat on the phone with their friends for hours. They still don't do their school work. You scold them for using any four-letter word; meanwhile you curse at me in front of them!"*

Harold: *"And you are totally innocent here? I curse for no reason? You are absent; I feel guilty for always being the heavy here. For you, they can do whatever they please. Not out of love or anything like that—you simply don't care. They eat too little or too much, no big deal; do they get to school on time? You hope so. Let me ask a question, what grade is Billy in? Don't laugh, just answer. You are laughing because you are not sure, right? Am I right?"*

In medieval times, a popular image, notes Joseph Campbell, that occurred in a multitude of contexts was the classic wheel of fortune. If we look at the mechanism of the wheel more closely, we can separate clearly the hub of the wheel from its revolving rim. Each has a particular place and function. We can analogize this wheel to the operation of human behavior: by being attached to the rim, we are either at the top moving down or at the bottom moving up. Alternatively, being at the hub means constantly remaining in the same place. In this analogy, the child, in the process of development, is situated at the rim of the wheel, whereas the parents remain steadfast at the hub. In this fashion, the parents enable the child's self to crystallize in the constancy of the relationship with them by setting certain rules and boundaries. Such constancy, however, is not synonymous with infallibility at all, but with remaining reliable and dependable. The child needs stable reference points. For the internal boundaries and the sense of stability to develop, children need that their parents are there steadily for them. If their essential needs are met, children, in return, help stabilize the marriage of their parents.

We require internal and external boundaries and structures to maintain our stability. That need is seen throughout childhood but is especially intense during the preadolescent and adolescent years. These internal and external boundaries can be environmental, such as finding comfort in one's room or in a walled-in garden. They may be psychological, whether derived from something as concrete as a specific principle to be obeyed—usually self-made—or as abstract as a sense of guilt that guides one's morality. Even though children may expressly complain about the limitations of such structures, they have a silent appreciation of their organizing importance. "I wish I weren't feeling so guilty," you may hear someone complaining, or "I wish I didn't care so much." Underneath these litanies lies an antithetical viewpoint: proud ownership of these moral qualities. Those structures define a child's boundaries, set limits, and thus are comforting. Children's dependency on us is inevitable; paradoxically, when children lose their sense of being independent entities, they experience anxiety and destabilization. They attempt to affirm their boundaries even when they are not being threatened. Unreasonable quarrels, provocations, betrayals, and many other inexplicable behaviors of a child result from the apprehension, or actual violation, of her perceived boundaries. It is the same with us adults. You may have heard friends or even yourself remarking, "I wish I didn't have to go work"; "marriage is too demanding"; "the kids are exhausting"; "friends are boring"; "life is too difficult"; "I hate deadlines." Yet the same person who enunciates those statements usually has no serious intention of yielding to any of these external influences, however negative, because they serve to provide reassuring boundaries and control.

Some people are so troubled without a definite structure that their search for structure becomes fanatical. They may engage in some rigidly defined activities with uncritical enthusiasm and unbalanced obsession, such as strict adherence to demagogic cults, radical political groups, or even neomilitary troops. Even potential danger does not deter these individuals from their zealous devotion.

At the extreme end of such a requirement for limits, some people prefer imprisonment to liberty. Their fragile self disintegrates with external intrusions, and they insist on defending their boundaries from even the natural environment. For such persons, everything in their world can seem to be intruding on themselves. The self, unless constantly defined, may appear to be dissolving into its surround: cars, trees, roads, ocean, buildings, and so forth. Children sometimes will do anything to avoid the sense of dissolution characteristic of that loss of self, including deliberately inflicting pain on themselves (or others). This pain, intended to sharpen a split between themselves and the environment, may range from mild self-injuries behavior (such as lip-biting, scab picking, skin peeling, or nail biting) to severe self-mutilation (such as head banging, wrist cutting). This pain serves as a somatic reassurance of where those children, precisely and at least corporally, begin and end.

Violation of Children's Boundaries Devastates Them, Disrupting Every Bond in the Family.

The use of a child for one's own emotional needs can occur with either parent, but actual sexual abuse is committed almost entirely by fathers. On the other hand, subtle emotional abuses by mothers are more commonplace. Bradshaw goes as far as to say, "The rule of thumb is that whenever a child is more important to a parent than the parent's spouse, the potential for emotional sexual abuse exists." In other words, the parent is using the child for his or her own needs. Continues Bradshaw, "Use is abuse."

The most frequent but seemingly natural abuse, by the maternal figure, takes the form of boundary infringement. Some parents seem to consider their children their property. These parents see nothing mistaken in invading their children's privacy (e.g., listening in on their telephone calls, opening their mail), intrusively controlling their lives, and perpetrating a form of victimization in the name of nurture. One adult once related that her mother had said to her, then a ten-year-old who kept her first diary while away at camp one summer, "If you love me, you'll let me read your diary." The consequence, at best, is the severance of the bond of trust between a parent and a child: the child attempts to extricate herself and flee from the blurred boundaries. At worst, the child identifies with the intrusive parents, assumes the character of these parents, and in turn victimizes others.

The child usually cannot victimize his parents and cannot even express infuriation and antagonism without guilt, which is even worse than fear. Alice Miller writes that children of abuse are in a worse condition than inmates of concentration camps. "The abused inmates of a concentration camp . . . are inwardly capable of hating their persecutors. The opportunity to experience their feelings, even to share them with other inmates, prevents them from having to surrender their self." This emotional luxury, however, doesn't exist for children. They dare not despise their parents because they fear losing parental love as a consequence. Thus children, unlike concentration camp inmates, are in an extraordinary bind—they are confronted by a tormentor whom they love and are frightened to hate, and someone they desperately require and whose love they crave.

Another common abuse is seen when a parent's marriage is unsatisfying and that parent consequently shifts attention onto a child. The result, however, is likely to be a further escalation of conflicts within the family, disruption of the marital bond, and, more damagingly, emotional abuse of the child by both parents. Usually one parent manifests a loving and protective function, while the other hides behind a jealous and angry one. The child may inadvertently fuel the conflict. The child's healthy triangulation in the family, however, is not a matter of winning against either parent; rather, it is one of competing safely with each in the emotional/sexual arena. Ultimately, it is comforting to the child that he will not be allowed to prevail.

One need not, of course, be concerned about preserving a marriage wherein children are sexually or physically abused. When it comes, however, to unintentional psychological harm emanating from subtle boundary violations or from establishing reasonable safety boundaries for children, one risks damaging the marriage. Parents' behavior and attitudes resonate multifold in children. They, in return, violate boundaries even more so than their parents and destabilize the whole family.

A Parent's Setting up Approval Competition among Children Generates Dislike between Them and Hate between Spouses.

Harold: *"No, they are not fighting, Judy; Billy is simply beating Rebecca any chance he gets. What is the matter with him? He is five years older, I mean my older brother never hit me or my sister. If anything, he was our protector."*

Judy: *"You three had a better mother, I presume!" she replied.*

Harold: *"That's for sure. But how do we stop him? Neither threats nor spanking are doing any good."*

Judy: *"Try strangling."*

Harold: *"If I strangle someone it won't be him, let me assure you."*

Judy: *"What do you want from me, Harold? First of all, don't get the idea that Rebecca is totally innocent. She taunts him and teases him. I have been telling you for some time that you began to spoil Rebecca with excessive gifts and attention. She has more dolls and toys than she has room for. She has more outfits than I do. Do you know that she is using Billy's closet because she has no space in her own even though she started with twice as much closet space? You take her to ballet, to shopping for jewelry. Who ever heard of a nine-year-old girl wearing diamond studs? You think these things escape Billy's attention? Why don't you take him to a ball game sometime?"*

Harold: *"Billy? Has he ever expressed an interest in any sport? Thanks to you! Furthermore, he doesn't really want to be with me. He hangs around with those creeps. You don't buy jewelry for a boy. But if I do, he would most likely wear it either in his nose or on his tongue. He is just a fat, lazy bum with no serious interest in school or anything else, except spending my hard-earned money."*

Judy: *"Harold, do you hear yourself talking at all? He is your child, too. You used to berate me for not loving him enough and now you berate him for not being lovable. The kid has an attention deficit disorder, he cannot focus, he gets impatient with himself. He thinks he is stupid already, and you are yelling at him."*

Parents can turn siblings against each other in spite of their love. The biblical children Cain and Abel were a case in point. In Genesis 4:1–8, so the narrative goes, these two sons of Adam brought offerings to the Lord: Cain brought some crops, as he was a farmer, and Abel, some choice parts of the first-born animals from his flock, as he was a shepherd. When the Lord approved of Abel and his offering and didn't approve of Cain's contribution, Cain became very angry, and later when they were in the fields together, Cain killed Abel. It wasn't rejection of his gift, nor even rejection of himself, that converted Cain's anger into murder, but God's approval of his brother Abel. Jealousy between siblings rarely results in murder, but if parents approve of or favor one sibling and disapprove of the other, they'll set the stage for murderous thoughts and fantasies, as well as antagonism and conflicts between the siblings. This is especially true when there are only two children in the family. The real hate meanwhile will germinate between mutually accusatory parents.

If a Parent Disapproves of Children, not Simply of Their Behavior, Children Will Split Spouses against Each Other.

Of course, parents will find that it is considerably difficult to approve of all children equally or at all times. Some children seem to, or actually do, excel in behavior, talents, love, or obedience. Nevertheless, parents must make an effort to differentiate the *behavior* of each child from the child himself. A parent may and should disapprove of some of the child's behavior but never confuse that with the entirety of the child. Any disapproval should never be expressed categorically, such as "You are fat" or "You are selfish." These are verbalizations that serve to negate the person per se. Rather, disapproval should target the child's particular behavior and be very specific, with potential accruable benefits from the requested change of behavior: "If you eat all that candy, you won't be able to play a good game" or "If you let your brother play with your toys, he'll let you play with his, and then you'll have twice as many toys to play with." Children need to be taught reciprocity. Comparably, punishment for naughty behavior should never be the threat of abandonment or, worse, actual abandonment. Fear of desertion for a child is worse than dying, as most children have very little concern with or appreciate the concept of death. A child, though, equates being alone with no longer being cherished. For a child, this feeling generates deep-seated anxiety and perpetuates, if not increases, the undesirable behaviors.

Parents Who Blame Each Other for an Adolescent's Behavior Are More Likely to Damage Only Their Own Relationship.

Harold: *"Does this kid look like my son? Purple, spiked hair, gold earrings, shirt sticking out of his oversized, baggy pants, which are hanging down to his knees, smelling of cigarettes and sweat! Does he wash himself at all? Is he going crazy?"*

Judy: *"Why are you asking me, Harold? He is fifteen years old. And what are you saying by "Does he look like my son?" Does he look like my son? Do I color my hair purple and wear bizarre outfits?"* she protested.

Harold: *"No, you are bizarre, though."*

Judy: *"What seems to be bizarre to you is normal to everyone else. You never understood me, and now you don't understand Billy. He is a typical teenager. Your darling Rebecca will get there too in a few years. Just wait. She is already into boys. The other day she wished she were dead because Chester didn't call her back. Apparently he likes Sandy more—that blond precocious girl that you have been eyeing!"*

Harold: *"Don't be ridiculous."*

Judy: *"You should see these ten-year-old kids e-mail each other. They are talking about whether oral sex is sex or not; whether one has to swallow or not; what it tastes like."*

Harold: *"Of course, you would have said, 'Never, it'll gag you,' if you were in their chat room,"* he said.

Judy: *"Can we ever talk about the kids without bringing the subject to us? The first night when you ejaculated into my mouth I almost drowned. Of course, I threw up. And why should I swallow it? What difference does it make to you after you come? Have you ever tasted your own sperm? You must have because you never kiss me on the lips afterwards. It tastes like crushed cockroach."* She put her two fingers into her mouth.

Harold: *"Yeah! What do you think your vagina smells like? It smells and tastes like rotten fish."*

Adolescents can destabilize your marriage along with themselves:

- Don't retaliate against their aggression; that is how they relate.
- Don't get withdrawn when adolescents reject you; that is how they develop their identity.
- Don't take their withdrawal and moodiness personally. That is how they establish their autonomy and learn to separate.
- Draw the line with major infringements of rules but don't fight every minor battle.
- Don't displace your frustrations, disappointments, or anger onto your spouse.
- Share your puzzlement and your feelings of powerlessness and helplessness with your spouse without attacking him or her.

The behavior of adolescents would be considered insane and unbalanced at any other time in life. Their negativism and peculiarities are essential in the formation of their selves. Adolescents spend enormous amounts of time talking on the phone, looking in the mirror, and attaching themselves to idealized popular figures, like movie and rock stars; they also alternate between abhorring their parents and emulating them closely. They suspect malevolent intent in an adult's demands, and they are suspicious, if not mildly paranoid, about others' intentions. They are easily slighted, and they fall into severe depressive moods over a "love" relationship; they can then turn expansive and grandiose on a dime, as they always complain that no one understands or appreciates them. Their arguments are symptoms of attempts to separate and, by implication, they are evidence of attachment. One minute, they never want to talk to their parents (or one parent) again; the next, they want to talk to you for hours. This ambivalence toward their parents can be mind-boggling and disorienting for parents.

Parents contribute to this state of confusion of adolescents by reacting with corresponding intensity: fear, desperation, control, guilt, anger. When adolescents, in turn, observe their parents' excessive and fluctuating reactions, they become further destabilized. What adolescents require at that phase is a lowering of the intensity of emotions, a buffering constancy, a reassuring stability. Simultaneously, her parents must assist the adolescent to disobey in minor, insignificant ways, while on her safe passage to facilitate autonomy and discover a separate identity. When adolescents are rebelling in these insignificant ways, they are demonstrating that their parents have made them comfortable enough to separate from them. Of course, when adolescents resort to major infringements of parental rules (e.g., getting into trouble with the law or serious abuse of drugs or alcohol), these adolescents are demonstrating just the opposite: their parents have made it so impossible and uncomfortable to separate and individuate, they must resort to extraordinary measures.

All adolescents suffer from merger and abandonment anxieties, but as their tolerance for anxiety is limited, they tend to act rather than reflect. Most of an adolescent's incomprehensible behavior is a confusing translation of some internal feeling directed into an activity. The most common manifestation is protest against something or someone. It is a search for identity by negation. This is the second individuation process. The initial one occurred during the "terrible twos," with its familiar retorts of "No," or "I can too do it," characteristic of the young child between the ages of one and a half to three years. That, however, is just a benign rehearsal for later adolescent rebellions and parent-child altercations. Based on their own childhood and others' experiences, parents instinctively recognize, and to some extent playfully accept, a child's self-assertion in the terrible twos, even though at times it may be quite exasperating. When we experience these rebellions in adolescence, however, we view them differently. After all, a supervised two-year-old cannot really get into too much trouble; an unsupervised adolescent, however, is more capable of action and can do considerably more damage. Some parents become quite frightened and react badly by imposing excessively strict and even unfair rules on their adolescents. This excessiveness, in turn, frightens these adolescents and makes them rebel even further. Consistent, fair rules are important for an adolescent's development; unnecessary and arbitrary ones impede his development. Sometimes a parent has to pick his or her battles.

The adolescent's anger and rebelliousness are as necessary as they are unpleasant to experience as recipient. What is particularly troublesome in adolescence is complacency: it is blind, unquestioning obedience, not negation, that usually interferes with the development of a sense of self. In the Old Testament story, God alerted Adam to the one forbidden fruit, with full knowledge—God is omniscient—that Adam would eat it. By doing so, says Joseph Campbell, "man became the initiator of his own life. Life really began with that act of disobedience."

Since the beginning of time, human beings have maintained a virtual compulsion to disobey certain rules and a natural tendency to transgress, both of which have served toward continued self-differentiation. What is essential, however, is that all participants survive. A person who had parents like Harold and Judy never fully recovers from this stage of development and embarks on all relationships with an unabated desire to transgress. They always wish to challenge, assume bad faith in every encounter, and engage others, especially authority figures, with negative emotions: anger, irritation, and an attitude of cynicism and devaluation.

The verbal altercation in the above vignette is a typical pay-off by adolescents to parents. Further, the undesirable behavior of adolescents fuels conflicts between parents in vulnerable couples.

Adolescent Identity Confusion Sets Off Existential Crises in One or Both Parents.

Adolescence is a stage for establishing a conscious identity, although it secures much of its foundation from the previous developmental stages. It represents both a sense of sameness and difference or distinctness. The broad term "identity" encompasses this dual and reciprocal relationship, insofar as it reflects both an enduring sameness within oneself as well as an equally steadfast contribution of some kind of essential nature from others.

The adolescent will reject any constancy derived from sharing that essential nature with adults, yet she can't find a consistent sameness within herself. Even the sense of time doesn't remain the same. Furthermore, the body is no longer the same body, feelings are quite different, and sexuality is overwhelming. Of

---

Adolescence is a "normal disease" but may generate "abnormal" reactions in parents:

- Adolescents experience a sense of emptiness and loneliness. Don't be put off with their appearance of bravado.
- Adolescents need peer validation. Let them have friends, even if you don't like their choices.
- Adolescents' passion and sexuality may evoke envy in you. Watch out for your vicarious enjoyment of their lives.
- Adolescents have a tendency to divide spouses. Don't share with them your negative feelings about your spouse.
- Help adolescents come home by letting them go.

course, one of the major developmental issues is the consolidation of a sexual identity, which can easily get more confused, especially when it is a component of a conflicted, ill-defined, or unintegrated sense of self. Until now, a child's identity is closely related to identification with his parents. In rejecting their parents, adolescents generate a vacuum that is difficult to fill quickly. For years they live with a sense of emptiness and loneliness, in spite of their outward activities and the appearance of bravado. David Elkind speaks of the need for the "personal fable" of the adolescent—a story she constructs about herself.

In addition to the continuity and structure provided by the family, adolescents also require peer validation, often by conforming to their peers in their development of a sense of self. Being loved and accepted by one's peers becomes particularly important in making choices, developing future plans, and possessing at least a rudimentary philosophy of life. Actually, adolescents who are able now to think abstractly are quite inclined to philosophic thinking in their own contrary fashion and, therefore, easily recruitable for religious or political activities. Once attached, they demonstrate sometimes not merely strong but even irrational and quite uncompromising fidelity and commitment to causes. The more the parents prohibit such activities, or *any* activity for that matter, the more the adolescent continues to do what is forbidden. The poet Carl Sandburg says of children, "Why do children put beans in their ears, when the one thing we asked the children not to do is put beans in their ears?" This need to rebel is even more typical of the adolescent. Elkind emphasizes that the power these alternatives have over an adolescent is in direct proportion to the extent to which that adolescent feels a lack of commitment from the parents.

An adolescent's agitation is compounded by the increased biological urges and drives of puberty. This is confusing because these forces are not stable, but selective, cyclic, and peremptory, as if wrongly wired. At any other phase of development, this agitation would be seen as pathology. Adolescent crises are characterized by an increasing agitation, an often profound psychosocial isolation, and a strong propensity for action. The extraordinary energy of an adolescent can lead the adolescent to search for adaptive and maladaptive experiences.

Adolescence is a "normal disorder." Anna Freud even compares it to a seemingly psychotic process. In the crises of those developmental years, the adolescent has both an expanding and contracting identity and seems to be veering toward total collapse. Yet in spite of the similarity of adolescent behaviors to episodes of neurotic or even psychotic symptoms, adolescence is not an affliction but a *normative crisis*. That is, it comprises a normal phase of increased conflict and disturbance characterized by apparent fluctuations in psychological strength. Within this conflict there is the more unquestionable capacity for a high potential for growth.

When parents have adolescent children, there can develop considerable strain on their marriage. Not understanding and thus not coping well with teenagers is extremely stressful in spouses' relations with each other. The adolescent's sexuality, aggression, and violation of mores not only generates anger, fear, disgust, disapproval, and despair but also may activate similar dormant feelings in a parent, prompting him or her to question the purpose and the value of marriage. There may also be vicarious enjoyment on the part of the parents for the adolescent's rebellious behavior. Likewise, adolescents may attempt to engage one parent in a peer relationship, often at the expense of the other parent. Adolescents may confide in one parent and directly express a wish that some secret not be shared with the other parent. This behavior obviously further weakens or even splits the parental bond and puts pressure on each parent.

Adolescent Sexuality Reawakens the Dormant Sexual Conflicts in the Marriage.

According to Susan Maushart, when children reach adolescence, spouses tend to like each other less.

Harold complained: *"You know, Rebecca has changed. She no longer cuddles with me; she never kisses me; when I try to kiss her she recoils; and if I keep after her she reluctantly extends her cheek for a quick peck, while keeping the rest of her body as far away as she can. Actually, 'reluctant' is not the word, 'disgusted' is more like it. I feel like I've lost her. I mean, what happened? She doesn't even want to talk to me, unless she has to, and she brushes me off quickly. Did you see all those signs she put up this afternoon on her door: 'No Intrusion!' 'Don't knock on the door when closed!' I used to just walk into her room. Now I can't even ask for permission to enter?"*

Judy: *"Welcome to the club, Harold! For years I told you about Billy's removing himself from us. In his room, which you don't care to enter, he has a sign that says 'A good parent is a dead parent.' He is always either with that bulimic girl or with that handsome boy, what's his face? They are always either in his room or in their houses. What if they are having sex? Mind you, she is only fifteen."*

Harold: *"What is to figure? Your fucking mother wouldn't even let us close the door when we were engaged. Look what that got us! We had to get married so that we could have sex,"* he said.

Judy: *"Are you saying that if we had sex before, you would not have married me?"* she asked.

Harold: *"Well, maybe you would not have married me. All I am saying is that having sex without your Nazi mother's prohibition was a major incentive. If you met me today, Judy, would you marry me?"*

Judy: *"You answered the question. Obviously you wouldn't marry me today and you would not have married me then either, if your cock didn't drag your brain. Since our honeymoon you have been complaining about me, for one thing or another. Why didn't you divorce me? I mean, I had no objection. You can still do that. If the kids were a consideration, well, no longer. They don't even seem to need us, or like us. One is shutting us out, the other wishes we were dead. So, why don't you do what you want? Just do it, Harold."*

Harold: *"Well, I could ask the same question of you. Why didn't you or don't you walk out? Financially, there is no problem, right? Do you know what I think? I think you need me as an opponent, but not as a lover or even as a friend. I guess I am sort of envious of kids' being in love."*

The sexuality of adolescents, as they move away emotionally from their parents, is one of the most common targets of couples' displaced conflicts. From adolescence on, love and desire are directed to strangers. If the person—the target of love—is too familiar, the adolescent develops a strong affectionate and platonic bond, simultaneously displaying some protective revulsion toward the opposite sex parent (e.g., Rebecca's discouraging her father's hugs and kisses that used to delight her when she was younger). Even with peers, platonic bonds lower tension, relax the mind and body, neutralize aggression, and desexualize the relationship.

If the target of love is not too familiar, the stranger is loved passionately and desired deliriously. This subjective state of mind is most comparable to our experience of eternal union. Such love—desiring the desire of the unfamiliar—requires that the other person remain a relative stranger. Purely romantic love, therefore, is sustained by mystery and can disintegrate upon meticulous inspection.

Parents Who Have Themselves Experienced Love Will Smile at Their Adolescent's Need for the Gaze of a Stranger and Marvel in the Eternal Recycling of This Miracle.

Nothing in nature is more miraculous than romantic love, says Deepak Chopra. He insists that turning lead into gold is trivial by comparison because these metals, however precious, require just a minor reshuffling of a few protons, neutrons, and electrons. Rather, if you hear the words "I love you" and your heart begins to beat rapidly (or even skips a few beats), you have undergone a much more daunting transformation. That is, an emotion in another person's mind has been metamorphosed into molecules of adrenaline rushing through your own bloodstream. This emotion activates receptors situated on the outside of your heart and in turn tells each cell that the appropriate response to love is to pump blood more quickly than normal. The body experiences that something extraordinary is happening. More specifically, believing that you are loved alters your entire emotional outlook and sense of self: in sum, you feel alive in the fullest sense of the word. In this exultant state, our being becomes fully present; at least it feels that way.

Being in love is the most exclusive form of an interpersonal relationship; it is that state of mind, that exultant sense, that once triggered, expands its domain. Feelings of ecstasy abound, with a sense that the universe is smiling upon oneself. That experience transcends the loved person and merges with nature, the universe. The loved one is just a chosen target, the initiator of self-abandonment. The lover projects his inner bliss onto everyone he encounters. As Anthony Storr tells, "All the world loves a lover, and a lover loves all the world." The only exception to this is the parents of adolescents.

Love is a truly universal concept. All nations, races, religions, and creeds experience its meaning. Its chronicles are embodied in the eternal poetry of all languages. These stories are often totally oblivious to reason, as the world continues to smile at its passionate excessiveness, objectionable transgressions, impracticality, and classic blindness. Even the selfish nature of love can be transformed into ultimate selflessness. The story of Admetus, found in Thomas Bulfinch's Greek mythology, for example, is what we expect from lovers: Admetus was granted by Apollo the special privilege to avoid dying, *if* he could find someone else who was willing to take his place. When he approached his parents, whom he thought would definitely be willing to die for him, both refused. Only his lover agreed to give her life to save his. This "divine madness," as Plato called it in "Phaedrus," reaches its apex in adolescent love.

Only after one develops a reasonable sense of identity does a genuine interpersonal *intimacy,* that is not just sexual, occur with others. Often, the drive for sexual intimacy commonly preempts the psychological one. Sexually active adolescents either avoid emotional intimacy or they gravitate to other extremes and become inseparable from another adolescent.

Such excessive attachment often focuses on an attempt to define one's identity by such things as plans, wishes, and expectations. Unfortunately, many young people, searching for their identity, decide to marry in the expectation of discovering themselves in another. If anything, the pressures of marriage and parenthood derail a person from finding the self.

Adolescents Need Intense Same-Sex Relations.

Man's longing is the longing—to be longed for.

—R. D. Laing

Same-sex attachment differs from both parental and passionate attachments. This attachment frequently gets confused with a sexual one in that it has no evolutionary motivation. An adolescent affectionate attachment—commonly with the same sex—is not inherent but acquired slowly; it is not orgasmic but develops silently. Nevertheless, the loss of this partner, that is, best friend, generates equally powerful emotions of grief and anxiety. Although such attachment conveys some remnants of the early bonds, it is more similar to a twin attachment—a kind of "induced twinship." Even a temporary absence of the other feels as if something—a portion of the self—is missing; an emptiness within envelops the person who can scarcely await being with the other, and not for a specific reason—just to be with him. All other social relationships become more meaningful and pleasurable when this "twin" attachment occurs; all accomplishments gain greater heights and all sufferings are better tolerated.

Long after the original self-confirming person (the mother) ceases to be in that role, we continue to project upon others certain self-affirmative attributes. To some extent, our mother's role as the provider of self-coherence continues through our internalization of her psychological presence. The yearning for someone else to know us intuitively, someone with whom we can identify as an extension of ourselves, as mother once did, however, still remains. Although this continues throughout life, we see it most prevalently and potently in adolescence.

In the early years, a child will experience himself as a cohesive, harmonious unit if he senses that others are joyfully and empathically responding to him. These other people are thus considered available to him as sources of strength and calmness. Another crucial role for these figures (usually mothers) is that of being able to comprehend so accurately the child's inner life as to be deeply attuned to his needs. In adult life, however, such attunement rarely occurs, although the wish for it remains forever. That fundamental desire to perceive someone who intuitively grasps our private self, who appreciates *specifically* who we are in all our uniqueness, reflects an illusion founded in childhood that we are often unwilling to relinquish. In reality, such a relation rarely exists in adolescence for it requires the other person's muting his own self and remaining in a primarily reflecting role. Adolescents don't listen to each other. Their conversations are more like parallel recitations. Their relationships are neither reciprocal nor mutual. They are often just parallel, the opposite of what parents may demand from their adolescent children.

Have Many Children; It Will Be Good for Your Marriage.

Kin love is proportionately strengthened by the number of one's siblings. Man is genetically programmed, as are most other animals, to protect his siblings and his clan, even if he has to endanger his own life to do so. Clearly, this is good for the preservation of one's personal genetics. The British biologist J. B. S. Haldane gives an explanation for this altruism:

> "Let us suppose that you carry a rare gene which affects your behavior so that you jump into a flooded river and save a child, but you have one chance in ten of being drowned. . . . If the child is your own child or your brother or sister, there is an even chance that the child will also have this gene, so that five such genes will be saved in children for one lost in an adult. If you save a grandchild or nephew the advantage is only two and half to one. If you only save a first cousin, the effect is very slight." Haldane adds, humorously, "But on the two occasions when I have pulled possibly drowning people out of the water . . . I had no time to make such calculations."

Contrary to common sentiment, large families provide fertile genetic ground for kin protection, with subtle and obvious manifestations of altruism. Competition and selfishness can sometimes decrease significantly with an increased number of siblings. As children's loving, selfless relation toward each other naturally extends toward their parents as well, there develops a remarkable feeling of union pervading the family. Even ordinary squabbles between spouses take a conciliatory tone. Of course, this identification from below is just a dividend of the earlier healthy emotional investment of the parents.

Don't Be Afraid of Making Errors as Parents; The Errors Stimulate Individuation in Children.

All of us, in our private moments, find something deficient or insufficient within ourselves and frequently blame our parents for our own deficiencies. Few of us present that attitude publicly, others go to therapists, and still others convert their lives into a litany against the past. It isn't that all parents are perfect and that children just need to complain. There are parents who are troubled themselves. They may be incapable of loving, insensitive, depressed, anxious, pessimistic, uninteresting, narrow-minded, too authoritarian, or too permissive, or otherwise inadequate as parents. Some of these traits may result from what they themselves had lacked in childhood—a generational inheritance transferred to their own children.

Independent of whether they deserve criticism, parents must realize that some of their own undesirable behavior toward a child is an evolutionary necessity required to facilitate separation. Our childhood habitat, no matter how awful it was, is still the only paradise we have ever had. It is also a prison, however, for our dependency. We require expulsion, if we cannot escape ourselves. Birds gently push their babies from the nest, in spite of their hesitations and even heart-wrenching protestations. In *Soul Mates,* Thomas Moore discusses that Adam and Eve were the first to be expelled from Paradise, and according to some tradition, their fall was even considered *felix culpa,* a "fortunate error." Through their errors, mistakes, bad judgments, conflicts, and emotional battles, parents invariably set the stage for children—postadolescence—to leave home. Adolescents commit their share of mistakes and undesirable behaviors to facilitate the expulsion. They often overtly devalue their parents. All of these errors of parents and children are fortunate errors—they assist in the separation process. Fortunate errors, however, can become unfortunate ones—if these individuation-specific conflicts between parents and children are perpetuated *after* the separation. If you keep grown-up children home and fail to allow their healthy separation, you may find your spouse may leave emotionally, if not literally.

You Can Go Back Home—and You Must.

For a complete development of a sense of self, adolescents must participate in a psychological return to their parents after the separation phase of adolescence. The permanent severing of familial relations, a kind of "parentectomy," is unfortunately misconstrued as a requirement for adulthood. A differentiation of our self from others is an important aspect of individuation and requires a *psychological* separation from the nuclear family. This is an extraordinarily difficult task. Frequently, a person remains too close within the familial environment, at least within familiar range. While the attachment, love, and sustenance provided by the family may make separation difficult, our excessive anxiety, guilt, self-doubt, emotional enmeshment, and dependency interfere with individuation. Nonetheless, the entire responsibility does not belong to the family. In fact, the child, with her own temperamental and biological makeup, must participate in and accept the separation as well.

Boys and girls have somewhat different paths toward their respective individuation. The ongoing development of female sexual identity requires that fundamental attachment to the mother remain. The development of male sexual identity, however, requires a continuous attempt to separate from mother. The special issues of separation for girls, therefore, as well as the issues of intimacy for boys, are potentially anxiety producing (if not disorienting, destabilizing experiences). Adolescents' attempts to sever the remnants of dependent attachment are tumultuous and uncompromising, frequently manifesting in powerful negative scenarios. The deeper the original attachment, the worse the psychological altercations. The outcome of the separation will determine the nature and quality of the adolescent's individuation.

Various stages are experienced as the developing child progresses from dependency (in-love stage) to counterdependence (power struggle) and, ultimately, to independence. At no stage, however, does a child or adolescent actually take leave of his parents completely. As each stage builds on the preceding one, an adolescent must have a successful negotiation of the early stages in order to have a better chance of establishing the foundation for sense of self. A completely differentiated and severed relationship with our family is not healthy or desirable: it uproots and disconnects. Instead, differentiation requires not only accepting one's roots but getting *reattached* to them without being dependent.

This return home is not being one with the family as we once were, but rather a softening of our boundaries with the family. It is a differentiated engagement, not an enmeshment. Differentiation comes to those individuated persons who are now individuated enough to remain involved without the fear of enmeshment. Although the main separation-individuation occurs within the formative years, attachment should remain forever. Other separations are lifelong processes because of the inherent threat of loss in every stage. Balancing the old attachments with new engagements tempers these losses. Adolescents who are able to return home psychologically to the members of the family, a second time around, come back without excessive dependency or guilt, without fight or flight, without being in love or in hate. It is a natural and healthy reunion. Welcome your adolescents and young adults wholeheartedly, for they will further ground your marriage. An adolescent who fails to separate successfully, and a family that resists such healthy separation, may very likely suffer the consequences when this young person eventually marries. That person may then bring an already enmeshed relationship to a new marriage and be less able to establish a solid adult relationship with a spouse.

Note

1. Letter to the authors from Dr. Margaret Hertzig, October 2003. These findings were not published but were presented in New York at New York University in the 1950s.

CHAPTER 7

Midlife in Marriage

Marital conflicts intensify during midlife as crises of maturation and self-realization. We are confronted with a reawakening of our vulnerabilities—it is our last stand. Unless spouses resolve their own personal conflicts, either spouse may target the marriage for personal discontent or see it as an obstruction to individual growth.

Feather Up: "Anatomy Is Destiny," but You Can Do Some Touch-Ups.

> In short, if you want a good sex life, you have to look the part.
>
> —Mae West, *Mae West on Sex, Health and ESP*

"Women who wear red Victoria's Secret panties during courtship," says Iris Krasnow, "put on beige Sears cotton underwear during marriage. Hardbodied male suitors become potbellied husbands." If anything, during marriage spouses need to pay *more* attention to their bodies and looks to remain attractive and desirable than during the courting phase. People are much more accepting of each other prior to marriage, more easily aroused and forgiving.

"Anatomy is destiny," declared Freud in "Dissolution of the Oedipus Complex"—but you can improve your advantage. A case in point emerges from consideration of the African widowbird. Malte Andersson, a foremost Swedish geneticist, studied this particular species. Observing that male widowbirds drag around spectacular and seemingly excessive tails, whose feathers can be longer than six feet, Andersson decided to examine what these tail feathers signify in terms of mate attraction. His experiment required that he deliberately alter some of the tails by artificially adding extra feathers or shortening some. He also left some other tails intact. He found that even the most dramatic and extravagant natural tail was no match for the female's attraction to Andersson's man-made creations. In effect, his newly created male widowbirds had outsmarted nature, even resulting in a revised widowbird mating season. The new elaborate birds were suddenly in great demand, quickly sharing their nests with available females, whereas the sheared birds were no longer desirable. Those male widowbirds, whose naturally long, beautiful tails would have otherwise made them the most desirable, had been replaced. The natural male birds were no more at the pinnacle of the mating hierarchy. Since the widowbird tails did not function as species protection and were useless as weapons (because the long-tailed birds were neither stronger nor fiercer), Andersson concluded that such sexual selection was simply about appearances. In other words, here females clearly favored certain elaborate male ornaments.

Likewise, Marion Petrie, Tim Halliday, and Carolyn Sanders studied peacocks and peahens. They concluded that the huge, elaborate peacock's train, just as Darwin had suggested, has evolved partly as a result of female preference. Females clearly prefer peacocks with the most elaborate trains. They noted that males are rarely seen to fight. Fighting would damage the peacock's tail, and males may be reluctant to engage in fighting to protect themselves, especially if a damaged train may result in lower mating success. In other words, the authors conclude that females could use the train as a means of assessing a male's performance in past contests, or, in other words, his fitness.

Baltasar Gracián's *The Art of Wordly Wisdom* explains that things do not transpire for what they are, but for what they seem. Although the story of the widowbirds is about the attraction of opposite sexes and the mating hierarchy, it is equally applicable to all relationships. An elegant self-presentation—clothing, hairdo, grooming, and language as our plumage—is important in pursuing a job or promotion, building confidence in others, and enhancing your social and organizational hierarchy.

- Men and women should pay more attention to their bodies and grooming during marriage than during the courting phase.
- Overworry about looks, age, and weight in midlife is a losing battle; grow old together and gracefully.

But somehow in marriage we tend to set aside that commonly known principle. Marriage is obviously more important than one's relations with others, or one's social or organizational standings, even one's job—though some dispute that. Are you taking it for granted?—Don't! Are you lazy?—Liven up. Do you have narcissistic entitlement?—Recover fast. Are you becoming uninterested in your spouse?—You need help.

Desperate Attempts to Stay Young Inevitably Frustrate and Depress You and Disturb the Marriage.

> The Lord said they'll live 120 years, humans.
>
> —Genesis 6:3

Sam: *"Since she turned forty, our life together has been transformed into a mission: how to keep her young, thin, and beautiful. She is so intensely focused on herself that it seems like neither I nor the children matter. If anything, we have become her entourage as assistants, timekeepers, weight watchers, mirrors, and cheerers.*

She had her nose fixed, her eyelids lifted, and her thighs suctioned a few times. She is always on the treadmill or doing stretching exercises or lifting weights with her trainer who more or less has checked in with us. She scrutinizes the calories and the content of everything she eats but still eats them. We have an extensive library of books and videos on food, cooking, exercise, dieting, plastic surgery, and beauty items. The only topics that she brings up are about various diet formulas and their relative merits, the nature of exercise, the best Botox dermatologists in town, skin creams, and shampoos. She constantly buys new outfits, taking their waistlines in and out as her weight fluctuates. She runs from stress reduction yoga and tai chi classes to her therapists; she has two—one individual therapist, the other, a group therapist who meets with group members individually as well. Then she complains that she is too busy and worries that she is ugly and too fat; she is getting old and tired.

Ironically enough, just watching her is exhausting me. And I see no end to this; if anything, it'll get worse. We have no joy in our life, only disciplined existence. Our life has become a treadmill itself; we are going nowhere. At times, I wish I had a wife who ate and drank without much thought, and who occasionally took a casual walk with me and even then, ran out of breath."

Within the last few centuries, the *average* life expectancy in modern societies has steadily increased. However, the *maximum* duration of life (life span) has not followed the same configuration. Three hundred years ago, only a handful of individuals lived beyond one hundred years of age; now, even though far more people live that long, the maximum life span today appears to be about the same. No matter how much we attempt to postpone aging, we find the death clock ticks at its own pace. Aging, though, may speed its rate; illnesses or accidents may harm its hardware, but the mechanism of the clock is relatively immune from external factors. Commonly, somewhere between the seventieth and eightieth year, for most humans, the dying clock seems to detonate, says Deepak Chopra.

The human body and, for that matter, animals' bodies, are perfect organisms. There are exquisite and intricate connections among various hormones and their multiple feedback systems in regulating the body's blood sugar, skin moisture, erection in men, lubrication in women, and orgasm in both, as well as in maintaining surfaces of joints, breathing patterns, heartbeat, blood pressure, digestion, and catabolism.

Our body's components, however, seem to possess a limited warranty. The wear and tear derives not necessarily from different but from natural and induced oxidation and the production of stress hormones, the glucocorticoids. Each species produces glucocorticoids (which are not by themselves harmful to the body) through the adrenal glands. On the other hand, under stress, the body pumps excessive glucocorticoids, especially cortisol, for no apparent reason, resulting in exhaustion, severe depletion, and even death, explains Chopra.

The excessive production of corticoids that cause the rapid aging and death in Pacific salmon is a potent example of this "no apparent reason." Chopra further notes that these young salmon spend their first four years of life at sea, swimming thousands of miles, until they unbelievably arrive at their destination—the exact freshwater lakes where they were born. After accomplishing this incredible journey upstream, through natural rapids and man-made dams, the mature salmon finally spawn. And almost immediately thereafter, alas, they perish!

Chopra explains that what prompts the salmon to age virtually overnight is an internal body clock, built into their DNA. The critical factor is cortisol, which is generally as potent a stress hormone in animals as it is in humans. In salmon, it becomes a death hormone, from its sudden massive release from the adrenal glands. This release of cortisol occurs even if the fish are removed from the sea before migration and are permitted to spawn in peak physical condition, rather than in an exhausted state.

Individual species have their own biological clocks that transcend environmental manipulation. Such aging clocks conform to their own inherent timetables, without regard to environmental influences. For example, after spawning, no special treatment or protection from external stress changes the fate of salmon. Nature, however, continues remarkably to balance an inordinate array of ingredients. The individual life span of any member of a species varies, while the overall life span of the species itself is preserved, for example, only one day for the mayfly or nearly a century for human beings.

Chopra soberly observes that the concept of a body clock is inevitably disturbing to the imagination: we liken it to a time bomb that is constantly ticking, while animals unknowingly await their own destiny. It is, in other words, an aging or death clock.

According to Seneca, "No man can have a peaceful life who thinks too much about lengthening it." People can live better, and maybe even longer, if they are not so preoccupied with living longer. We might expect that we would fatigue from our unrealized worries about health, work, life, or death and that our neuroses would crumble away from sheer exhaustion. Unfortunately, not. In the words of E. M. Cioran, we continue to fear "to have accomplished nothing and to die overworked." In fact, most likely we may have accomplished plenty but died overworried.

When both spouses overworry about their looks, weight, age, and death, they may forfeit their joyful existence. They may feed into the neuroses of each other, preempting other priorities, primarily zestful living. The major reason we may want to live a longer and healthier life is to enjoy what we have—life as it is.

If only one spouse, however, is so preoccupied, a marital conflict ensues. The clash of their lifestyles, if not their life philosophy, manifests in every aspect of their daily living. Spouses accuse each other of excessive self-concern and narcissism, and they exhibit harsh intolerance and ignorance of each other. Marriage becomes a field of attack and defense and determination to convert your spouse into your own way of being, albeit unsuccessfully. Our advice? Don't try too hard! You might alienate your spouse. Trying too hard to look young, as with Botox and plastic surgery, is a losing battle. Your efforts should go toward looking the best and healthiest for your age.

It Is Common to Displace Personal Midlife Crises onto the Marriage.

A Very, Very Brief History of Marriage
1963 Niagara
1999 Viagra

—Judith Viorst,
Suddenly Sixty and Other Shocks of Later Life

Sam's wife Linda gave a surprise party recently to celebrate his fiftieth birthday. This wasn't exactly a surprise to him as she had left plenty of evidence during the preparation for it: bills, telephone messages, her frenetic state and coyness, the children's conspiratorial tone of voice, and so forth. He wished she hadn't fussed so much about it and spent all that money for nothing:

> Sam: *"What is there to celebrate? I look like my father; my gums have receded up to the roots of my teeth; my hair is limited to my sideburns; my eyes are failing—I can't even read a menu in restaurants, so I ask the waiters what is good that night and just order that. The firm is an upper-class, three-card monte: I sell hopeless stocks to the public, and when the company collapses, we help a vulture buy it for a song. I make money either way. I am not worried about it at all. Every business is a con game. I am only worried that my body has changed. I am always constipated, no matter how many prunes I eat. The constipation has caused hemorrhoids, which then has caused anemia. Now I have to take iron pills and B^{12}, on top of another twenty pills: vitamins, antioxidants, two different cholesterol medicines. Oh, I forgot the Metamucil, which makes me gassy and bloated all day long. It is awfully uncomfortable, and I've got to be careful whether I am with a client or in a movie theater, because the smell of my whole body is different. Even my fart has changed. I cannot stand it. It is so foul.*
>
> *Even my orgasms are different. Only a few drops of ejaculation spurt out. It feels like it's going backward. I don't get the total release that I used to get. Afterward, I feel unsatisfied, if not a little discomforted. I try again, hoping that the second time around the whole thing would come out. No. The same, a few drops. The psychiatrist I saw thought that I am depressed and gave me Zoloft which made matters worse. Now I can't even have an erection, and if I even get there, I can't ejaculate at all.*
>
> *What do I think is my problem? I am not depressed. I am just unhappy, period. Both girls are grown-up now and living their lives. My wife and I are like two ships passing in the night. There is no tension between us; there are no fights—well, occasionally. We both work hard, come home, have either take-out dinner or cook something simple, watch a little television, and go to bed. In the morning, back to the same routine. Have you ever seen the movie* Groundhog Day? *It is like that. I feel like I'll continue doing the same thing, seeing the same friends, and one day, I'll just die.*
>
> *What should I do? Dump the whole thing, the job, Linda, and go to some small island in the Pacific, buy a hut, and live among the natives. Perhaps get a teaching job in a small college in the Midwest, live on campus, maybe remarry, this time a young student; I don't know. I would do something like that if Linda didn't exist, died or something. I feel guilty even*

saying that. The occasional fights that I mentioned usually come out of my provoking her to throw me out. But she isn't going to do that. For menopausal women, options are even more limited. So, I am resentful. Here I am sacrificing my life because she has no alternatives.

Have I talked to her about this? Yes, she says, 'Go, I'll survive, don't worry about me. Do you think it is fun to have you around, always complaining about yourself, me, and everything? Go!'

Why don't I take up the offer? Because I am not sure whether that is what I want either."

This is the lamentation of a man in middle-age individuation, getting ready to make his marriage the target of his discontent. Humans go through three major normal individuation phases: childhood, adolescence, and middle age—each with its own built-in crises. Although these crises reflect internal personal struggles, they manifest themselves within a social context. The individuation phases of childhood and adolescence have a counterpoint—the family—whereby the child and adolescent individuate via separation from significant others within the family. Middle-age individuation, however, has no such counterpoint. The person does not have to individuate from anyone and certainly, specifically, not by separation from a spouse. He or she is expected to maintain strong allegiance to the spouse while going through a crisis. Frequently enough, however, a spouse is conveniently used as a counterpoint to individual crises. Marital conflicts then ensue and supercede personal ones. Divorce doesn't resolve the individual impasse; it only delays and exacerbates it. If anything, internal problems worsen with the additional stresses associated with the dissolution of the marriage. Middle-age individuation must fold on itself; it is a kind of separation from the self, a self that had defined the person until then, and quite often falsely—such as the image of an eternally youthful and immortal person or one with unusually high expectations.

- A marriage may become a target for the dissatisfaction of one spouse in midlife.
- Undiagnosed or untreated psychological disturbances, such as anxiety or depression, are common factors in the deterioration of a marriage.
- Spouses with personality disorders, such as narcissism and sociopathy, are particularly vulnerable to midlife difficulties and may cause havoc in their marriage by their behavior.

Adults become confused in midlife because of their gradual realization that they have limitations as human beings. Carl Jung wrote of the vulnerability people experience around age forty, particularly if one holds onto youth and refuses to embrace midlife. The task of midlife is to begin to take stock of one's life and focus on one's work. It is the time when both men and women express their own mature uniqueness as individuals. It is the time to come to terms with these limitations.

In contrast to the future-looking hopeful expectation of adolescence, those in middle age view the future as worse than the present; this is partly the result of both men and women beginning to experience major physiological transformations heralding, sometimes with great consequence, inauspicious changes. In turn, these changes result in serious psychological effects. For women, the impending end of the childbearing years in the perimenopausal time, followed by actual menopause, is a well-known stressful physiological marker.

> Linda: *"I began to experience changes in the past year, just after my forty-eighth birthday. Believe it or not, at first, I had no idea what was happening. Initially, it was just that I couldn't sleep through the night. It never even occurred to me this could be the beginning of menopause. My periods were still coming. At first, I would get up every couple of hours for no reason at all. I had always been a good sleeper. Sometimes, I would go back to sleep, sometimes, not. Then the hot flashes began. But initially the hot flashes were so subtle. I thought it was just the heat in the building. I would feel like I was burning up, then later, I would be cold. Then, I would start awakening from sleep covered in sweat—this would happen five or six times each night. I would awaken exhausted in the morning. The sweats sometimes continued during the day. I had to start dressing differently. I would be the one with a sleeveless blouse on in the middle of winter. And my moods—unbelievable! I would find myself crying for no reason. I'd be watching some silly commercial on TV, and I'd start getting choked up and even begin to cry.*
>
> *Finally, I realized what was happening. I guess I was just denying that this was all menopause. My periods started getting less regular too, and when they came, bleeding was very heavy. And I now notice how dry I am—I just can't get lubricated during sex. And I feel my mind is going too. I just can't remember things the way I used to. I feel I am just not that sharp mentally.*
>
> *Sam, of course, who is not the most sensitive even under the best of circumstances, has no tolerance for any of this—which just makes everything worse. He really just doesn't get it. And he keeps wanting sex, which now hurts. I don't have much interest in him most of the time now. I feel so irritable and angry. And this whole controversy about taking hormone replacement! What a mess! I don't know what to do.*

Sometimes, I even feel I want out of this marriage, but where would I go? The girls are mostly grown and out on their own. I feel nobody needs me—especially not Sam."

Gail Sheehy has suggested that there is a man's menopause, which she calls "manopause." Though not as hormonally based as it is for women, it is more gradual and elusive than female menopause. Yet it may share comparable prevalent symptoms, including irritability, sluggishness, and mild to moderate mood alternations. In addition, physically, a man may notice a decrease in muscle mass and strength, and psychologically, a lowering of his overall sense of well-being, increased vague anxiety, and a specific one—problems of gaining and sustaining erections. Such events as losing one's job or being disregarded for promotion in midlife, as well as nonspecific losses of power and control and other defeats, decrease already naturally declining testosterone levels and contribute further to a loss of sexual interest and confidence.

The arrival of middle age heralds other signs of aging: the loss of one's eyesight, hearing, teeth, hair, physical shape and stamina, sexual attractiveness, and even intellectual rigor. While decline hurts a man's pride, he still desires to live forever, and his fear of death encourages him to confront his ultimate fate. This age is his last chance to find himself before losing it. Joseph Campbell notes about Dante: "in the middle years of his life, he was lost in a dangerous wood, in which he was threatened by three animals that symbolized pride, desire, and fear. Then Virgil, the personification of poetic insight, appeared and conducted him through the labyrinth of hell, which is the place where those fixed to their desires and fears remain, unable to pass through to eternity."

Middle age is a period of life when we find it unendurable to experience outer losses. If we cannot shift the focus onto an inner search for the meaning of our existence, we frequently blame the marriage for our unhappiness. If anything, it is the other way around; personal unhappiness is frequently the cause of marital discord. Undiagnosed or untreated psychological disturbances, especially anxiety and depression, are common factors in the deterioration of marriages.

Our misery is related to that of a sense of entitlement for a vague concept of "happiness." Its inevitable absence condemns us to a childlike search and chronic disappointment—a vicious circle of self-addiction, depriving us of finding what makes one obtain a joyful and serene grown-up life.

A Narcissistic Person's Self-Addiction Deprives Him of a Spouse's Help.

Sam: *"Linda thinks that I am simply a selfish person, period . . . that I am only interested in myself, the whole middle-age crisis is nonsense, that*

I have been in the same crisis since she met me, that I am addicted to my-self, that I only talk about myself.

I am the only one of us who went to an Ivy League school; I think I am interesting, maybe a little peculiar, but still interesting. Linda and the girls all are vanilla ice cream. They are only interested in talking about their hair, their skin, their weight, and potential husbands.

I am making all the money for the indulgences of all three women. Yes, Linda works but her salary is insignificant in comparison to my income. Once, I tried to tell them the how and why of a hostile takeover. Not only were they not interested in listening, but they accused me of being im-moral, if not actually criminal. Can you believe that? My own family!"

Linda may be correct in her interpretation of her husband's psychological state. Any crisis, especially a middle-age individuation crisis, compounds the personality traits of the individual. Persons with narcissistic traits are addicted to themselves. They are the center of their own universe. No one else, nor anyone else's feelings, matter as much. They are typically insensitive to others, not empathetic, and downright selfish.

The word "addiction" is commonly used in conjunction with matters "from without," whether drugs, shopping, alcohol, gambling, work, even sex. Alternatively, addiction "from within" receives little attention, even though it causes as much, if not greater, damage to the individual suffering from it. Despite the ostensible distinction between the two, in some ways all external addictions are consequences or different manifestations of self-addiction. In either event, to be addicted means to surrender yourself to something obsessively. It is a compulsive habit, an acquired pattern of behavior that has become and feels nearly, if not totally, outside of your control. In its extreme form, psychological addiction compounds physiological addiction, causing cravings for the substance or object in question, as well as withdrawal symptoms in its absence.

When it comes to self-addiction, the subject (the addict) and the object (the matter of addiction) are the same. Maybe for that reason, in our society self-indulgence is relatively well tolerated, if not encouraged, by most psychological and pseudotherapeutic tenets of our times. A profusion of contemporary books condones self-preoccupation and self-centered behaviors and lifestyles. Selfishness at the expense of others—malignant selfishness—thus becomes a legitimate, if not highly desirable, character trait. Even though there may be some concrete gains in ardently pursuing self-interest, a person in this pursuit inevitably experiences vacuous isolation.

The cessation of self-addiction (it requires a long and arduous journey) may initially generate some confusion and disruption of the pathological status quo, but it eventually results in a special contentment. With the addiction removed,

> Survival of marriage in midlife demands full engagement:
>
> • In midlife, see your spouse as your life-witness, not your adversary.
> • In midlife, cultivate independence and attachment: a cointerdependence.

a person whose previous characteristics were seen in the addictive cycle (e.g., grandiosity, holding court, seeking praise or envy, diminishing others, self-preoccupation) begins to appear pathetic.

The Spouse Is a Life-Witness, if Nothing Else.

Remember, particularly in midlife, the words of Robert Louis Stevenson that by marrying, "You have willfully introduced a witness into your life."

> Sam: *"At times I feel like I am about to grasp what I really want; but I consciously stop pursuing. In that fleeting moment what I want is to run away from Linda and the girls. How did I get here? I have forfeited myself by becoming a husband and father.*
>
> *Do Linda and our daughters really have me as husband and father? I always have one foot out, psychologically. If I fully commit myself to them, I feel, I would be missing something elsewhere. That something I could never formulate. Women, money, other places were only temporarily distracting. I am not fully there either. I seem not to want what I have, but what I don't have, and I don't know what that is. Wherever I am I want to be elsewhere, but I don't know where that elsewhere is. I don't have a specific place or woman in my mind. Wouldn't I be better off living alone?"*

Just as there are near-death experiences as one briefly hovers on the brink of dying but doesn't die, some people exist in a manner in which they do not experience life fully. They are on the brink of living. Such near-life existence is a state where a person feels alienated, not only from himself but from others. In the formation of the self and maintenance thereafter, we need others. As Tzvetan Todorov states: "The very being of man is a *profound communication . . .* he is all and always on the boundary; looking within himself, he looks *in the eyes of the other or through the eyes of the other.*"

Interestingly enough, a woman, although this custom is changing, as we have noted, has usually taken the last name of her husband. His name is no longer his alone but her name too. His life is living in the context of a family. His health, his job, and his successes and failures have witnesses and sometimes judges. We fully live our personal lives only in engaged relationships. Marriage is full engagement.

A Marriage Requires Transparency to Your Spouse.

> When I am weak, I am strong.
>
> —2 Corinthians 12:10

Sam: *"No, I never shared these thoughts with my wife. I don't think she would appreciate them to begin with, but also I don't want her to see me confused; after all I am supposed to be the man of the house. Linda thinks I am too self-preoccupied anyway, so she most likely would dismiss these thoughts as just another example of my 'narcissism.'*

Furthermore, I've got to figure all this out myself. I mean, you can't really rely on others for life questions. Linda and I may easily get divorced; the girls are already gone. Speaking of selfishness, I only hear from them when they need something. Do I ever call them? No. What for? Since they discovered other men they hardly relate to me. This year both of them came to the surprise party with their boyfriends and after a procedural hug they just deserted me.

That night, after we came home Linda said 'You know, you were not very social. All your friends and family were there for you, but you weren't there. I can tell from your glazed eyes. Where were you? This was your moment of being recognized by everyone, including your children. You couldn't wait for it to be over.' She was right. When I told her how impersonal her and my daughters' toasts were, she replied, 'Because we don't know you. If you go on like this, at your funeral I am going to say: 'Sam! We never knew you.'"

Intimacy is a kind of reciprocated psychological striptease. It means exposing our vulnerabilities to our self and to another, and enabling the other to do the same comfortably. Sam, who avoided any intimate relationships, defended his position by his private axiom: "One is born alone and dies alone." Like Sam, we all assert our own pronouncements that explain our idiosyncratic forms of avoiding love and intimacy.

During midlife, cultivate a wholeheartedly supportive relationship:

- Expect illnesses, losses, and other adversities.
- Be more attentive and nurturant during life crises.
- Generously comfort your spouse when in stress.
- Tame even your reasonable demands during your spouse's difficult times.

Love is a kind of "sugar-coated neurosis," Sam said, quoting his old analyst. "Men and women belong to different species," this analyst professed. These statements may all be true but may also be used as "fear defenses" against love: the fear of failure in love; the fear of being found out and rejected; and especially the fear of losing the loved one. In *Soul Mates*, Thomas Moore says people who love are always faced with separations, if nothing else, then with the inevitable separation of death such that "love is always laced with death." These fears will deprive a person of two significant anchors: twoness and oneness—intimacy with someone else and self-intimacy.

Personal and interpersonal grounding requires being aware of and sharing our weaknesses, including these fear defenses, with intimates. Most of us disavow any vulnerabilities, claiming not to possess any. We must not deny such vulnerability but, rather, reclaim it. Social demands of invulnerability in males inflict unnecessary aloneness and emotional isolation as inevitable side effects of being "strong." At times of stress, some individuals experience total collapse from the pressure of this posture. Frequently, we are astonished to learn of a severe breakdown, suicide, or other destructive behavior (toward self or others) in a person we thought of as the Rock of Gibraltar. The best two preventive measures against the total breakdown of one's psyche are: first, claim your vulnerabilities by incorporating them as part of yourself and, second, share them with your intimates. Nonintimates, by definition, are likely to consider such sharing a burden. If the afflicted person fails to expose his weaknesses spontaneously and his intimates fail to facilitate the process, he will experience an emotional divorce.

Self-Knowledge Is a Precondition to Intimacy with a Spouse.

Sam: *"'We never knew you?' I never knew myself. I mean I have some idea but not really. I think Linda knows me as much as I know myself, well may be a little less. But I don't know her that well either. I am not all that interested in getting to know her. If I spend too much time with her, I'll be short-changing myself, or if I get to know her better I couldn't leave her, if I needed to.*

Do you know what I mean? I want my options to be open. Equally, if I knew myself I would be frozen in time. I can no longer surprise myself. I don't want to be found by myself or by others. Being lost has the potential of going further, or at least thrashing around to seek. But being found and understood is like dying. What else is there to do?"

Sam is in such a quandary because he doesn't realize that "there" is within himself. Only by going to himself simultaneously can he go somewhere with others. *Intimacy* is the sharing of our emotions and thoughts with another person. Before we can achieve such an interpersonal intimacy, however, we must gain a sense of self-intimacy. Some people explore relationships with many others—sort of a "platonic promiscuity" (Edward Hoagland's term)—anticipating that through them, they will develop an ability to be intimate. A relationship is beneficial, but the deficiency within cannot be totally ameliorated from the outside.

A Person Needs to Be in Synchrony with His or Her World in Order to Be in Synchrony with a Spouse.

Sam: *"It isn't just my family. I don't feel part of the firm or my neighborhood either. The firm is a cash cow; it exploits me and I exploit the clients. Is there a moral to the story? There's no moral, and it is fine with me. Because I never thought that there was one. So there is no disappointment here at all. If anything, it validates my point of view: there are no permanent friends or enemies, only permanent interests. I can't say and do that for Linda and the girls, for they seem to have certain moral fiber and genuine feelings, commitments. I wish I were single, so I could really let myself loose in the world. My family's existence, to some extent, restrains me from doing really selfish things or things that I would just do for kicks: like burning down the house, poisoning the dogs in the neighborhood, or sleeping with anyone I wanted. I was going to say cheating the firm and clients; well, I already do that. I need some über stimuli to get engaged, to feel alive. It is not enough that I win; someone has to lose and lose big."*

In order to be stable, the self, that is, the totality of one's makeup (i.e., emotions, thoughts, perceptions, and sensations) needs *cohesion* and *coherence*. *Cohesion* is an internal process involving the integration of these various elements of the self in synchrony with each other. *Coherence* is an external process of synchrony with the outside world. It is a process of internalizing the attributes of our culture and environment. Under the best circumstances, internal cohesion and external coherence synchronously participate in the adaptive development and formation of our identity.

As Kenneth Gergen describes, contemporary Western man is the reluctant recipient of two major cultural and societal inheritances: the nineteenth-century romantic (passion, creativity, moral fiber, and personal depth) and the twentieth-century modern (reason, rationality, and conscious choices). A romantic view of the self is essential to the formation of deeply committed relations, dedicated friendships, and profound life goals and purposes. It provides the inherited makings of a *collective soul.* The modernist view of the self is reasonable and predictable, and it makes educated choices such as the rational selection of marital partners—in short, the inherited makings of a *collective mind.* In both the romantic and modernist views, the self is in synchrony with its respective world and the temper of the culture. Those nineteenth- and twentieth-century people who failed to develop internal cohesiveness and external coherence suffered from a multitude of neurotic disorders.

Contemporary man, that is, twenty-first-century man, assumes either of those two inheritances—romanticism and modernism—whenever it is convenient. Sam is not in total synchrony with or committed to either of them. In short, his self is under siege; here, competing meanings create the danger of no meaning at all. The diversified voices of humankind are forcing him to face a multiplicity of sometimes incoherent selves. He doesn't even recognize what he desires. Sam is an example of ultimate isolation. Such isolation, providing neither inner cohesiveness nor external coherence, is responsible for his pervasive feelings of emptiness and profound inner disturbance that he experiences in marriage as well as at work.

Nineteenth- and twentieth-century mental disturbances—neuroses—are conflicts within a person. Says Jung, "The neurotic is rather a person who can never have things as he would like them in the present and who can therefore never enjoy the past either." As unhealthy as they may appear, neurotic symptoms, that is, hysteria, hypochondriasis, conversion, and so forth, only indirectly affect other people. In our era a person may not have such discrete ailments but may experience other, more diffuse, symptoms such as anxiety and depression. More commonly, he will show the hardened traits of a personality disorder, such as a narcissistic character disorder. It is the disturbance of our era—a condition from which the afflicted person suffers indirectly, whereas others in his life suffer directly. A neurotic person actively participates in his own suffering, as his established *complaints* simultaneously function to soothe him and make him feel intact. People like Sam, who do not evolve psychologically and fail to tame their narcissism, cause suffering to their spouses, as *other people's* pains and complaints simultaneously function to soothe and make them feel whole. Often, they make others feel bad as a way of feeling better themselves. In the process, people like Sam turn their marriage into soul murder.

The Emperor Has Too Many Clothes: A Narcissist Slowly Murders the Spouse's Soul.

Sam: *"Oh, my father? He was my idol. Everyone considered him a small-time crook. He wasn't. He was a big-time crook in a small pond.*

My other idol is President Clinton. Now there's a big crook, in the biggest pond. I love him. He turned all the stupid rules of society and the family upside down. He cheated on his wife, his staff, his own government, his own court and came out laughing. He beat his own system. I love it. What is he really saying? The whole thing is bullshit: marriage, fatherhood, screwing others, young and old; lying under oath. There is no crime or sin unless you get caught. You apologize and pay your fine and then carry on as usual. Don't you love it? What other fucking meaning does one have to search for in life, except recognition that the whole thing is meaningless. You only feel empty if you seek a meaning in life, and if you don't believe there is one, then you don't feel empty. Well, I am not sure what I am saying either. Anyway, you got the gist of it."

The last few decades have seen yet another transmutation in our culture, whereby we observe sociopathic traits in addition to narcissistic characteristics. Neuroses of the early-twentieth century—for better or worse—were the result of excessive guilt, with family and religion providing the prohibitive structure. As these weakened and lost their prohibitive influence, many no longer felt the signature affect of guilt. With decreased anxiety and guilt come moral idleness and decay (and hence sociopathic behavior).

There is a small subgroup of people, usually men, who have these sociopathic, as well as narcissistic, traits. These are the people like Sam who violate the rules of others. They may lie and steal and cheat and deceive, whether at home or at work. Spouses have to be vigilant about these men since, characterologically, they cannot be trusted. Further, these men often tap into the masochistic (wish for punishment) needs of their wives. For these men, the spouse is something owned, and the marriage is something to be manipulated to serve their own interest. Their wives then fall prey to their charm and lies and deception, especially if these women earlier had been victims of psychological or physical abuse themselves. Sometimes, a spouse has similar character traits. In this case, her marriage will less likely survive unless she can extract some compensation or benefit of her own from the marriage.

In Peter De Vries's *Reuben, Reuben,* the protagonist says "Marriage is corrupting." Here, it is the narcissistic sociopaths who corrupt marriage, among other things. They even corrupt counseling since they lie and deceive in therapy as well. Such a person should be put under total psychological receivership.

While *personal fatherlessness* (a man's actual absence or, even worse, his presence as an idealized father without ethical values, a so-called negative hero) is responsible for the moral decay in a specific family, *collective fatherlessness* (Thomas Moore's term in *Care of the Soul*), has had the same effect on a national scale. The influence of the traditional family, as well as organized religion, is in decline. They might have induced excessive guilt, but they also provided support and structure. The demands of religion may have contributed to the formation of a severe conscience, but they also afforded a sense of belonging and meaningful context to life. With the decline of the influence of organized religion and an intact family structure have come severe disturbances of the self and the unleashing of unrestrained impulses, sometimes with total imperviousness to others. The narcissistic sociopath—the prototype illness of the last few decades—vulnerable to pervasive feelings of emptiness, and invulnerable to feelings of guilt, began to search for an anchoring philosophy and discovered it in the nature of a capitalistic equivalent: "Everything has a price and can be bought or sold. The primary principle is to win, the truth is what one says it is. One is what one says one is." This philosophy contributes to the making of a false self. Fear (or more aptly, fearlessness) has replaced guilt. Legality has replaced ethics, and the modus operandi becomes how to maneuver the system.

> Sam: *"The problem with me is I can play many roles, but I am simply impersonating those roles. I am doing things to find what I want. So I fall between the cracks. I am not like you, serenely settled down and wanting nothing. Well, at least that is how you present yourself."*

A narcissistic sociopath can be thought of as an actor whose stage is the world. In contrast, a normal person is dependent on his inner life for his self-presentation, which ranges from a transient mood to a deeper, more persistent sense of his existence. To some extent, realness versus impersonation, "being" versus "seeming," are universal struggles. Except in narcissistic sociopaths, one's presentation of falseness is not designed primarily to deceive others but rather reflects a natural mutability characteristic of an unformed self. The establishment of one's "being" is a lengthy process of transformation during which many configurations are stand-ins for one's real essence. In fact, one may be more accurate by talking about "becoming" rather than "being," the former implying something that is active and dynamic, the latter something that is static. Unfortunately, for some people like Sam "seeming" remains the only self. They remain inauthentic and alienated. To some extent, every person plays a determined role in a myriad of social and work situations. Praise of such adaptation and almost chameleon-like behavior may be useful, only if there is also a real self that resides behind the adaptive or even deceptive mask. For Sam, there is no real self underneath.

> Sam: *"My younger daughter says 'I can't hang my hat on you.' I never heard such an expression; it must be one of those college expressions. Anyway, she means, I guess, that I am not a steady, solid presence in her life; a sort of illusive character that she can't place. Welcome to the club. I can't hang my hat on me either. I don't believe in anything. My wife, the family, work, religion, or government—or myself. So, where do we go from here? How can anyone be earnestly a wife, a child, to me?"*

Some people effortlessly capitulate to society's familial and social order, with the hope of "becoming" by association. They may appear to be in earnest—not sociopathic—as long as they remain within some collective selfhood. Some others, like creative people, manage relatively to disregard much of the social order. Their selves are intertwined with their work, and they feel no need for an independent self as long as they are creative, at least in their own eyes. Most others fall somewhere in-between. They can neither yield to society and thus be in a deceptive unity with it nor can they disregard it. They are dangerous to themselves, and they suffer from all sorts of symptoms of maladaptation.

Coindependence: A Healthy and Mature Relationship between Spouses

> Sam: *"I don't complain—to my wife, my children, my friends, my colleagues—about their inaccessibility. They are fine as they are, as far as I am concerned. I didn't know my parents that well either. I didn't care then, I don't care now. I mean, every one for himself, right? If my wife died, let's say, my life would change a little bit. I'd get another wife who, incidentally, would have the same complaints about me as Linda: 'I don't feel you really love me; you never listen to my problems; you never help me out; you never praise me!' Linda has to go to the hospital for an operation. They found a growth, most likely a fibroma, in her uterus. Doc-*

tors think that it isn't dangerous, but it could become so. So they'll try to scoop it out from below if possible. If not, they'll take the whole uterus out. Does that mean that there'll be no vagina either? Actually, it is okay with me. The idea is grossing me out. Could she be pregnant at the age of forty-nine? Anyhow, she is hysterical and also angry. Am I worried? Of course not. She is the one having the operation. Isn't that ridiculous? Do I care? Of course, I got the best surgeon and a private room. What else am I supposed to do? She is constantly talking about it and nothing else. The girls are also in a panic. I guess it is a woman's thing. Now both of them are calling me everyday to get a daily report about her mental state, and Linda is clinging to me worse than ever. I'll tell you, marrying a woman isn't the best deal I ever made. As a class of beings, females are too dependent."

Contemporary Western societies, alas, can be characterized by an excessive promotion of isolated and disconnected individuals, generated in the name of independence. Although self-esteem, self-confidence, sense of security, and worth develop within the context of dependent relationships with our own parents, we are still in need of confirmation from others for the remainder of our lives. Healthy connections provide nurturing interdependence. It is not necessarily pathological that one partner has more dependency needs than another, as long as the other is not in need of equal reciprocation. We can perceive unhealthy dependency when it manifests as one partner demanding togetherness with the other at all times: constantly needing reassurance, seeking undue encouragement or problem-solving assistance in social or work situations, or urging frequent expressions of love in order to soothe his or her anxiety and insecurity. "Codependency" is the term given to even unhealthier relationships, wherein destructive and self-destructive behaviors are perpetuated or encouraged by one or both parties.

Self-mastery is a progression from determination by another to self-determination. Self-mastery, however, should never reach the point of detachment from others. Independence is not freedom from relations, indifference to others, or immunity from emotions and impulses. Taken to such extremes, the person who achieves this kind of independence devoid of attachments reduces himself to the abstract existence of an uninterested spectator.

Independence without attachment becomes a vacuous imperturbability. Dependent attachment, on the other hand, becomes tiring, and codependent attachment is subversive. None of these is grounded in a healthy existence. What is desirable and viable in relationships is relative independence and attachment, a *cointerdependence*, that is, the cultivation of independent selves while simultaneously meeting each other's dependency needs. Cointerdependence is a state in which both individuals have an independent existence, yet at the same time, maintain healthy dependency on and attachment to each other. Leo Buscaglia quotes Zen Buddhist Sensai Onimito as wisely advising:

> Pattern your life after the giant bamboo. The exterior, though smooth and lovely to the touch, is tough and resistant to the sword. Within, it is soft, pliable, with much empty space for continued growth. It grows neatly and ordered, never cluttered. Alone, it rises tall and straight, always upward to the sky. There, it spreads its beauty to the sun. It leans on nothing. It makes its own way, perhaps near others, a part of others, but very much dependent upon its own strength and force.

Blind Trust: It Is Better to Trust and Get Hurt, Than Never to Trust and Never Get Hurt.

> There is no pain equal to that which two lovers can inflict on one another.
>
> —Cyril Connolly

The adage "trust is gained" situates the "accused" in a position to prove himself trustworthy—not just guilty until proven otherwise. The mistrusting person, however, doesn't do justice to himself either. Chronic suspicion and vigilance rob a person of the dignity of good relations, as well as an optimistic naiveté that contributes to a joyous life.

Linda's operation was successful and uneventful. The fibroid, though, was too enormous and entrenched into the walls of the uterus so that Linda required a radical hysterectomy (the removal of uterus, ovaries, and fallopian tubes). After surgery, one strange and unsuspected complication emerged. She became very mistrustful and intolerant, especially suspicious about her husband's fidelity. She had always wondered about Sam's loyalty, but she either tolerated his indiscretions or didn't concern herself much about them. Now, however, she was on

---

- Extramarital affairs can occur at any phase of a marriage, but they must be understood in the context of that particular marriage.
- Sometimes, affairs occur when a spouse is experiencing personal vulnerabilities, such as health or job security, during midlife.
- No marriage is immune from extramarital affairs; sometimes affairs are more about opportunity than love or even dissatisfaction with a spouse.

his case. As she was formulating her suspicions, Linda became more and more depressed, angry, and paranoid, even in her own eyes: she believed Sam was having an affair with his twenty-seven-year-old assistant, Grace.

Sam and his wife would often socialize with the employees of the firm. Linda's first suspicion began when she smelled an unfamiliar perfume on her husband the day she was discharged from the hospital. At the first social opportunity, under the disguise of a long, friendly embrace, she sniffed Grace's hair and neck thoroughly and convinced herself that this was the woman to whom the perfume belonged. She then began to monitor her husband's calendar, as she looked for gaps or unidentified blocks of time, and got duplicates of his telephone bills and called all suspicious numbers. When she failed to find Grace's phone number on the telephone bills, she concluded that Sam wasn't senseless enough to call her at home. They must be using a third party to communicate, she thought. Every night she checked his discarded underwear for a vaginal smell and, even though she preferred not to, would have oral sex with him simply for the sake of exploring his genitals for some evidence. Whenever he was out of town, she called his room at odd hours to see whether he was there and to test his availability for having long conversations with her. If he appeared eager to get off the phone, she was sure that Grace was there. She went so far as to call security to alert the hotel that her husband was about to commit suicide; she requested that they should enter his room to stop him by force, if required. When they did so, they discovered that he was not in his room. She hired a detective to follow him and bug his office. Linda even managed to catch a few conversations of his with Grace but said that "they were so coded that it was impossible to decipher them." Interestingly enough, Sam, for the first time in his life, wasn't having an affair with anyone. It was not necessarily out of loyalty; he was experiencing erection problems and not telling anyone, including his physician.

Linda, on the other hand, was so consumed with her suspicion that she could not even specify what she really wanted from him or from their marriage. She revealed that she had no desire to make love to him and didn't even like him that much. What was the reason for such an intense preoccupation, if not obsession, with whether her husband was having an affair? When asked that question, she insightfully replied, "It's because of the *memories* of hurts"—betrayals to the naiveté of her childhood. Her parents were never truthful with her, even about insignificant matters, and whenever she confronted them with their falsehoods, they accused her of being paranoid. But now she was suspicious not only of Sam but also the housekeeper, gardener, store clerks. She was even wondering about her daughters' motivations.

The childlike naiveté that some fortunate people possess results from their early experiences with trustworthy adults. The adult world may not justify such optimism or innocence. A trusting predisposition, however, generates a more propitious outcome by attracting the benevolence and affection of others. In fact, contrary to common suspicion, trusting people rarely get cheated and, if so, only by the most unscrupulous. Mistrusting persons, on the other hand, set the stage for unconscious urges in others to deceive and manipulate them, with the conscious rationalization that such mistrusting individuals deserve what they get. Mistrusting, therefore, seems to be a challenge to, if not an actual encouragement or recruitment of, betrayers.

People who were psychologically abused, which is sometimes worse than physical abuse because of its undetectable and chronic malignancy, inevitably lose their trust. The consequences reverberate forevermore, since mistrusting one's parents removes all one's potential for optimism. In fact, these psychologically battered children become chronically anxious, waiting vigilantly for the next deprivation, abuse, or betrayal. This pessimism extends to all their relationships, such that even as adults they cannot believe in anyone's genuine feelings or accept behaviors made in good faith. At the same time, they will in turn manipulate everyone, almost indiscriminately, to procure some trust or love, even though they really don't believe it exists. They may even be excessively generous to others, but inconsistently; at times, they are also extremely petty and selfish, especially if there are some signs that love is forthcoming. The child whose natural vulnerability is violated or exploited gradually learns—the painful way—not to become vulnerable.

Occasionally from such a wounded child, there emerges a creative regeneration. This requires a great number of corrective experiences—a matter of having the good fortune of longer-term association with trustworthy people. The danger is in the grown-up's imprinted tendency to seek similar, untrustworthy relations, which mirror her early experiences and thus repeat the original trauma. In turn, this later trauma validates the pessimism and cynicism resulting from these earlier relationships.

For Linda, Sam was such a repetitive relationship. She knew from the beginning that he couldn't be trusted but still went along with the marriage. Now, she was sure that Sam as well as her parents were untrustworthy people. "Did I almost lose my life to open my eyes?" she cried. No, she lost her false naiveté that denied her early betrayal of her parents, which was later compounded by the incorrective experience of her husband. Narcissistic sociopaths naturally promote expanding suspicion, if not full paranoia, in their spouses.

Extramarital Affairs Do Not Have to Destroy a Marriage: They Must Be Understood in the Broad Context of a Marriage Itself.

According to Gerald Early, in a relationship ledger, spouses tend to keep "strict accounts with a relentless memory. Nobody ever forgets a single moment of embarrassment, and nobody ever forgives a single moment of cruelty." Sexual betrayal is one of these points of embarrassment and an unforgivable act, in spite of its common occurrence. It need not be. Extramarital affairs must be understood within the context of a specific marriage.

Robert Wright explains that years ago, in the nineteenth century, for example, or even as recently as the 1950s, men would confine their sexual dalliances to prostitutes or women they would not consider marrying. In other words, those women would be completely different from their wives and usually not a threat to the marriage. Now, however, with more women in the workplace, men (and, for that matter, women) tend to meet other suitable partners. Instead of infidelity being "sheerly a sexual outlet" these days, Wright notes it is often a "slippery slope to desertion."

Shirley Glass, in *Not Just Friends,* speaks of the "new crisis of infidelity" where both men and women are exposed to new temptations, often in the context of a work relationship. She feels that no marriage is immune and that affairs can happen in good marriages. Affairs are therefore sometimes more about opportunities and crossing boundaries and less about love. They are, of course, more apt to occur when a spouse is experiencing personal vulnerability. As more and more women like Grace enter the workplace, there are more opportunities for them to meet men and begin affairs. Likewise, as more and more men, as well as women, change jobs over time, move from one location to another, or even travel more frequently for a job, they are exposed to more potential temptations. Resisting those temptations goes against genetics for both sexes and will depend on the strength of the marriage and the realistic understanding each sex has about marriage at a particular time in its course.

Psychoanalyst Henry Dicks suggests that "benign infidelity" may be a "self-healing, even a necessary crisis in the growth process" of a couple. That may be so, provided that the other spouse understands and remains within the boundaries of fair reciprocity and maintains what Ivan Boszormenyi-Nagy and Barbara R. Krasner call some "residual trust." These authors believe loss of trustworthiness or merit is rarely absolute. They accept that each relationship contains an invisible slate or "ledger of give-and-take," what Peter Kramer calls a "trust fund." Kramer says, "Strong balance sheets make stable marriages. But if one partner continually overdraws the account, the other will feel justified in retaliating or leaving."

De Vries ventures into the subject of extramarital sex in *Reuben, Reuben:*

> Adultery made Mopworth if anything a better husband. Mellowed by pleasure, thankful for it (his ego of course soothed by the sense of romantic conquest), he went home a more kind and generous man, twice as willing to deserve the gratitude on deposit for him there by "pitching in" after dinner and bathing the children. "Another woman," or man, is low on the list of causes for divorce. Infidelity has

probably stabilized more marriages than it has shaken. It is from its
discovery that the trouble arises.

We may look at extramarital sex not only from legalistic, moralistic, and
other damaging perspectives but also from its potential benefits. Says Louise De-
Salvo: "My experience told me I needed to think about adultery differently. Until then, I believed that having sex with someone other than your lawful partner
necessarily ruins a marriage. But this wasn't true in mine. However hard it was,
my marriage—and I—were better off because of it."

That was not the same case for Sam and Linda. Sam didn't just deceive
Linda with extramarital sex; he deceived her as to who he was. Eventually, Sam
moved out. He had to move out. Linda made it impossible for him to stay. It was
as if she were paying him back for all those years of infidelity, chronic blaming
and complaining about her, his indifference to her and the children's suffering,
and, most important, his dishonesty with them.

> Sam: *"I found a nice apartment at the hotel. All service included. There
> is a wonderful restaurant downstairs, and every night there is some per-
> formance by a cabaret singer. A little lonely, but maybe that is what I
> need for a while. The girls totally took their mother's side and more or less
> excommunicated me. It is really funny, not ha, ha, funny, but it is the
> first time in my life that I am innocent and look what it got me.*
>
> *Anyhow, I called Grace. I told her how I got evicted because of her and
> that she now had to fill the role after the fact. She was delighted to oblige.
> Did you not say when one vagina closes, the other opens? Now, now, don't
> get defensive, I know what you really said."*

Relations to others are dependent on self-relation. In each phase of our lives,
we may need to relate differently, to the same people and possibly to different
people, since our relation to ourselves changes. In that sense, all relationships are
time limited. When that fateful time comes, both parties will inwardly know that
the relationship is dead; and it is time to mourn the loss. Sam wasn't mourning
the loss of his relation with his wife and daughters. One can lose only what one
has had. Unless he figures out how to find his authentic self and tame his narcissistic sociopathic traits, he'll inflict himself in a similar pattern on the next
woman, who will probably be another victim of an abused childhood.

CHAPTER 8

Marriage as a Cause of Illness

Marital stresses can cause physical illnesses and they, in return, place further stress on a marriage.

Time-Released Trauma of Marriage

Cynthia Heimel, in "Beware of Mr. Right," wonders why we are not even telling, if not shouting, the awful truth of marriage: "How do marriage counselors sleep at night, knowing all they know about marriage and not screaming it to the world? They should stand on their rooftops in their pajamas with megaphones, shouting, "Citizens! Heed my words! Never marry! Marriage is bad! Marriage is a bloodbath!"

We would add physicians to the list of marriage counselors who equally keep mum about the truth of marriage—that a large number of patients' physical sufferings derive from stresses in their marriage. The medical profession acknowledges that more than 30 percent of patients who seek help do not have any actual physical illnesses. Their complaints are simply physical manifestations of their psychological stresses. Often physicians identify this phenomenon, simply reassure the individual about the absence of disease, and offer some placebo-like remedy for the symptoms. Seasoned practitioners go one step further and inquire into the nature of the patient's stresses: are they work related or home related? Are they financial or legal worries? Physicians prescribe antianxiety and antidepressant medication when indicated and advise their patients about well-recognized problems of living, often quite successfully. They may refer some recalcitrant situations to psychiatrists.

Many patients who seek individual therapy are suffering from difficulties with relationships. They are somatizers when they present with physical symptoms, real or imagined; they tend to manifest either the fear of an illness with noncorresponding symptoms or the wish for an illness with (eventually) corresponding symptoms.

- Spouses in marital distress may present with physical symptoms.
- Spouses in marital distress may express the fear they have an illness.
- Spouses in marital distress may express the wish for an illness (i.e., wishing for a medical or honorable discharge from the marriage).
- A spouse's symptoms are pleas for recognition of the stress he or she is experiencing in the marriage.

The first one, the fear of an illness, occurs in the early stages of stress when one of the spouses begins to experience anxiety and depression accompanied with some physical complaints, often involving a specific target organ such as hyperacidity in the stomach; skin lesions; impotence; vaginismus; sleeplessness; weight gain or loss; asthmatic attacks; and so forth. At this stage the patient's symptoms are pleas for recognition of the stress she experiences. No physician should dismiss such a patient by declaring that she is perfectly healthy. Here, neither a compliment nor reassurance is being sought. Even simple recognition that the patient's symptoms emanate from her marital problems and that appropriate measures are required to address these problems is relatively effective. If unattended, these psychosomatic symptoms may gradually develop into actual illnesses.

The second form of a medical presentation of marital stresses, the wish for an illness, is potentially more dangerous than the previous one. The wish for an illness is a form of request for a medical, that is, honorable, discharge from life. When spouses subjectively experience that their attempts to find a solution to the marital conflicts reach an impasse, their bodies and their minds begin to deteriorate. More accurately, such an individual will actively participate, if not attempt, to effect her demise. The nature of this participation is usually very subtle, in the form of self-neglect, poor sleep, poor hygiene, bad eating habits, lack of exercise, and perpetuating the stressful situation. If left unattended these patients may eventually succeed and predispose themselves to develop a fatal or, at least, devastating illness—cancer, heart attack—corresponding to their wish for a serious illness.

Ironically, both groups—the fearers of illness in the form of psychosomatic symptoms and the wishers for the illness in the form of self-neglect—desire good marriages. They do so, however, in a self-destructive fashion. Neither the fear of nor the wish for illness can improve a marriage; if anything, each seriously compounds conflicts between spouses, as each imposes additional physical, financial, and psychological burdens on the partner.

On the other hand, it is beneficial for spouses to maintain their physical and psychological fitness in the midst of their marital discord. Such expedient maintenance of body and mind heals actual illnesses, whether related to the marital problems or not. In fact, those individuals who remain physically and psychologically fit are less likely to fall ill with serious diseases. If they do, they tend to recover, and recover rapidly and completely. They are neither anxious nor depressed, and they have a better opportunity of enjoying a good marriage or terminating a bad marriage without undue stress. Understanding of and adherence to the principals of physical and psychological fitness should be one of the requirements for obtaining a marriage license, if not for graduation from kindergarten!

A Woman Thing: The Illusion of Marriage

Women are more likely to suffer psychosomatic illnesses in marriage, partly because they may enter marriage with greater expectations than men. These expectations inevitably turn into major disillusionments. Once confronted with the realities of marriage, some women convert their despair into physical distress.

Pamela Paul, in *The Starter Marriage,* says, "we assume that once you're wed, the rest falls into place—the beautiful home, the gourmet dinner parties attended by other witty, vivacious couples, the glorious pregnancy—with a trouble-free, healthy baby. . . . The kids who always do their homework and get into prestigious schools, the fabulous family vacations . . . ultimately, home fires burning into the golden years. All you need to do is marry; the attendant rewards are waiting."

Rarely does it happen that way.

In a 1999 article in the *New York Times,* Peter Godwin speaks of the American obsession with marriage, as evidenced by the enormous wedding industry. He says, "Indeed, it's no coincidence that our interest in marriage's storybook representations grows just as fast as our practical evidence of its failures." Our American "penchant" for serial marriage, he adds, "is a perfect testament to the repeated triumph of hope over experience." Godwin also scoffs at our obsession with how happy we are in marriage—how we are always trying to gauge our own happiness to others. To Godwin, it is a "self-indulgent exercise," an outgrowth of the Declaration of Independence, which emphasizes our "pursuit of happiness."

Hundreds of books published every year on the subject of marriage each provide a point of view as to how to make marriage work—or more lasting, interesting, intimate, equal, sexually exciting, and romantic. These books, says Lynn Darling, "offer calm reason and logical interpretation; they teach strategy and negotiation. They attempt to protect us from chaos. . . . But a real marriage is a hideous Victorian pile: overstuffed and wildly eccentric." Both Pamela Paul and Lynn Darling may exaggerate both the illusionary expectations of women from marriage and the harsh reality to follow, but only in degrees. That is why marriage is particularly stressful for women. It must be, for they initiate over 60 percent of divorces. "Knowing how important relationships are to women, this is a dramatic walkout-strike," says Dalma Heyn.

The Incredible Shrinking Woman

> The true index of a man's character is the health of his wife.
>
> —Cyril Connolly

In William Congreve's play *The Way of The World,* a gentleman named Mirabell falls in love with Millamant, an eligible niece of an old and wealthy widow, whose consent to their marriage is required if Millamant is to inherit her fortune. After a complicated plot of blackmail, the old lady agrees to grant Mirabell his wish to marry her niece. Millamant states all kinds of conditions before she will consent to "dwindle" into the role of wife. Interestingly enough, Mirabell offers only a few minor conditions and anticipates being "enlarged into a husband."

A dwindled or enlarged marriage, no matter how well negotiated, forces its participants into a different status from where they were prior to their union. That change alone is stressful but gets worse by the negative consequences of the change. Women sometimes are most affected by these changes in marriage. Dalma Heyn shares her experience that many women felt something was "very wrong" even as they were walking down the aisle. "Not with the relationship, necessarily, but in the stunning dissonance between what they were supposed to feel and what they actually felt. They had the unmistakable sense that life as they knew it was forever ending." She calls this dissonance "marriage shock." "I do" becomes "I should." In *Against Love,* Laura Kipnis makes the same point about both sexes, namely that marriage is about rules and prohibitions and expectations, or as she says, "a catalogue of strictures, commands and punishments so unending you begin to wonder why no one has yet evoked the Geneva Convention."

Marriage is especially stressful for women:

- Women suffer frequently from depression, anxiety, and psychosomatic diseases, partly because they have high, if not unrealistic, expectations about marriage.
- A woman's own identity is diluted by marriage (e.g., assignment of domestic duties, losing her own last name).
- Children make women further dependent on their husbands.
- A woman further may compromise her employment skills and opportunities when she becomes a mother.
- If a woman leaves a marriage, she will usually suffer financially.

Women attempt to minimize the impact of chronic, seemingly mild stresses within marriage. Isolated from an overall pattern, they can appear too insignificant for strong emotional reactions. For example, a woman may say, "We don't really have major difficulties in our marriage: we are very loyal to each other, very attached, and very concerned about our children. We have an agreeable life together." Then the "buts" will follow: "He is always finding something wrong in whatever I do"; "he is always angry"; "he does not like my friends"; "he never gives me credit"; "he always diminishes me in front of our friends"; "he doesn't make me feel desirable"; "he never compliments my work"; "he is always demanding"; "he is arrogant and puts me down"; "he is constantly criticizing me"; "he makes me feel useless"; "he makes me feel incompetent"; and so forth.

These complaints are not necessarily objective statements but rather reflect a woman's subjective experiences. They do not—and need not—be validated by others. We must also, however, be careful to distinguish (without disqualifying) our spouse's objective behavior from our subjective reactions. Epictetus said, "It is not events that disturb the minds of men, but the view they take of them." That view is commonly distorted by our earlier experiences. As we have emphasized, traumas experienced in our formative years especially alter our subjective experience of contemporary events and muddy all our later perceptions. That is why at times symptoms do not necessarily correspond to pathology nor is the pathology necessarily consistent with precipitating factors. A present stressful situation becomes considerably more stressful if it has an historical precedence. Past stresses resonate with present ones and intensify their impact. For example, marital conflicts that parallel what we had experienced between our parents when we were children are more stressful to us than otherwise. That is why some self-reflection may be useful. Your spouse's arrogance may be stressful, but more so is

---

Marriage is especially good for men:

- Married men are physically healthier. Insurance companies consider them a better risk.
- Married men are psychologically healthier. National statistics validate the lower rate of suicide, depression, alcoholism, and so forth.
- Married men are often financially successful. Credit lines, banks, and mortgage companies attest to that.
- Married men are stable and productive. Employers will tell you so.
- Married men live longer.

---

your sense of diminishment as a response. Your spouse's selfishness is inherently stressful but more so is your feeling deprived, especially when these feelings are reminiscent of ones you had previously experienced.

A Trapped Jolly Giant

On the other hand, marriage has had a bad press among men. Jessie Bernard tells us that it was not until the middle of the sixteenth century that books like *The Prayse of All Women* and *The Defense of Women* appeared. Before that, books focused on marital discord, and even after, other books criticized women as "when married, querulous and gossipy, not willing to mind the house." Continues Bernard, "Thus, for centuries men have been told—by other men—that marriage is: no bed of roses, a necessary evil, a noose, a desperate thing, a field of battle, a curse, a school of sincere pretense." But he adds: "The male clichés could hardly have been more wrong." It turns out, however, despite all these negative charges, that marriage is actually beneficial for most men.

Bernard stresses that on almost every index—demographic, psychological, or social, married men do better than never-married men. And employers, bankers, and insurance companies all know this! Men need to acknowledge that they are often very well off in that "female-designed trap." Contrary to common belief, men don't do well when their wives leave.

Women, on the other hand, are not as well protected. Psychology professor Shelley E. Taylor, in *The Tending Instinct,* explains that women are usually the ones in marriage who are responsible for managing the conflicts and difficulties within a family. Many of the family burdens fall on them. Men, she says, enjoy the advantages of the support women provide while being protected from any of the stresses inherent in family life. Taylor believes that both men and women have a strong innate caring and cooperative instinct. She calls it the "tending instinct." Women, however, especially as mothers, play a more central role in tending to others, and men, in marriage, benefit from this.

Monkey Mind: Negative Emotions within a Marriage, If Prolonged, Will Deplete and Exhaust the Body.

"I do have real medical problems. I don't know why my doctor thought that I should have a psychological consultation. I have very high blood pressure that causes headaches and occasional dizziness. I am worried that I am going to burst an artery or something and get paralyzed. I guess the doctor is getting a little impatient with me; I seem to be either not responding to his medications or having terrible side effects.

So, how would you feel if you were in my situation? I feel as if I am sitting on a powder keg. The doctor's office gave me an appointment three months from now. Well, I may not be alive by then! What kind of medical practice is that? When I told the receptionist that I need to be seen right away, she said, 'Then you should go to the nearest emergency room.' Can you believe that? So, I let her have it. If that is why I should be seen for psychological evaluation, then it is ass backward. If they took care of me properly, I wouldn't be upset; if I weren't upset, my blood pressure wouldn't go up and I wouldn't get tense and yell at people. Excuse me, I've got to go to the bathroom . . .

Sorry, the last few months I get this spasm in my lower abdomen and a sense of urgency. What comes out is mostly liquidish bowel movement. That is why I cannot focus on my job or even on conversations, because I keep constant vigil. I have to be no more than twenty feet away from a bathroom when cramps start. A couple of times I soiled myself.

Do I have other symptoms? Don't ask! I don't sleep well; I lost my appetite, though I gained a few pounds. I don't know how that works. No, I have no stress at work; I am just not as effective. Sex? No. I haven't had sex for over a year. My wife and I are having some problems. We are seeing a marriage counselor. I am not sure whether I am rooting for reconciliation or divorce, honestly. If it weren't for the kids, the marriage would have ended long ago. The counselor is very understanding. Do I drink? Yes, only when I come home at the end of the day and have two, occasionally three martinis, just to unwind."

Our body functions poorly when confronted with psychological stresses. It gets disorganized internally in response to external disorganizers. "There is a noteworthy term in Buddhism," writes Herbert Benson, "that depicts this mental chaos, *papañca.* It means 'monkey mind.'" Its analogy is to monkeys who jump repeatedly from one tree limb to another. Comparatively, the human mind can leap from thought to thought, with no interruption. When this "monkey-mind" phenomenon occurs, there is usually excessive brain activity that overloads the brain. That manifests as difficulties in concentration, interference with new learning, and difficulty falling asleep. Moreover, the body's muscles—internal and external—may start to clench, that is, in the colon, diaphragm, neck, back, eyes. This muscle tension repeatedly dispatches a distress signal to the brain, which in turn can perpetuate a vicious circle.

Furthermore we are subject to a host of pathological repercussions. For example, during stress, the body may require a repetitive need for more forceful blood flow that can cause sustained increases in blood pressure. This process, in turn, can cause enlarged and strained hearts and, worse, strokes and other types of sudden internal bleeding. The equally repetitive pumping of adrenaline throughout the body can induce anxiety, irritability, and even hypersensitivity to pain, as well as digestive system problems.

Intensive negative engagement with others, as in fighting or hating, depletes considerable psychological and physical energy, even though ostensibly we seem visibly animated. The brain struggles to maintain a considerable state of arousal and corresponding level of energy to cope with stress against its natural tendency to lower excitement. The brain will induce the continuous release of cortisol and noradrenaline to perpetuate this state of arousal. Ironically, in such a state of mind, we may feel very creative, while not creating, and very productive, while not really producing. In fact, business, family matters, and physical health may all get seriously neglected or badly managed.

The body naturally strives for a low level of activity in order to conserve energy, which it needs for repair and rebuilding itself. M. Scott Peck likens that process of "winding down," to the currents of a stream, which naturally flows downhill. It requires arduous work to reverse this process, that is, to return to equilibrium. In fact, if we want to bring the water back up the hill, we require energy from somewhere else: one energy system replenishes another. That is why people sometimes feel somewhat relieved when a love affair ends, in spite of the pain of the loss, or when they reconcile with their enemies. Their minds experience events as an elimination of a tremendous burden: their bodies and brains can return to their main business of maintenance.

Only in this wound-down state of equilibrium can the body focus on self-care and renewal. Approximately 90 percent of a cell's energy, notes Deepak Chopra for example, normally operates in manufacturing required DNA and

RNA and toward building new proteins. Nonetheless, this process of building ceases when the brain perceives any form of threat. The normal method of metabolism that typically builds the body (i.e., anabolic metabolism) reverts to its opposite form that breaks down tissues (i.e., catabolic metabolism).

This catabolic metabolism demands a concurrent rise in adrenaline which, itself, can cause a host of responses, such as an increase in blood pressure, increase in muscle tension, rapid breathing, a suppression of sexual desire and hunger, and the halting of digestive processes. At the same time, the brain becomes unusually alert and the senses more acute. The stress response is essential in dealing temporarily with the immediate situation; if permitted to continue uncontrolled, its effects on catabolic metabolism can be profound, with every manifestation of stress arousal producing dangerous effects on health.

The adaptive survival value of the old brain—and the amygdala (the emotional brain) within it—is in the immediate processing of information and reaction to a dangerous natural environment. In a normal social environment, the amygdala is also capable of generating maladaptive responses, such as the common panic attacks people experience in theaters, planes, crowds, or in intimate interpersonal relations. People may experience impotence, vaginismus, blushing, cold sweats, rage, excessive aggression, or even total collapse. These reactions are predetermined by our emotional brain and paired with certain stimuli having little to do with the actual current circumstances. Sometimes these memories are not even conscious. They may be specific to the original stimulus, but nonspecific to newer ones (e.g., premature ejaculation with a new mate because of an earlier experience with another one).

Some people, like the person in the above vignette, who experience social stress, go directly to the bar for a drink or take tranquilizers to calm down the amygdala. That only works temporarily. Though there are genetic components to alcohol and drug abuse, alcoholism and abuse of tranquilizers may be seen as a result of stress in the marriage. If marriage counseling fails to improve physical health (improving communication is not sufficient) and fails to stop the maladaptive coping mechanisms, (e.g., drinking) the couple may require a temporary separation.

The Stress of Marriage Can Damage the Immunological System.

> Men and women are infinitely ingenious in their ability to find new ways of being unhappy together.
>
> —Lawrence S. Kubie

"She is Dr. Jekyll and Mrs. Hyde. I don't know what I am going to find when I get home. One day she is sweet and loving, calls me at the office and tells me how much she loves me, that I am the kindest and the most generous of all men, handsome and strong. Another day, she is angry, if not hostile; screams at me at the top of her voice that she hates me, that she hated me all her life but now more so, because I am inconsiderate, rude, and the stingiest man she ever met—an ugly brute. In either situation, I never know what I have done to deserve the praise or the damnation.

Ahchoo! I seem not to be able to shake this cold. The doctor thinks that it may be an allergy to be lasting for so long. Anyway, don't worry, it is not contagious. Neither my wife nor children have gotten it. It is no big deal, except that with all that sneezing and coughing, I am developing a sort of mild asthma. I consulted another doctor who thinks that my coughs are coming from the irritation of my air pipe from acid reflux. I don't know why I develop too much acid in my stomach either."

Throughout our lives, our bodies are constantly in a low-level chronic battle for survival. The physiological system for survival operates in a very similar fashion for both genders. An intricate neural/hormonal structure is the basis for a highly sensitive communication system in the subcortical area of the brain that maintains autonomous functions. Its roles include repairing injuries and fighting invasive agents and pathogens (germs). The strength of this reparative power is what distinguishes one person's illness from another's: the battle between our protective immunological system and the diseases that attempt to overwhelm it determines the outcome.

Because of illnesses and naturally occurring or self-induced toxins, the body can never suspend its defenses, at least not completely. The immunological system is like the National Guard on weekend alert. This low-level alertness cannot prevent certain illnesses, such as viral infections, but when mobilized in full force, it can and usually does overcome most diseases. The immunological system, however, cannot maintain this high level of arousal in order to prevent illnesses. In fact, the chronic fatigue that can result from such vigilance may be worse than the potential disease itself. If the anticipatory vigilance is limited only to a brief interval, the body can cope well. Chopra discusses some experiments with rats: when they were warned in advance of an oncoming shock, they displayed a decreased stress response compared to rats given no such warning. On the other hand, when rats were subjected to unpredictable shocks, they remained constantly vigilant and hence chronically stressed.

All illnesses, mild or grave, generate a generic response from the immunological system: the immunological system is not illness specific or illness tailored. Under the chronic stress of marriage, therefore, it can make serious quantitative and qualitative errors, especially in midlife as the body ages. It can fail to protect when it should, and it can proceed to attack when it shouldn't. The former type of error reflects either one of total omission or else an inadequate response, such as an illness or a disease process that might have been prevented but instead progresses to a deteriorated condition. The latter type of error reflects one of commission or overresponse, whereby, for example, the body's reaction to minute chemical changes is out of proportion. In other words, the body's response is greater than it ought to be and misdirected, as in the case of autoimmune illnesses. Nonetheless, the body's degree of responsiveness should approximate the optimum, that is, sufficient to counter pathogens, yet not so great as to attack the body's own structure in the process. Therefore, what an individual requires is a fit and well-trained, well-rested body, whose defenses can be mobilized at immediate notice. Foremost, that requires the absence of chronic stress. Acute problems in marriage, no matter how stressful they are, are usually effectively counteracted by the immunological system. Much less severe, chronic stresses in ongoing marital conflicts, however, will inevitably exhaust the body's defenses. Even a relatively minor disease, such as the flu, can substantially incapacitate or even kill a person if his immunological system cannot launch an appropriate counteroffensive within a given time frame.

When reality becomes intolerable, we numb our psychological pain via a host of defense mechanisms. People who are subjected to seemingly mild traumas, such as continual disapproval by a spouse, tend to age faster and begin to languish. There is preliminary evidence of this finding in physiological research: Chopra notes that placing a mouse on an electric grid and administering shocks to it can kill the mouse, even when the shocks are not lethal. Rather, the mouse's stress response (simply by administration of very mild shocks at random intervals) is on alert. Each time this occurs, the body of the mouse deteriorates gradually. After a few days of such stress, however, the mouse will die! On autopsy, the tissues of the rodent will display many signs of accelerated aging. Since the shocks themselves were mild, Chopra insists that it was the mouse's reaction, rather than any external stress, that killed the mouse. In other words, Chopra explains that the mouse's body essentially killed itself. It is similar with humans. In a chronically disapproving marriage, the disapproved of spouse ages and begins to deteriorate.

The results of stress are not limited to one component of our bodies even though they may manifest with a single encapsulated symptom. A depressed person's tears are found to contain chemical traces different from those in tears of joy! Sooner or later, the entire body founders with chronic stresses: the brain's output of neurotransmitters can become depleted, hormone levels can drop, the sleep cycle will be interrupted, and platelet cells in the blood will be disturbed. Strokes, heart attacks, cancer are opportunistic diseases awaiting the vulnerable.

Bodily symptoms of marital stress intensify in midlife as the body ages:

- Everyone has her own target organs of distress—this distress manifests itself in symptoms such as headache, asthma, stomach acidity, skin lesions, impotence, sleeplessness, weight gain, weight loss, and so forth.
- These symptoms are often unresponsive to standard medical treatment.
- These symptoms are often situational (being away from the spouse ameliorates the condition).
- Patients present symptoms as a signal of their distress. If understood correctly, they'll quickly reveal their marital problems.
- Patients may fear the worst (i.e., "Am I dying?" "Do I have cancer?").
- Patients may wish the worst (i.e., "I wish I were dead").
- Chronic stress depletes the immunological system and makes the person vulnerable to all sorts of diseases ranging from an ordinary cold to cancer.

Fighting on Too Many Fronts Weakens, If Not Defeats, the Best Army.

History has documented countless examples of powerful armies defeated when they engaged in battles on many fronts simultaneously. The immunological system is equally vulnerable if it encounters multiple conflicts, such as conflicts in marriage as well as work. Even one additional minor conflict on one front can catapult the entire army into defeat when it is already engaged elsewhere. Likewise, infections can compromise disease-controlling mechanisms not simply at the precise initial site of the disease but can disseminate to multiple locations as well. Both viruses and bacteria can induce the proliferation of cancer-infected tissues. Viruses, especially, are particularly prone to damage cells because they are not so sufficiently different from an ordinary single gene in a human cell. A virus may easily find a niche on a chromosome and settle there as if it belonged there. Once established, a virus can cause havoc by interfering with the normal machinery of the cell, attacking the body's immune system, and thus impairing the ability to prevent disease. As with bacteria and larger parasites, viruses can also manufacture toxins that weaken cellular-control mechanisms.

Although this is observable at every age, those over fifty have to be more vigilant because the regulation of cell growth, like virtually every other aspect of biological adaptation, becomes less effective with increasing age. In fact, cells themselves age. As the various major systems of the body deteriorate (e.g., digestive, respiratory, cardiovascular, excretory), cells are less able to remove waste products and toxins. An inevitable result is that the body is less effective in controlling the occurrence and spread of deleterious cells (e.g., cancer).

Illnesses in the midst of marital conflicts tend to demoralize people. There is also a progressive decline in the stress response that is a concomitant with the process of aging. In general, older people take considerably longer to recover from stress, and they are less tolerant of major traumas, such as the death of a loved one. It is relatively uncommon for a young person to die of grief, for example, but more commonplace in the elderly. In fact, it is not uncommon for the surviving spouse to die within a year of the first spouse's death. This is seen especially in men in long marriages, after the death of a wife. Decline in the capacity to recover from trauma is not simply a linear process. Rather, it changes exponentially. In fact, notes Chopra, one year of old age can produce as much deterioration in the stress response as two years of middle age! For very old people, such deterioration may occur in only six months. With this geometric progression, older people may forfeit their ability to recover completely. Even mild stresses, such as a minor fall, a mild illness, or even losing a small amount of money, can become insurmountable.

It is very important, therefore, to treat even the most ordinary illnesses, so that they do not become chronic. A long-standing, untreated sinusitis, for example, can impair a strong immunological system and make the body vulnerable to more serious internal and external invasions. Interestingly enough, as we have said, people who are in the middle of serious marital conflicts tend to neglect their actual physical ills. These are the people who favor their ailing status and present themselves to doctors' offices—in search of that medical discharge from life.

Spouses who are about to leave their marriages tend to stay once a seriously life-threatening disease is diagnosed in their partners. Whether out of guilt, pity, or sense of responsibility, they table their decisions in order to see their partners through the treatment. A grateful patient who feels relieved from the immediacy of abandonment may begin to invest in remaining sick in order to keep the spouse in the marriage. Such secondary gains not only prolong the recovery of the patient but further result in deterioration of the relationship with the self-sacrificing spouse. He or she might be simply expecting a quick result—full recovery or death. When neither of these results happens, the spouse feels trapped in the nurse-spouse role indefinitely. A healthy spouse's own "shoulds" and "musts," or other principles, sooner or later begin to take their tolls and make both spouses resentful.

Too many principles, and even too much compassion, especially when imposed from within, can be counterproductive in navigating through life's stresses. Occasionally, we need to question those principles. Too many rules about what we "must" do can be as stressful as having no rules. The burden of submitting to so many demands—even if self-imposed—can be intolerable. There was a TV program that featured families of quintuplets, in which each set of parents was asked, "What is the most important thing you've learned for maintaining sanity?" The *prominent* message that came across repeatedly was: "Don't have too many rules." With so many stipulations, and a comparable number of rules that can—and will be—constantly violated, there is only one conclusion: you will experience continual stress, if you attempt to respond to innumerable demands, even if they are your own. It is worse if you are subjected to the "musts" and "shoulds" of your spouse.

On the other hand, if the psychological stress is reduced through a genuine reconciliation or through an amicable separation (while still remaining supportive), you will increase your chances of recovery. Even in a severely compromised body there is still a fighting chance. In fact, even after a tumor has been clearly detected and is producing discernable symptoms, natural control mechanisms, especially immunological processes, are operative nonetheless. They just require enhancement. Slowing the progression of maladaptive growth or containing the multiplication of unrestrained cells to other locations is still a possibility. Retarding cancer growth may allow a person to live an extended and healthy life, even if the patient is never fully cured.

Numbing Fatigue Is the Most Stressful of All Fatigues.

"I guess I am just tired of being attacked at home and at work. There is no place to escape. I used to get at least some respite at work. The drive to Manhattan, as awful as the traffic is, used to lift my mood. Then, I was going some place where no one yelled at me or made excessive demands. I did my job, did it well, if I may say so, and people left me alone. But now things have changed a lot. Young kids are taking over. They are arrogant and foulmouthed. I took two hours off to go to the dentist—I need gum surgery—this guy, who isn't even the big boss, screamed at me in front of two other kids: "Where the fuck were you for the whole afternoon?" When I told him why it took so long, he puckered up his mouth and coyly said, "Have them pulled out, man. It would improve your performance." Everyone chuckled.

It isn't, of course, just that—the whole field has changed. I couldn't make the transition to computer models, and I don't want to. Once, I was the most sought-after draftsman; now I feel like I am simply being tolerated. I know it's not all that true, but I can never match these kids' technolog-

ical wizardry. It takes time to do authentic work; these kids are like machines themselves. By the time I finish one drawing, they have a dozen. I just don't fit. On the way home I am more depressed. I have nothing to look forward to, except my wife's finding something to yell at me about."

There are three kinds of fatigue, note both Betty Friedan in *The Feminine Mystique* and John Lagemann in "Why Young Mothers Are Always Tired": good, bad, and numbing. In *good* fatigue, the brain fatigues from overwork, even if the work performed is within its domain. The brain recovers by shifting focus into sensual and bodily experiences, such as walking, eating, conversing, lovemaking, listening to music, or going to movies—a kind of downtime. Here, the brain's natural proclivities are not challenged, and the brain can overwork, even though it eventually gets overloaded. *Good* fatigue is a mental whiteout. It is like rallentando in music, a gradual slackening of tempo, a winding down.

If, however, the brain performs a task to which it is not suited, fatigue sets in immediately, accompanied by an acute sense of defeat. This is *bad* fatigue, a mental blackout. No amount of rest or recreation can refuel that brain to return to the identical assignment and successfully complete it. The task may require a different kind of brain, usually the left brain. People with right-brain predomination or, worse, those with attention deficit disorder, suffer considerable mental fatigue. Most people adaptively retreat from the task by declaring themselves incompetent, further damaging their self-esteem.

The third kind, *numbing* fatigue, has nothing to do with either the amount of the work or the nature of the work. The brain is neither overworked nor overwhelmed, but rather chronically depleted. A steady dose of repetitious, unrewarding, or mindless activities prompts the brain to enter a state of cruise control. It is simply idling, however. This is the mental gray-out of chronically tired individuals. A classic case is the woman who complains bitterly that she is "just

---

There is "good," "bad," and "numbing" fatigue in marriage:

- Good fatigue is like a mental whiteout. Marriage rarely suffers from it. It is the kind of fatigue we see from productive and creative work.
- Bad fatigue occurs when we have a sense of defeat. It is a mental blackout. Bad fatigue and bad marriages tend to go together.
- Numbing fatigue occurs when we are chronically depleted from unrewarding activities. It is the mental gray-out of chronically tired housewives.

a housewife," with all the negative connotations of the term: the waste of talents, the household drudgery, the feelings of (or actual) loss of her attractiveness, underutilized intelligence, and diminution or loss of her very identity as a complete person. A prototypical description is that one's mind gradually becomes blank and can't concentrate. In short, it's like "sleepworking."

In the 1950s, Harley C. Shands, Jacob E. Finesinger, and Arthur L. Watkins spoke of people who complained of having "no pep, no initiative, no zest, no enthusiasm." These people also spoke of being "fed-up" and weary. Often this feeling of fatigue came in the context of changes in the person's life, such as marriage and childbirth. The researchers saw the symptom as a danger signal closely related to anxiety and depression. Shands and Finesinger conducted a classic study on persistent fatigue. None of the one hundred patients studied had chronic fatigue as an isolated complaint. The fatigue became crippling.

Marriage rarely suffers from good fatigue—the mental whiteout. When, however, both spouses enjoy and are good at what they do, their fatigue, at the end of the day, is easily converted to relaxation or poured into some energizing activity.

The man in the above vignette suffers from bad fatigue—mental blackout. He neither enjoys what he does nor is he any good at it at this point in his life. Bad fatigue and bad marriage tend to go together. It is difficult, at times, to figure out what preceded what, but they definitely compound each other. A husband who comes home every night complaining about his work may receive sympathy for a while, but in the long run, his chronic complaints will tax even the most devoted wife's nerves. Depression and anxiety are contagious. Even the most loving spouses, out of self-protection, eventually distance themselves from chronically unhappy people. One wife, for example, once shared that her husband kept a count of days until retirement. He had over fifteen thousand days to go, which clearly demoralized her each time he joked about it.

Psychological Bends: The Ills of Emerging from Marriage

> Even had his love lessened, he was bound to her now by a hundred ties of pity and self-reproach.
>
> —Edith Wharton

"All my friends, everyone including my doctor, all said that if I got rid of her, most of my medical problems would disappear. The day that I actually left the house and moved into an apartment, I felt very good for a few hours. In spite of carrying my stuff up a two-floor walk-up, lifting

various boxes and luggage, I felt neither tired nor had any coughing or asthmatic attacks. But that very same night all my illnesses were back: my stomach churning, spasms, head pounding, you name it. Now, is it possible that my marriage isn't the cause of my sicknesses? Is that sort of true, true, or unrelated? I don't even feel good about our separation. I am confused. In fact, I am ashamed to tell you that part of me wants to go back to her. My father used to get drunk and leave regularly but always came back a few weeks later and resumed receiving abuse from my mother.

My friends are encouraging me to go out a lot, introducing me to women, giving me tickets to the theater and Madison Square Garden, all that. I have no desire to do any one of those things. If anything, I sit home by myself and worry about my health. I occasionally have severe chest pain. I have lost quite a bit of weight, I don't sleep well, my spasms are getting worse. Do you think I have colon cancer?"

Severe traumas, especially those lasting for a long time, rather than being discrete events, leave their imprints on our psyches—emotional numbness and confusion. Viktor Frankl, in an extreme example, has described his and fellow inmates' experiences after being saved and liberated from a concentration camp:

> We came to meadows full of flowers. We saw and realized that they were there, but we had no feelings about them. The first spark of joy came when we saw a rooster with a tail of multicolored feathers. But it remained only a spark; we did not yet belong to this world. In the evening when we all met again in our hut, one said secretly to the other, "Tell me, were you pleased today?" And the other replied, feeling ashamed as he did not know that we all felt similarly, "Truthfully, no!" We had literally lost the ability to feel pleased and had to relearn it slowly.

Frankl likens this liberation numbness to deep-sea divers in a decompression chamber, a kind of psychological counterpart of the bends. Long lasting chronic traumas accumulatively generate analogous stresses that require decompression chambers.

Separated couples go through such an experience. For a while they feel enormous anxiety and a sense of being lost. They often have the impulse to run back into marriage, no matter how awful it was. This is especially so for couples who have been married more than six or seven years. Couples generate common traits—a mixture of their individual traits—partly through enmeshment, partly by identification. All of this helps them to maintain their joint identity. Furthermore, they grow dependent on each other, no matter how undesirable each may seem to the other. In that sense, some marriages never end. Even after separation or divorce, couples seek reasons to perpetuate their conflicts with each other and maintain contact.

CHAPTER 9

Redefining Marriage

There is no such a thing as "marriage" but rather "marriages." Consider them all before you proceed with divorce because there is only one and final divorce.

Whose Marriage Is This Anyway? Husband's? Wife's? Children's? Society's? Religion's?

Husbands, wives, children, in-laws, relatives, friends, as well as religion, the legal system, and society, all have their own claims on, ideas of, and expectations from marriage. Sociologist Jessie Bernard said that anyone discussing the future of marriage has to consider that there really are two marriages in every marriage, that is, the husband's and the wife's. Bernard emphasizes that these two marriages do not always coincide. In fact, as Susan Maushart says, "It is more accurate to speak of three marriages—His, Hers, and The Kids."

These three marriages all have different expectations from one another. Children are often the major beneficiaries of the marriage. Men and women may have the same, as well as different, expectations in entering marriage. For example, men expect an easy access to sex and women may expect an easy access to affection, and provision for and protection of their children. The "gradual untethering of motherhood from marriage," however, emphasizes Susan Maushart, will have considerable impact ultimately on the structure of the family and, of course, on marriage itself.

Both men and women fail each other relatively in their expectations and sometimes find themselves sorely disappointed. Why then, when so many marriages, after all, end in divorce, do we still keep getting married and even remarried? Katha Pollitt sees marriage, at least in the United States, as a social welfare system: for many people, marriage is a means to health insurance and pensions and help with their children, which is especially true for women. This practicality makes our penchant for marriage understandable, at least for some. Various other practicalities play an important role when we marry as, all the while, we know the odds. Mopworth, a character in Peter De Vries's *Reuben, Reuben,* has an explanation: "though the institution was widely considered no longer to work, people continued to go in for it because there was nothing better, and besides one has invested all that bother in courtship, from which there is no place to go but forward. The whole thing was like one of those plays of which one has read bad reviews but to which one has already bought tickets. One goes anyway."

Until of course, one can no longer tolerate remaining, sometimes even as early as at the end of the honeymoon. In *Coming to Life,* therapist Leston Havens expresses a thought recognizable to many couples: "Most loving couples begin their relationship with a stern resolution to honor and respect, and yet they have hardly left the church before the slowness of one or the haste of the other, the disappointment of one expectation or the unwanted fulfillment of another, reveals the snarling beast."

Not only do couples often have dissatisfaction with each other in first marriages almost immediately, but we find this kind of dissatisfaction in second or third marriages as well. What is even worse, the odds that the divorced will remarry are good, but the odds of succeeding in a second marriage less so. Census statistics indicate that remarriages fail at a higher rate than first marriages and last a shorter time. In fact, the more often you marry, the less likely your marriage will succeed. Judith Wallerstein and Sandra Blakeslee in *What about the Kids?* note that 75 percent of divorced men will remarry, often within two years. They note that about 50 percent of women will remarry after divorce but not as quickly. What is quite striking is that second marriages result in divorce about 60 percent of the time!

Despite our penchant for marrying, however, we are becoming increasingly suspicious of each other. The whole subject of the prenuptial contract is based on the notion of a lack of trust between spouses. We are entering the marital contract with safety clauses that protect (usually one spouse more than the other) us should the union dissolve. Since there is about a 50 percent chance of divorce, it is a brave and perhaps legally foolish couple who does not have a prenuptial arrangement. This is especially true when one member of the couple is marrying for the second or more times and children are involved.

How this arrangement is handled, however, can have far-reaching consequences for the couple. Sometimes, the prospective spouse who favors the prenup waits until the week of the wedding for the other to sign. The psychological coercion involved is akin to abuse and inevitably damaging to the marital relationship. A spouse can rarely overcome the effects of such manipulation. Years later, that spouse will remember the process with resentment and bitterness.

It is even more disappointing if couples learn nothing from their first experience and repeat the same maladaptive dynamic in their subsequent marriages. That is why psychiatrist Peter Kramer, in *Should You Leave?* says that he leans toward encouraging reconciliation when he counsels couples, in part because he has not been impressed that second marriages are much better than first marriages. Kramer adds that when a second marriage does fare better, it is because the couple has learned from mistakes of the first. This is especially true for "starter marriages"—a term by Pamela Paul for those first marriages that result in no children and dissolve after a few years.

Divorce counseling is as important as marriage counseling. If a marriage cannot be saved or should not be saved, couples still may need some help in separating and divorcing. This help is not in the legal sense for there will be plenty of lawyers involved, but rather in the psychological sense. Otherwise, the same couple who suffered in marriage will inevitably continue to suffer in divorce. Wallerstein and Blakeslee, in *What about the Kids?*, note that couples can fail at divorce just as they have failed at marriage.

"Why" to Marry Should Precede "Whom" to Marry.

> The dread of loneliness being keener than the fear of bondage, we get married.
>
> —Cyril Connolly

Charles Darwin, after a long and methodical deliberation, ultimately decided to marry. It is noteworthy that he first decided to get married and then tried to figure out whom he should marry. He figured out that the alternatives to marriage were worse. Interestingly, apparently, Darwin had an unusually happy and lasting marriage. The couple had seven children who lived into adulthood, and as Robert Wright says none of these children ever "penned a 'Darwin dearest' memoir."

Darwin is not alone in his priority or the sequence of his decision. Commonly, first we decide to get married and then look for someone to marry, though on the surface it might be the other way around. *Why* precedes *whom*.

That is why those who are not ready to get married regret they wasted many marriageable partners. These people are either not mature enough to take on the responsibilities of marriage (then rightly postpone the decision regardless of the missed opportunities) or they are so otherwise engaged in their work and other endeavors that they forfeit a relationship that might have led to a good marriage. Those who decide to marry a specific person before contemplating why they should get married justify their decision in practical terms: long-enough engagement, legitimization of sex, pressure from families, formalization of the commitment and the habit, and so forth. We are of the opinion that if "who" precedes "why," divorce might be more likely. Especially when the "who" to marry is chosen purely on the basis of sexual attraction. Hacker, in *Mismatch,* agrees.

Romance the Chores of Everyday Life— It Survives All Other Romances

> After ecstasy, the laundry.
>
> —Zen saying

"Love begins as a sonnet, but it eventually turns into a grocery list. Therefore, you need someone with whom you can go to the supermarket," says Joel Achenbach in "Homeward Bound." Men's and women's romantic feelings toward each other are time limited. They rarely last for the duration of the marriage. Couples who create a new ground for their togetherness during their passionate stage are able to survive the sexual boredom that may invariably ensue with the fading of romantic interest within a few years.

Michael Vincent Miller, in *Intimate Terrorism,* believes that passionate relationships are "both too fierce and too fragile" to support decades of married life for couples to rely on. He also believes that romantic passion alone fails to cushion couples from the "domestic messiness" of everyday life. He describes "a romance of the ordinary": taking care of children, maintaining the house, organizing social life, cooking, eating, cleaning, exercising, doing the taxes, and yes, going to the supermarket together. Obviously the majority of couples do not succeed in romancing the ordinary enough to survive, because they have no concept as to how and why to make the shift. But as if failing each other in their realistic expectations is not enough, spouses do also have totally unrealistic expectations: perfection. Barbara Ehrenreich, in "Why It Might Be Worth It (to Have an Affair)," portrays such unreasonable expectations with witty questions and an answer, though a little slanted toward her own gender:

Q: Santa Claus, Darth Vader, Batman, the Perfect Man, and the Perfect Woman are driving along together when they suddenly get a flat. Who changes the tire?

A: The Perfect Woman, of course—the others are make-believe characters.

Ehrenreich contrasts love with marriage: "love is something wild and crazy, while marriage is sober and sane." We expect love to be everlasting and blissful. For marriage, however, she says, "we demand something far harder to find—the perfect, all-purpose Renaissance man."

Divorce is the solution, when the marital conflicts are related to characterological mismatches:

- Feeling contempt and disgust toward your spouse or being subjected to your spouse's contempt and disgust.
- Finding yourself complaining and being critical of your spouse or being subjected to your spouse's criticism and complaints.
- Finding yourself vilifying your spouse or being vilified by your spouse.
- Becoming entrenched in believing that your spouse is the cause of your inner deadness or being blamed for the same by your spouse.
- Finding yourself abusing or humiliating (physically or sexually) your spouse or being humiliated or abused by him or her.

But the "perfects" don't often want to go to the supermarket; they are more inclined to go to divorce lawyers' offices. Those people need to come to terms with the relative failure of their unrealistic expectations and face squarely the total revision of their idealistic views of marriage; otherwise, they fall into another romantic illusion, this time fueled with despair and rage: the divorce. What is tragic is the fact that these divorces are neither really desirable nor inevitable. Divorce is definitely not the solution to the problems of marriage as an institution.

The Marital Ghetto: The Legitimate Reason for Divorce

Sometimes couples inhabit a "marital ghetto," which Michael Vincent Miller defines as "the human equivalent of a balanced aquarium, where the fish and plants manage to live indefinitely off each other's waste products." This degree of negativity in marriage, if allowed to run rampant, is lethal to a relationship. John M. Gottman and Nan Silver highlight "criticism," "contempt," "defensiveness," and "stonewalling" as the "Four Horsemen of the Apocalypse." These four behaviors bode badly for a marriage. Contempt implies disgust. At its worst, decay and even death in marriage are a real possibility—the death of the soul. That is where one of the spouses effaces her "self" (usually a woman) to accommodate the union. In *Learning to Be Human,* Leston Havens gives an example of Marilyn Monroe as the ultimate prototype of such compliance— embodying others' wishes. "A photographer of Marilyn Monroe remarked that it was unnecessary to tell her how to pose or where to stand; she appeared wired in to the other's intentions. (Monroe remarked that she was a different person with everyone she met.)"

Divorce is not the solution, when the marital conflicts are related to generic differences between men and women:

- Don't constantly entertain the idea of divorce—an escape-hatch mentality preempts your staying power and natural commitment to working on the marriage.
- Come to terms with the fact that there is no such a thing as a perfect marriage but only a "good-enough" one.
- Hang in there. The best and most enduring love is the love at last sight.
- The ultimate solution is not in leaving or staying in a marriage but growing up.

Solely pleasing the spouse almost exclusively and sacrificing all of your needs may ultimately lead to resentment sufficient enough for divorce or even psychological or real suicide. The vast majority of divorces are initiated by women. "Men prefer to make a marriage so unbearable," says Karen Karbo, "that a woman has no choice other than to leave; in any case, a man almost never leaves a marriage unless he's got someone to leave it for."

Even so, where does the blame lie? Divorce is bad enough, but individuals tend to blame their partners and convince themselves that the next person will be better. Self-blame for the breakup compounds their individual sense of failure. At times one of the partners may be solely responsible for the failure of the marriage (e.g., abusive spouse), but commonly it is the result of reciprocal failure of the couple in their adjustment to each other and to the institution of marriage.

What are valid reasons for divorce? You should consider divorce when you or your spouse feel ongoing contempt, disgust, and lack of respect for each other or are made to feel that way in marriage; you are constantly complaining about the other or are subjected to such chronic complaints; you vilify the other or feel vilified; you believe you are responsible for your spouse's feelings of inner deadness or you are made to feel that way; you are chronically abusing or humiliating your spouse or are humiliated or abused by him or her. In other words, divorce seems a course of action when you do not feel safe both metaphorically and in reality with your spouse: when you have lost all trust in him or her and when your marriage no longer feels like a safe haven. This issue, of course, is one of degree. We all feel misunderstood at times and experience empathic failures on the part of a spouse toward ourselves. When these feelings and experiences, however, become chronic and overwhelming and part of the fabric of the marriage itself, they signal a time to consider divorce.

Irreconcilable Differences Exist between Men and Women; They Should Not Be the Reason for Divorce.

> There is no absolute reality in marital conflict, only two subjective realities.
>
> —John M. Gottman and Nan Silver

Irreconcilable differences in marriage emanate partly from the irreconcilable differences between men and women that we have discussed previously. These are the John Gray *Men Are from Mars, Women Are from Venus* issues that are often not solvable. They are there at the beginning and during the marriage and also will remain there after the divorce. If you cannot live with the opposite sex, simply don't get married to someone of the opposite sex.

Differences between our idealized concept of marriage and its reality are sometimes responsible also. Pamela Paul explains that marriage is a "coveted ideal because we've made it one," where we have placed considerable pressure on the institution. Paul believes that marriage today is less about creating a family, and more about becoming two well-rounded and happy people.

Someone who isn't well-rounded, fulfilled as an individual, or happy or simply content, however, may expect all that from union with another person, who may or may not be suffering from the same illusion. "Why do you expect to be happily married when you are not individually happy?" asks the protagonist in *Reuben, Reuben*. "Every magazine has an article with Nine Keys to it, or Seven

Steps, as though the quest had any more sense to it, or any more hope of fulfill-ment, than the search for El Dorado. . . . How do you expect mankind to be happy in pairs when it is miserable separately?"

So we expect from marriage a sense of fulfillment and purpose. Adds Paul, "We want marriage to make us feel intellectually stimulated, emotionally ful-filled, socially enhanced, financially free, and psychologically complete." It is no wonder couples feel disappointed with each other and think divorce is the solu-tion.

Marriage, in fact, has potential for all these things, but it is also depriving, self-limiting, intellectually dulling, frustrating, and at times terrifying. Karen Karbo interviewed a number of women athletes who engage in "extreme" sports such as sky surfing where they jump out of an airplane and surf the air currents as they free fall, and extreme skiing, where they descend mountains steep enough that a fall means certain death. To these women it was marriage and having chil-dren that were terrifying.

It Is the Reconcilable Differences That Cause Divorce. Don't Jump to a Conclusion. Try to Reconcile in Good Faith. You Can Always Get Divorced Later.

Solvable, not unsolvable, problems bring couples to an impasse. It is almost in-evitable that you will experience miniconflicts almost on a daily basis. How you handle the conflicts and how you eventually recover from the emotional im-pacts of them and, more important, whether you can use the process to build on your relationship determines the future of your marriage. Ivan Boszormenyi-Nagy and Barbara R. Krasner talk about maintaining an account of fairness in the distribution of burdens and benefits between spouses, what they call a "ledger of merits." The ledger is a kind of balance sheet of the merits and debts the couple accumulates. Just how much entitlement or indebtedness each spouse has at any time depends on the fairness of give-and-take that exists be-tween them.

A lack of balance in the ledger of merits may manifest in a number of ways in the daily life of spouses, even in the most trivial ones. For example, a husband may have brought a chronic illness into his marriage. A wife may have children from a previous marriage. Both spouses obviously may have been aware of these factors when they married, but later these issues become sources of resentment and discontent. As a result, instead of dealing with these matters directly, a couple may argue over mundane events like dishes left in the sink or who forgot to lock a door. Gottman and Silver call that building of trust, good faith, and mutuality "a couple's 'emotional bank account.'" Couples who turn toward each other are "building up emotional savings" that can buffer them in rough times, when they're faced with a major life stress or conflict. Gottman and Silver identify eight signs of such gridlock, including talking without making headway, feeling rejected by your partner, and experiencing no sense of humor or affection from your partner, but rather more frustration and hurt. Eventually, you vilify each other and disengage.

Before you reach that stage of disengagement you should do some soul searching and find out how and why you contribute to causing and perpetuating conflicts within the marriage. At times, these factors are simple and on the surface and you may be able to figure them out if you confront yourself honestly. At other times, your motivation to undo the relationship is deep and complicated and requires the hand of a seasoned psychotherapist.

If the problem between spouses is primarily a communication issue, simultaneous counseling of both spouses by the same therapist with joint meetings may be useful, especially when both spouses wish to preserve the marriage. When it comes to resolving fundamental conflicts through communication, Gottman and Silver found that discussions in couples' therapy invariably ended on the same note on which they had begun. Exploration of communication problems between spouses has a limited value and is potentially inflammatory if they focus on unchangeable gender differences. In good hands, however, most marriages are salvageable.

Iris Krasnow tells of her sister, who specializes in family law and hears the "suffering and wreckage of divorce" in her work daily. This attorney strongly recommends counseling for a couple if she sees any evidence, any hope the marriage might survive. Divorce can always proceed later. We concur. Once divorce proceedings are under way, there is less likelihood couples will reconcile. Quoting her sister, Krasnow says, "The work on a marriage needs to be done while you're married." That counselor phase, even if it has only a modicum of a chance of being successful, should precede the lawyer phase, and the lawyer phase should be combined simultaneously with divorce counseling. Pamela Paul even goes so far as to say that the process of divorce can strengthen a spouse's belief in marriage.

Interestingly, California economists Gordon Dahl and Enrico Moretti note in David Leonhardt's article that couples who have children are less likely to divorce if at least one child is a boy. They found that this result occurred in every decade since the 1940s, and it happened across the country though more so in whites than in blacks, and more in couples with a high school education rather than a college education.

> Weave yourself to each other by weaving yourself into the world:
>
> • Belong to a religious congregation.
> • Join social and avocational clubs.
> • Identify with or work for a missionary organization.
> • Engage in your local institutions, such as politics and schools.

If You Attain Psychological Hermaphroditism, You Won't Need to Divorce.

Most flowering plants are hermaphrodites: they possess both male and female reproductive organs. Yet, there is very little battle of the sexes in the garden. There are only heavenly colors, shapes, and smells, inviting joy and excitement. This situation seemingly operates well as long as there is no need for concern about genetic mutations or other defects and vulnerabilities of an inbred system.

Because of nonhermaphroditism, the world is cacophonous. The so-called battle of the sexes, though, is rarely about sex itself. Rather, however, it is about the nature of the relationship between men and women and how very different men and women really are. They accuse each other of not listening, of listening but not understanding, or, if understanding, of not appreciating or accepting. Most of the conflicts between spouses don't pertain to sexual relations per se, but to different perceptions, ways of thinking and doing, and about priorities and sensibilities. Men and women *are* different. Nongender behavior is simply a politically correct wish. In *The Proper Care and Feeding of Husbands,* Laura Schlessinger speaks of the "sadly mistaken and destructive belief that there is a unisexuality," a belief that men and women have no differences.

The classic complaints about marriage do not mean necessarily that people should get divorced. They are just complaints, the way that one may complain about the weather. In this sense, a complaint is a wish that it were sunnier. The more a couple stays married, the less likely the couple will get divorced. This is partly because spouses transform each other to the point that a kind of natural "psychological hermaphroditism" evolves. Complaints within the marriage decline as the couple adapts to each other's contrary qualities, and the dissatisfactions with each other are replaced by self-complaints. In this way, a vague unhappiness about themselves substitutes for a well-defined unhappiness they may have had about the marriage. Through this unintended cultivation of psychological hermaphroditism, couples gain perspective on each other that comes from incorporating some of the contrary qualities of the other sex. They transcend themselves and reach a tolerance of their own shortcomings, whether original or acquired in marriage. They learn to weave themselves to each other, as well, by weaving themselves into the world.

It Is Normal to Remain Ambivalent about Being Married and to Whom.

In general, our ambivalence is all-encompassing. We are of two minds about almost everything, ranging from the most significant to the most trivial matters. Although ambivalence is always the state of our minds, we see it best exposed in conflictual relationships. One of the common complaints that couples have of each other, for example, is that the other one never makes a decision, never says exactly what he or she wants, and then ends up miserable and victimized by someone else's decision. Under such ubiquitous circumstances, "What would you like to have for dinner?"—a simple question—may get the same response as "Shall we have children?" And the equally ambivalent answer will similarly be, "Whatever you like"; "Either way is fine with me"; "You decide"; "Well, I'm not sure"; "Let's wait and see"; or, perhaps more provocatively, "Why ask *me* to decide?" It is in the nature of the subjective mind to be ambivalent. The ultimate ambivalent being, Kierkegaard called himself a "subjective thinker." Apparently, in his native city of Copenhagen, so the story is reported by William Barrett, perhaps apocryphally, the street urchins used to run after Kierkegaard yelling, "Either/or? Either/or!"

Man's variable and ambivalent human nature is most aptly depicted in T. H. White's *The Once and Future King*. One tale from this notable book dates from ancient days, when all of the earth's creatures were still in the same embryonic form. One afternoon God called all the little embryos together and informed them that they could choose what form they wanted for themselves. All the embryos changed into different forms except the embryo that was to become a man. After much consideration, that embryo couldn't decide how he wanted to change his form. Instead, the embryo left it up to God, who was, in fact, delighted, after all, to have that decision left up to Him.

Ambivalence is a natural conflict between our old and our new brains. Our complicated brain represents our new brain, the cortical system. We still have an old brain too, similar to other mammals, that has stayed intact and unchanged no matter how developed our new brain has become. This old brain in us and in all animals, as Joseph LeDoux has explained, controls our emotions as well as all

Cultivate soulfulness toward each other:

- Forgive and forget transgressions. Forgetting is as important as remembering.
- Find endearing aspects of your spouse's "faults."
- Provide emotional shelter during your spouse's failures and disappointments.
- Encourage each other to succeed but do not demand success.
- Avoid envy and unfriendly competition.
- Provide and demand equality and a peer relationship.

involuntary activities, that is, breathing, heartbeat, digestion; it knows what it wants and makes automatic decisions based on external and internal perceptions. Its principle is to survive, to identify its requirements and enable itself to get them as soon as possible.

The new brain, the highly developed cortical brain of humans, differentiates us from the rest of the animal kingdom. It evaluates perceptions, makes complicated judgments, anticipates others' reactions. The principle of the cortical brain is also to survive and to get what is required, but it, unlike the subcortical brain, also cultivates social, political, and altruistic concerns. Moreover, it delays, and even at times negates, our primitive urges that collide sharply with the demands of the old brain. Humans, therefore, envision the world in two dissimilar ways. On every subject presented, humans take two conflicting postures simultaneously—corresponding to these two brains. We are conscious as a cortical brain (the rational adult) of what we must not desire when our old brain (the instinctual animal) demands. Freud actually divided these two brains metaphorically into the "ego," or rational brain, and the "id," or the brain of the drives and wishes and the irrational. That's why the history of mankind has long revealed the innate need of the human psyche to tell two kinds of tales about the nature of things. Even the Bible begins with two different tales of Creation as James Hillman reminds us. Despite your two minds about everything, cultivate soulfulness toward each other.

Marry, Nonetheless; It Is the Best of All Options.

As society changes, so will the concept of marriage. Choose one type or perhaps invent your own marriage contract with a reciprocating partner. But marry! In his autobiography, Charles Darwin wrote of his struggles with the question of whether to marry. In a paper headed "This Is the Question," Darwin attempts to deal systematically with the subject by categorizing the pros and cons of marriage, and he reaches a remarkable conclusion that is still relevant over 150 years later:

MARRY

Children—(if it please God)—constant companion, (friend in old age) who will feel interested in one—better than a dog anyhow—Home, and someone to take care of house. . . . These things good for one's health. . . .

My God, it is intolerable to think of spending one's whole life, like a neuter bee, working, working and nothing after all.—No, no won't do.—

NOT MARRY

No children, (no second life) no one to care for one in old age.—
Freedom to go where one liked. . . . Choice of Society *and little of it*. Conversation of clever men at clubs.—
Not forced to visit relatives, and to bend in every trifle—to have the expense and anxiety of children—perhaps quarrelling.
Loss of time—cannot read in the evenings—fatness and idleness—anxiety and responsibility—less money for books etc.—if many children forced to gain one's bread.—(But then it is very bad for one's health to work too much)

Then he sums up:

"It being proved necessary to marry . . . if one does not marry soon, one misses so much good pure happiness. . . . Cheer up—One cannot live this solitary life, with groggy old age, friendless and cold and childless staring one in one's face, already beginning to wrinkle."

Darwin's thoughts, as would be expected, are logical and practical. We see a wistful longing for a wife, on the other hand, in John Barth's novel *Chimera*. Here a king confesses to one of his concubines of his yearning for a wife. He says he has had many and all kinds of women:

"Tall and short, dark and fair, lean and plump, cold and ardent, bold and timid, clever and stupid, comely and plain—I bedded them all, spoke with them all, possessed them all, but was myself possessed by nothing but despair. Though I took many, with their consent, I wanted none of them. Novelty lost its charm, then even its novelty. Unfamiliarity I came to loathe: the foreign body in the dark, the alien touch and voice, the endless *exposition*. All I craved was someone with whom to get on with the story of my life, which was to say, of our life together: a long friend; a loving wife; a treasurable wife; a wife, a wife."

Marry:

- A spouse is a life-witness: without such a lifelong companion, we are unbearably alone.
- Children bring additional purpose and meaning to your life in the form of responsibility and continuity.
- Marriage furthers social engagement; it is a source of pleasure and liveliness.
- Marriage has practical advantages of safe sex and sharing responsibilities, chores, finances.

The king did get married and his kingdom prospered. In fact most men, as we have said, prosper in marriage. Marry, especially if you are a man. In marriage man is hardly a slave. Men do very well in every aspect of life, all sources seem to agree. Maushart explains that marriage increases men's wages and reduces substance abuse and drinking. Marriage also fosters community and church involvement, as well as philanthropic activities. Jonathan Rauch calls marriage "*the* great civilizing institution." Women, though, do not flourish necessarily as well in a marriage, professionally, physically, or psychologically. Nevertheless, when marriage is good, it is even good for women.

Actually, every marriage is an ongoing rehearsal. There is no finished product. That is to say there is no such a thing as "being married" but rather degrees of "married," whether to one spouse forever after or one of many. Although the specifics of each marriage are different, we cannot improve on Darwin's reasoning. So you should marry with the full understanding of the

Marriage is an institution for adults:

- Don't seek happiness in marriage; bring your own.
- Don't seek meaning and purpose in the marriage; bring your own meaning and purpose.
- Don't seek marriage for intellectual and social stimulation; bring it.
- Don't seek unconditional acceptance from your spouse; don't expect to give unconditional acceptance in return.
- Don't seek salvation in marriage for your personal problems.
- Marriage is neither hell nor heaven; it is mundane real life.

limitations of the person you are marrying as well as those of the institution of marriage itself.

The Marriage Cure: Idealize Certain Aspects of Your Spouse, Deservedly.

Marriage is limited in what it can provide: it cannot make you what you are not. Marriage is another expression of ourselves. It might tap your potential (e.g., parental affection), but it cannot create much *de nouveau,* nor provide complete satisfaction—for either men or women.

In effect, Betty Friedan was saying the same thing, though with a somewhat different emphasis, in the early 1960s when she wrote her classic *The Feminine Mystique.* Then, Friedan took offense with women's colleges who were educating women to be wives and mothers only, rather than scholars. She reports that one group of students took to calling this a "WAM"—"wives' and mothers' education." This is, incidentally, well portrayed in the film *Mona Lisa Smile.* Friedan's view was not that women should forsake being wives and mothers but that satisfaction and fulfillment, for most women, do not come exclusively from the role of housewife. Friedan felt that marriage should be seen without the "veil of overglorification." Friedan recognized that women she had talked with felt a sense of discontent with their husbands and continually irritated with their children when they saw marriage and motherhood as the only fulfillment in their lives.

Our point is that neither women nor men should make their marriage the focal point of their happiness and satisfaction. Marriage cannot, and should not, be all things to all people. You particularly must stop regarding marriage as your private wellspring of salvation or happiness. "Thinking you get happiness everafter is a ticket to divorce," says Iris Krasnow. She says there are four things she would say about marriage: it can be hell; the grass may not be greener elsewhere; savor the highs because there will be lows; and since no one is perfect, "you may as well love the one you're with." We can amend Krasnow's four conclusions with four of our own: marriage is neither hell nor heaven; it is mostly mundane; the grass may be greener elsewhere, but that is not where you are; hang in when down, because highs may be around the corner; and love your spouse for his or her imperfections.

Such love at last sight grows naturally if you don't run out on the relationship. Hang in there through crises and adversities, and fight it out when needed. Furthermore, a little effort to look at your spouse without a jaundiced eye, but with an appreciating one, goes a long way. Everyone has some positive aspects to them. If not apparent, seek them out, deliberately, and you'll find that many qualities of your spouse's will surprise and delight you. This recognition creates invisible ties of loyalty and affection. Equally, in adversity, understanding goes a long way in mutual empathy and accountability.

Most marriages are salvageable:

- Seek marital counseling early. You may find each other through successive approximations.
- Differentiate your personal problems from those of the marital ones and get individual help.
- Learn to love your spouse's imperfections.
- Don't expect total honesty and loyalty.

Focusing on the positive aspects of the spouse, instead of having a chronic litany about his or her failings, helps considerably in building self-esteem and, in return, ensures affectionate reciprocation. Framing your spouse's faults in a charitable light or interpreting them in an encapsulated form generates a life story for you as a couple and your own life-witness.

In both "A Leap of Faith?" and "The (Mental) Ties That Bind," researchers Sandra L. Murray and John G. Holmes found that couples' abilities to idealize their partners—the *relationship illusion*—predicted greater satisfaction and less conflict in marriage. Partners create stories they tell themselves and the world about each other whereby they tend to exaggerate the good qualities and minimize (or even perhaps, deny) the bad qualities of their partners. Wallerstein and Blakeslee's research in *The Good Marriage* is confirmatory. Even in the so-called good marriages, spouses were not always completely loyal or honest with each other. Some spouses who shared with Wallerstein and Blakeslee certain secrets potentially damaging to the marriage did not share them with their partners, nor was such information necessarily discovered by the spouse. For example, some spouses were absolutely convinced that their husbands or wives had never cheated on them when, in fact, these partners had confessed the opposite to the authors. In other words, the spouses were able to maintain the *relationship illusion* of loyalty about each other, whether warranted or not.

A less dramatic form of putting a positive slant on one's spouse came from a woman who initially complained of a lack of verbal expressiveness in her engineer husband. She eventually came to recognize his virtue through the following construct: "He works with machines; they don't talk. But I know he loves me; he is a silently loving man." You may even take greater poetic license in weaving and reweaving the tales of virtues of your spouse without stretching its fabric too much. It may strengthen your marriage.

There Is No "Marriage," but Rather "Marriages."

Some attempts have been made to recognize the fact that not only the romantic ideal but all other aspects of marriage—its nature, formalities, length of commitment, and so forth—require reevaluation. Should there be qualitative degrees of being married? Should there be quantitative degrees, that is, renewable marriage contracts with term limits, as it were?

Based on their study of happily married couples, Wallerstein and Blakeslee, *The Good Marriage,* divide marriages into four types: romantic, rescue, companionate, and traditional. The authors note that a marriage does not always fall into one type or another, but many of the couples they studied did. Some marriages were hybrids of more than one type.

The *romantic* marriage has a lasting, passionately sexual relationship at its core. Noteworthy, only 15 percent of the authors' sample fell into this category. A couple in a romantic marriage often "shares the sense that they were destined to be together." These couples maintain exciting, sensual memories of their first meeting and courtship.

The second type is the *rescue* marriage, where the couples' early experiences have been traumatic. The authors call these couples the "walking wounded," where healing is a central theme of the marriage. Incidentally, they believe that every second marriage, whether romantic, companionate, or traditional, should be considered, by its very nature, a rescue marriage. It rescues a spouse from the trauma and unhappiness of the failed earlier marriage.

The third type is the *companionate* marriage. This is the most common form of marriage among younger couples today. Say Wallerstein and Blakeslee, "At its core is friendship, equality, and the value system of the women's movement, with its corollary that the male role, too, needs to change." A major factor in the companionate marriage is the couple's attempt to balance a work investment with an "emotional investment" in their own relationship with each other and the children.

The fourth type is the *traditional* marriage. Here there is a clear division of roles and responsibilities: the woman takes charge of home and family while the man is the primary wage earner. Wallerstein and Blakeslee explain that women in this form of marriage define their lives in "terms of chapters of time," such as before marriage and children, when children are young, and so forth.

Steven Nock proposes the "challenge of reinventing marriage." He considers six normative characteristics of legal marriage (individual free choice; maturity, age eighteen; heterosexuality; husband as head; fidelity and monogamy; and parenthood) designed for the era of women's dependency on men. Women's independence challenges these rules that originated from outside the marital union. Nock offers cohabitation as an alternative to marriage. Cohabitation, for example, offers freedom from the rules of marriage since, as he says, there are no boundaries regarding cohabitation. But he also sees that complete independence is not a viable solution either. Two great soloists do not always make a good duet.

Sarah Lyall notes that some European countries are ahead of the United States in granting legal rights and status to couples who don't necessarily want to commit "till death do us part." She explains that countries such as France and Portugal are taking what she calls a more "pragmatic" approach to marriage by taking into account changing attitudes of their populations. These countries are giving "alternatives to marriage," sometimes with specific names, such as the *pacte civil de solidarité* or *PACS,* in France.

Cohabiting couples, whether heterosexual or homosexual, may enjoy being exempt from the rules of traditional marriage, but they also suffer from their absence. Whereas marriage obviously provides a template to follow, cohabitation does not. Rauch emphasizes that marriage is a legal contract between two people and the community. It is a "life-altering boundary." What gives marriage its power and mystique is the community support and social expectations marriage engenders.

Your marriage is not fraudulent if it seems different. There is no such thing as "marriage" but rather "marriages" like other heterogeneous institutions, such as education or business:

- Yours may be primarily a "marriage of passion." Expect a great deal of emotional upheaval. It is the shortest of all marriages.
- Yours may be primarily a "marriage of parenthood." Expect sexual frustrations, but this marriage lasts longer.
- Yours may be primarily a "marriage of companionship." Love and sex are not necessarily important aspects of the relationship, but liking and respecting each other are. It is for keeps.
- Yours may be a variation on one of these or a combination or an entirely improvised one.
- Your marriage may also start in one form and morph or evolve to another type. Most commonly, marriage evolves from passion to companionship.

Given the extraordinarily high rate for failure of marriage and the equally unsatisfactory alternatives, as well as the sheer quantity of scholarly and self-help books published on marriage, we want to approach the subject somewhat differently: to recognize that there is no such thing as "marriage" but rather "marriages." Marriage may not be a homogeneous concept but rather a heterogeneous one, in the way that other institutions are, such as education or business. There are many categories of education, or classifications of business partnerships, for example, that serve heterogeneous purposes. This typology may be seen as a non-romantic approach to our most romantic of institutions. It may, however, be a more realistic one.

We propose three prototypes of marriages distinguished from each other by their own alternative boundaries and durations; their own purposes; and their own specific rules and principles originating from within those particular unions. They are distinguished from within, rather than from without, by society and religion. In Edith Wharton's "Souls Belated," the protagonist objects to his having to conform to the external authority of marriage, as defined from outside: "don't you see what a cheap compromise it is? We neither of us believe in the abstract 'sacredness' of marriage; we both know that no ceremony is needed to consecrate our love for each other."

Many marriages can be labeled fraudulent by the standards of conventional marriage. Spouses blame themselves or each other and become chronically unhappy. If anything, it is conventional marriage that requires scrutiny. Here, then, is an attempt to reinvent and reframe marital unions from within. We divide marriages into essentially three categories: a *marriage of passion*; a *marriage of parenthood*; and a *marriage of companionship*. These three prototype marriages are not absolutely categorical. They may unfold and morph into each other. Furthermore, they are not age specific, but rather somewhat age related: they demand different expressions of loyalty, expectations, behavior, and commitment from the two partners. Each may result in a time-limited or renewable, long-term agreement, or both.

Reinvent Your Marriage Again and Again.

The *marriage of passion* is usually short-lived, not more than a few years' duration. More typical of the young, this marriage can actually occur at any age. As first marriages, these marriages of passion are sometimes the *starter marriage, training marriage, rehearsal marriage, practice marriage*. The couple just wants to be together, in an almost driven, compulsive way. They are head-over-heels in love with each other, and marriage just seems a logical next step, often to legitimize sex and to appease their families. Having children may be on the minds of the couple, but starting a family is not the immediate focus. Love and sex and passion are on their minds. If there is not much else the couple has in common, each may find the other bored after a period of time as the novelty wears off. It is rare for such passion to continue beyond a few years, at best, especially in the context of mundane daily life. These marriages may end in divorce eventually if they do not transition to something more sustaining.

Sometimes, second marriages result from such passion, often at the expense of a first marriage. This is often the marriage that can result from an affair when either or both of the partners are initially married and end their marriage to be with this other person. In this case, the partners are not necessarily thinking their goal is to raise a family. They are driven by passion. Children may become a product of the relationship, but the idea of having children is not usually the reason for the marriage (unless pregnancy results accidentally).

These second marriages, when they are driven more by passion than anything else, are particularly vulnerable to failure. When the relationship began during a first marriage, this relationship evolved in the context of a web of deceit. Especially when there are children from either or both of the couples' first marriages, each spouse enters this second marriage with considerable guilt regarding the breakup of the family and its effects on their previous spouses and children. Further, each spouse may have less tolerance for the other spouse's children, no matter how sensitive he or she hopes to be. If there is little else in this second marriage beyond passion, this marriage may not survive very long. Sometimes, this second marriage results in a second set of children, and when failure occurs the cycle of guilt intensifies.

The second category of marriage is the *marriage of parenthood*. These are the marriages where the couple clearly plans on having children. That is the couple's goal and immediate focus of the marriage. Sex may be seen, especially for the woman, as a means to conceive a child, rather than something enjoyed passionately. Whereas sex for the marriage of passion is a recreational commodity, sex in this marriage is primarily a reproductive commodity. Once children are conceived, one member of the couple, usually the woman, may lose interest in sex with the spouse. If a couple has difficulty conceiving in this category of marriage, there is considerable strain on the marriage itself. The woman is usually expected, or actually desires, not to seek a career or other responsibilities and puts a hold on her career as she is so focused on her children. The man is expected to be a good provider. Each spouse sees the other as primarily good parent material. If the woman continues to work and advance her career opportunities, she may feel particularly torn about her responsibilities to work and family and may feel more conflicted about her marriage.

The marriage of parenthood may last many years, not only through the decision to have children, but through the children's growth and education as well. These are the marriages that may be most vulnerable when the children leave home. Unless there are other goals in the marriage (e.g., focusing on grandchildren or developed common interests), the couple may find the marriage exhibiting considerable strain after completion of the goal of raising the children.

The third category of marriage is the *marriage of companionship*. Certainly, this marriage can also occur at any stage but is more common in older age. This may be a second marriage that occurs after the first spouse dies or leaves, and loneliness for the other is unbearable.

Sometimes, this type of marriage is the transition from either the first (passion) or second (parenthood) category of marriage. Here, the spouses genuinely like each other. They enjoy being with each other and sharing their ideas. They also have similar interests. Sex may or may not be a part of their relationship. This marriage may likely last until the death of one of the spouses.

These three prototypes of marriage are not absolute categories, as we have said. Some marriages, particularly successful, long-standing ones, may evolve over time from one into another—mostly toward companionship. Some others have elements of all three simultaneously.

Appreciating, though, that there are different reasons for marrying at various times in one's life, and that there are actually different kinds of relationships that evolve over time, may enhance a couple's satisfaction with each other. Accepting that one cannot be all things to another person, particularly at every point in one's life, enables each spouse to gain a greater, overall perspective of the institution of marriage.

The Question of Same-Sex Marriage

Obviously, we have focused our book on heterosexual couples. One of our main arguments is that men and women are fundamentally different in their social outlook and their biological wiring. The considerable differences between men and women result in inevitable difficulties when they live together in marriage. Rauch emphasizes that not one same-sex couple has ever married legally or even hoped, until recently, to marry. Same-sex marriage, therefore, has been impossible to study. This is soon to change: Massachusetts has just become the first state to allow same-sex marriages.

The topic of same-sex marriage is a highly charged one and gets to the core of the very definitions of marriage. Is marriage solely a legal contract empowering individuals with rights? This is one of the arguments for same-sex marriages and analogous to issues of interracial marriages in our not so distant past, as discussed by David Moats in *Civil Wars*. Is marriage a spiritual contract with God? Is there something sacrosanct about heterosexual marriage? Clearly, same-sex couples can feel just as married and have just as many difficulties and joys of being together as heterosexual couples, particularly if they have been together for many years. Does calling the union of same-sex couples anything other than "marriage" make it a "separate but equal" institution? As authors like Jonathan Rauch and Davina Kotulski note, "civil union" is not marriage, but an inferior substitute that many who study same-sex relationships call "marriage-lite." Kotulski make the point that "domestic partnership" sounds more like a "housecleaning service than a term of endearment." All of these designations may endow same-sex couples with certain rights but not necessarily the burdens and responsibilities of marriage, and so it is not the same thing.

Geoffrey Nunberg, a linguist from Stanford, explains that the word "marriage" has such a charged meaning for people because it is what linguists call a "performative notion." In other words, it is something that can occur merely by pronouncing certain words in a specific setting—"like christening a boat." It must be a very specific setting, though: it must take place in front of others.

Nunberg believes, in the end, that the meaning of "marriage" will be determined by "popular usage, rather than edicts or courts." He notes that meanings do change over time and adapt to people's changing attitudes. Some dictionaries already define words like "couple" and "family" differently, and he explains that an upcoming edition of the *Oxford English Dictionary* will change the definition of "marriage" to make it more inclusive: a union involving "two people."

The very nature of "marriage" may very well change over this next decade. Whether its nature will be determined by popular usage or the courts remains to be seen. It may even take a Constitutional amendment as some are suggesting, or at least a repeal of the Defense of Marriage Act of 1996. This act, signed by President Clinton, states the federal government does not recognize same-sex marriages.

Even television shows find the need to comment on the issue. The dramatic series *Law and Order* had an episode that dealt with legal custody rights of same-sex couples. Says prosecuting attorney McCoy, "I say, let them get married. Why shouldn't they be as miserable as the rest of us?" Attorney McCoy's cynical comment notwithstanding, we believe that marriage, however it is eventually defined legally, and when properly understood and appreciated, does not have to lead to chronic dissatisfaction and even misery.

Tending the Base Camp While Climbing the Mountain in Marriage

> Marriage is more than the sum of two spouses.
>
> —Steven Nock

Success in marriage is analogous to success in mountain climbing: successful mountain climbers appreciate that they must expend at least as much time, if not more, in tending to their base camp as they actually do in climbing mountains.

Their survival is dependent upon a base camp that is sturdily constructed and well stocked. As M. Scott Peck has pointed out:

> A common and traditionally masculine marital problem is created by the husband who, once he is married, devotes all his energies to climbing mountains and none to tending to his marriage, or base camp, expecting it to be there in perfect order whenever he chooses to return to it for rest. . . . In contrast, an equally common and traditionally feminine marital problem is created by the wife who, once she is married, feels that the goal of her life has been achieved. To her the base camp is the peak. She cannot understand or empathize with her husband's need for achievements and experiences beyond the marriage.

Marriage is mountain climbing in tandem, with a mutual tending of the base camp. There are considerable "how to" teaching materials, technical formulas, and manuals for it. These all emphasize the importance of the synchronicity of the couple; in marriage, as in music, each instrument continuously influences the other. Even the best efforts by one member of the couple may sabotage the music of the other.

The Specific Nature of Your Relationship in Marriage May Be Time Limited: Your Relationship with Your Spouse Is Timeless.

"I hate divorce" says the Lord.

—Malachi 2:16

The Old Testament quotes the Lord as saying He hates divorce. So do *humans*. Even though all the people interviewed by Pamela Paul believed that divorce might have been the solution for themselves, they wanted to protect their children from that experience. It is not the recommended process for any kind of personal growth. She adds, "Divorce is not the lesson we want to teach."

As noted by Marsilio Ficino, Pythagoras, who believed in the harmony of the spheres and the eternal recurrence of things, asked that we not permit a friend to go easily. Rather, we should remain with a friend as long as possible, until we are compelled to abandon him completely against our will. That wisdom is rarely practiced in the dissolution of a marriage today. Unfortunately, even couples who were married for a long time, had wonderful times together, raised children, and considered themselves each other's best friend often attempt to sever the relationship completely after the divorce.

Friendships are our most precious possessions. As is in all love relations, we do not appreciate their full value until after they have disappeared. The manner in which we lose them has enormous impact on our psyche. Some people accumulate enough anger, resentment, envy, and disappointment to justify the abrupt ending of long-standing relationships, or they allow them to languish through indifference. Relationships do not have to survive forever, even if so promised. They must be permitted, however, to have their natural lives and deaths.

However, when divorce becomes inevitable, that is, when there is an emotionally and sexually dysfunctional, abusive, or dead relationship, then we need a constructive philosophy of disengagement. This enables the psychological survival of all the parties involved, especially when there are children.

Karen Karbo repeats an oft-married matron's comment: "Honey, marriage is forever, but divorce is for life." We need therefore, to divorce better if we keep having a penchant for divorce. We, as well as the person with whom we have spent some years together, deserve the same respect and dignity of disunion as that of union. Especially, we need to acknowledge that one can never totally get divorced, specifically when there are children involved. Even when there are not children, the person whom we once loved and with whom we lived will remain in the recesses of our mind for the rest of our lives.

"My mother remained married to my father for long after they were divorced," says psychotherapist Leston Havens in *Learning to Be Human*. He, in fact, proposes a ceremony of divorce congruent with his concept of being human. "Do you take this spouse as your former spouse, for better or for worse: to be met at every graduation, marriage, and funeral."

Divorce is formidable and agonizing even when it is fully justified. It becomes more so if one or both of the spouses have had attachment and separation conflicts in their early developmental stages. The divorce is particularly excruciating when the spouse experienced as a child the divorce of his or her parents.

The loss of the present relationship evokes memories and feelings of abandonment, and it compounds the pain and makes it unbearable. At times we are unable to allow the other person to leave, even when long overdue, because of the reactivation of this earlier pain. Once the emotions develop a life-or-death quality, we cannot acquire enough distance to evaluate our reaction. Because of a regression to a primitive state of merger (such as that of the earliest infant-mother bond) on these occasions, we invariably feel as if we could never survive the separation. This fear, however, is only legitimate for the defenseless infant. Because the emotional mind cannot differentiate age—the unconscious has no concept of time—it experiences the danger of abandonment, even though the cognitive mind can argue convincingly of the irrationality of the fear.

Every termination is a little like dying. At the end of a relationship, however, we maintain our capacity to relate. As painful as it might be, having once loved enables us to be receptive to future relationships. It requires some time, though, for the psychological disengagement from that particular person (albeit not so effortlessly). We then have the possibility to connect with someone else, provided that we do not expect the identical relationship to be recaptured. The original bond can never be completely replaced or substituted, even with the same person a second time around.

Our relationship to others is a reflection of our relationship to ourselves. In each phase of our lives, we relate to ourselves and thus to others differently. As Thomas Moore says in *Soul Mates*, relationships "initiate us into ourselves. They shape our lives, not only the story line of our biographies, but also the character of our souls." The more we relate, the richer our souls become; the more we connect with other souls, the easier we can permit some relationships to dissolve. As we are increasingly able to accept that a particular relationship may be time limited, we can develop relationships that become timeless.

Epilogue

They lived long, and were faithful to the good in each other.

—Wendell Berry, "A Marriage, an Elegy"

We need to come to terms with ourselves, our cherished ones, and the nature of marriage, itself. We need not always desire to be someone else or to be with someone else. Such frustrating lamentations only leave us chronically dissatisfied.

There is no perfect marriage, just as there is no perfect person. We may aspire to such ideal destinations, but this concept of "perfection" is a dangerous myth. Comparing our marriage with some idyllic form generates unnecessary and unjustified unhappiness in those of us who may have a good-enough or, even, very good marriage. Says Judith Viorst, in *Grown-Up Marriage,* "The risk is that we fail to understand how much real misery there can be even in the very best of marriages." And Voltaire said, "Sometimes the best is the enemy of the good." Nonetheless, people reach different levels of approximating their respective ideals.

Similarly, we judge our spouse's accomplishments, maturity, and behavior. These are just ideals. We hold ourselves and our spouses to that mythical view of maturity, and inevitably failing to measure up, we indulge in a chronic litany against them or in derogatory self-accusations. We always imagine ourselves to be richer, better looking, smarter, and deserving of a superior mate. Inspiration can be a double-edged sword. Although it may give us an impetus to go forward, it may also rob us of contentment. Failures in a marriage are relative failures and, as all other failures, they are an inevitable part of the human soul. At times, such descents facilitate an ascent either for us or our spouse. Such an ascent is not an

221

exact point of arrival; rather, it is a process and it has nothing to do with perfection. It is primarily desiring and appreciating what you already possess. This is a lifetime enterprise, a journey toward a destination—which we can only approximate. Viewed from this evolving perspective, we can visualize ourselves as succeeding only relatively. More satirically, someone once said, from the "inexhaustible curriculum of self-improvement one never graduates." Life is—and should be viewed as—full of undershootings as well as overshootings but always progressing toward a fated destination.

Who is ever up to his destiny? Joseph Campbell raises this question in regard to Hamlet. None of us is immune from this query. Our destiny is somewhat cultivated if we incorporate elements from all who preceded us, whether based upon Shakespeare or our kindergarten teacher or this book of ours. "A good mind that is cultivated is a composition, so to speak, of all minds of former ages. It is the same mind cultivated throughout all that time," said Bernard de Fontenelle, a French writer and philosopher in the late 1600s.[1] This collective mind is like a full-scale orchestra, wherein individual instruments need only to synchronize themselves. Our personal lives may seem an improvised solo performance, full of wondering, replete with loss. It need not be so, however, if we are receptive to the experiences and wisdom of others.

A Finale for Two Violins

> Love seems the swiftest, but it is the slowest of all growths. No man or woman really knows what perfect love is until they have been married a quarter of a century.
>
> —Mark Twain

As we get older, we begin to appreciate the harmony and preciousness of being cherished by one person with whom we have shared life, after many others have more or less deserted us. This is similar to the last movement of Haydn's 1772 Symphony No. 45, in f-sharp Minor, *Farewell*. Apparently, so the anecdote goes, Haydn wrote this symphony in the manner requested by his musicians, who were performing out of town and expressed to him their wish to return home as soon as possible to their spouses and families. Describes music critic Michael Steinberg, "The music resumes, and one by one, instruments play farewell solos and leave. . . . The survivors play the gently pathos-filled slow music again. The cello leaves, then all the violins, but two, then the viola." The two violins remain to play a haunting melody "leaving us somewhere between tears and a smile."

Similarly, in the final movement of a successful marriage, life together continues after children, grandchildren, friends, colleagues leave, one by one, to return to their own homes. Husband and wife remain alone as life-witnesses to each other, as the two violins faithfully continue to play a melody full of tears and smiles.

Note

1. Leonard M. Marsak, trans., "Discourse Concerning the Ancients and Moderns," in *The Achievement of Bernard le Bovier de Fontenelle,* part III, 1688, *The Sources of Science* #76 (New York: Johnson Reprint Corporation, 1970), 1–8.

Bibliography

Achenbach, Joel. "Homeward Bound." In *Here Lies My Heart: Essays on Why We Marry, Why We Don't, and What We Find There,* foreword by Amy Bloom, ed. Deborah Chasman and Catherine Jhee, 50–56. Boston: Beacon Press, 1999.

Ahnert, Lieselotte, and Michael E. Lamb. "Shared Care: Establishing a Balance between Home and Child Care Setting." *Child Development* 74 (4) (July/August 2003): 1044–49.

"Al Furqan." In *The Koran,* 205–209. Translated by N. J. Dawood. 5th rev. ed. Baltimore: Penguin, 1990.

Altman, Stuart A. "Dominance-Submission: A Field Study of the Sociobiology of Rhesus Monkeys, Macaca Mulatto." *Annals of the New York Academy of Sciences* 102 (2) (1962): 338–413.

American Academy of Pediatrics: Committee on Psychosocial Aspects of Child and Family Health. "Coparent or Second-Parent Adoption by Same-Sex Parents." *Pediatrics* 102 (2) (February 2002): 339–40.

Andersson, Malte. "Female Choice Selects for Extreme Tail Length in a Widowbird." *Nature* 299 (October 28, 1982): 818–20.

Angier, Natalie. *Woman: An Intimate Geography.* New York: Random House, 2000, 45, 160, 167.

Apter, Terri. *Why Women Don't Have Wives: Professional Success and Motherhood.* New York: Schocken Books, 1985, 33–34.

Ban Breathnach, Sarah. *Simple Abundance: A Daybook of Comfort and Joy.* 1995, 1999. Reprint, Sydney: Hodder Headline Australia, 2002, Nov. 27.

Barash, David. *The Whispering Within: Evolution and the Origin of Human Nature.* New York: Harper & Row, 1979.

Barash, David P., and Judith Eve Lipton. *The Myth of Monogamy: Fidelity and Infidelity in Animals and People.* New York: Henry Holt, 2001, 7–8, 12, 36, 46, 83–84, 174.

Barr, Ronald G., and Megan Gunnar. "Colic: The 'Transient Responsivity' Hypothesis." In *Crying as a Sign, a Symptom, and a Signal: Clinical, Emotional and Developmental Aspects of Infant and Toddler Crying,* ed. Ronald G. Barr, Brian Hopkins, and James A.

Green, 41–66. Clinics in Developmental Medicine, #152. Suffolk, UK: MacKeith Press, 2000.

Barrett, William. *Irrational Man: A Study in Existential Philosophy.* Garden City, NY: Doubleday, 1962, 152.

Barth, John. *Chimera.* New York: Houghton Mifflin, 1972, 52.

Barthelme, Donald. "Critique de la Vie Quotidienne." In *Sadness.* New York: Bantam, 1974, 3–4, 7.

Bayot, Jennifer. "For Richer or Poorer, Wedding Costs Grow to Credit Card Limit." *New York Times,* Sunday, July 13, 2003, National Section, 1, 13.

Belsky, Jay Michael, and J. Rovine. "Nonmaternal Care in the First Year of Life and the Security of Infant-Parent Attachment." *Child Development* 59 (1988): 157–67.

Benson, Herbert. *Timeless Healing: The Power and Biology of Belief.* With Marg Stark. New York: Simon & Schuster, 1997, 80, 128–29.

Berger, Peter L. *A Far Glory.* New York: Macmillan, 1992, 193.

Bermant, Gordon, and Associates. "Sexual Behavior: Hard Times for the Coolidge Effect." In *Psychological Research: The Inside Story,* ed. Michael H. Siegel and H. Philip Zeigler, 76–103. New York: Harper & Row, 1976, 76–77, 89, 94.

Bernard, Jessie. *The Future of Marriage.* New Haven: Yale University Press, 1982, 5–8, 15–16, 17–19.

Berry, Wendell. "A Marriage, an Elegy." In *Collected Poems: 1957–82.* New York: North Point Press, 1987, 152.

Blum, Deborah. "The First Week: Pathway to Survival Holds Peril." *The Sacramento Bee,* October 8, 1989, Main News, A17.

——. "Is Mother's Milk Key to Child's Growth, Future?" *The Sacramento Bee,* July 8, 1996 Main News, Section A1.

——. "'Natural Born Killers' May Be More Than a Movie Title." *The Sacramento Bee,* A1, Main News, October 19, 1995.

——. *Sex on the Brain: The Biological Differences between Men and Women.* New York: Viking Press, 1997, 18, 22, 24–25, 27, 28–29, 46–47, 56, 86, 100, 109, 114–16, 124, 141, 143, 176, 179, 180, 184, 217, 235.

Booth, Alan, and James M. Dabbs Jr. "Testosterone and Men's Marriages." *Social Forces* 72 (2) (December 1993): 463–77.

Boszormenyi-Nagy, Ivan, and Barbara R. Krasner. *Between Give and Take: A Clinical Guide to Contextural Therapy.* New York: Brunnel/Mazel, 1986, 66, 338, 342–43, 417.

Bradshaw, John. *Homecoming: Reclaiming and Championing Your Inner Child.* New York: Bantam, 1990, xi, 42.

Bulfinch, Thomas. "Admetus and Alcestis." In *Bulfinch's Mythology,* ed. Richard P. Martin, 162–63. New York: HarperCollins, 1991.

Buscaglia, Leo. *The Way of the Bull: A Voyage.* Thorofare, NJ: Charles B. Slack, 1973, 11.

Campbell, Joseph. *The Power of Myth.* With Bill Moyers. Edited by Betty Sue Flowers. New York: Doubleday, 1988, 51, 115, 118, 151.

Canivet, Catarina, Iren Jakobsson, and Barbro Hagander. "Colicky Infants According to Maternal Reports in Telephone Interviews and Diaries: A Large Scandinavian Study." *Journal of Developmental and Behavioral Pediatrics* 23 (1) (February 2002): 1–8.

Carrell, Laura and Huntington F. Willard. "X-Inactivation Profile Reveals Extensive Variability in X-Linked Gene Expression in Females." *Nature* 434: (03479) (March 17, 2005), 400–404 (Letters to *Nature*).

Carroll, Lewis. *Alice's Adventures in Wonderland* and *Through the Looking-Glass*. With introductions by Will Self and Zadie Smith. New York: Bloomsbury, 2003, 357, 380.

Choi, Susan. "Relationships: Identity Crisis." *Vogue,* March 2004, 286, 290.

Chopra, Deepak. *Ageless Body, Timeless Mind: The Quantum Alternative to Growing Old*. New York: Harmony Books, 1993, 137, 151, 152, 153, 157, 160–2.

Cioran, E. M. *Anathemas and Admirations*. Translated by Richard Howard. New York: Arcade, 1991, 85.

Clifford, Tammy J., M. Karen Campbell, Kathy N. Speechley, and Fabian Gorodzinsky. "Sequelae of Infant Colic: Evidence of Transient Infant Distress and Absence of Lasting Effects on Maternal Mental Health." *Archives of Pediatrics and Adolescent Medicine* 156 (12) (December 2002): 1183–88.

Congreve, William. *The Way of the World*. Edited by Brian Gibbons. London: A & C Black, 1994, 81–82.

Connolly, Cyril. *The Unquiet Grave: A Word Cycle by Palinurus*. Introduction by Cyril Connolly. A Karen and Michael Braziller Book. Rev. ed. New York: Persea Books, 1981, 4, 11, 16, 57, 64.

Cowan, Caroline Pape, and Philip A. Cowan. *When Partners Become Parents: The Big Life Change for Couples*. New York: HarperCollins, 1992, x, 32, 37, 59, 109, 198, 205.

Coward, Noël. *Private Lives*. London: Methuen Modern Plays, 2000, 32, 56.

Critser, Greg. *Fat Land*. Boston: Houghton Mifflin, 2003.

Crokenberg, Susan C. "Rescuing the Baby from the Bathwater: How Gender and Temperament (May) Influence How Child Care Affects Child Development." *Child Development* 74 (4) (July/August 2003): 1034–38.

Cunningham, Allan S. "Breastfeeding: Adaptive Behavior for Child Health and Longevity." In *Breastfeeding: Biocultural Perspectives,* ed. Katherine A. Dettwyler and Patricia Stuart-Macadam, 243–64. New York: Aldine de Gruyter, 1995, 248–49, 251.

Curb Your Enthusiasm. Produced by Larry David, Jeff Garlin, and Gavin Polone. HBO, 2004. Television program, season 4, episode 39, "The Survivor."

Dabbs, James Jr., M. Timothy, S. Carr, Robert L. Frady, and Jasmin K. Riad. "Testosterone, Crime, and Misbehavior among 692 Prison Inmates." *Personality and Individual Differences* 18 (5) (1995): 627–33.

Dallos, Sally, and Rudi Dallos. *Couples, Sex, and Power: The Politics of Desire*. Buckingham, UK: Open University Press, 1997, 139.

Darling, Lynn. "For Better or Worse." In *Here Lies My Heart: Essays on Why We Marry, Why We Don't, and What We Find There,* foreword by Amy Bloom, ed. Deborah Chasman and Catherine Jhee, 178–202. Boston: Beacon Press, 1999, 182, 189, 197.

Darwin, Charles. *The Autobiography of Charles Darwin, 1809–1882*. Edited by Nora Barlow. New York: Norton, 1958, 231–34.

———. *The Expression of the Emotions in Man and Animals*. Introduction, afterword, and commentary by Paul Ekman. 3rd ed. New York: Oxford University Press, 1998, 43.

Dawkins, Richard. *The Selfish Gene*. Oxford: Oxford University Press, 1976.

DeSalvo, Louise. "Adultery." In *Here Lies My Heart: Essays on Why We Marry, Why We Don't, and What We Find There,* foreword by Amy Bloom, ed. Deborah Chasman and Catherine Jhee, 57–60. Boston: Beacon Press, 1999, 58.

Dettwyler, Katherine A. "Beauty and the Breast: The Cultural Context of Breastfeeding in the United States." In *Breastfeeding: Biocultural Perspectives,* ed. Patricia Stuart-Macadam and Katherine A. Dettwyler, 167–215. New York: Aldine De Gruyter, 1995, 195, 201.

De Vries, Peter. *Reuben, Reuben.* New York: Little, Brown, 1964, 80, 102, 313, 332–33, 386, 412.

de Waal, Frans. *Chimpanzee Politics: Power and Sex among Apes.* New York: Harper & Row, 1982, 88.

Dicks, Henry V. *Marital Tensions: Clinical Studies towards a Psychological Theory of Interaction.* New York: Basic Books, 1967, 168.

Dowd, Maureen. "Incredible Shrinking Y." *New York Times,* July 9, 2003, Section A, 21.

———. "X-celling Over Men." *New York Times,* March 20, 2005, 13 (Sunday, Op-editorial page).

Dowling, Colette. *The Cinderella Complex: Women's Hidden Fear of Independence.* New York: Summit Books, 1981, 16.

Dunbar, Robin. *Grooming, Gossip and the Evolution of Language.* Cambridge: Harvard University Press, 1996, 21, 35.

Dwyer, C. M., W. S. Dingwall, and A. B. Lawrence. "Physiological Correlates of Maternal-Offspring Behaviour in Sheep: A Factor Analysis." *Physiology and Behavior* 67 (3) (September 1999): 443–54.

Early, Gerald. "Monogamy and Its Perils." In *Here Lies My Heart: Essays on Why We Marry, Why We Don't, and What We Find There,* foreword by Amy Bloom, ed. Deborah Chasman and Catherine Jhee, 61–67. Boston: Beacon Press, 1999.

Edelman, Gerald. *Wider Than the Sky: The Phenomenal Gift of Consciousness.* New Haven: Yale University Press, 2004, 38–39.

Ehrenreich, Barbara. "Why It Might Be Worth It (to Have an Affair)." In *Here Lies My Heart: Essays on Why We Marry, Why We Don't, and What We Find There,* foreword by Amy Bloom, ed. Deborah Chasman and Catherine Jhee, 6–8. Boston: Beacon Press, 1999.

Einstein, Albert. *Collected Papers of Einstein,* vol. 5, *The Swiss Years: Correspondence, 1902–1914.* Trans. Anna Beck. Princeton: Princeton University Press, 1995.

Einstein, Albert, and Leopold Infeld. *The Evolution of Physics: The Growth of Ideas from Early Concepts to Relativity and Quanta.* New York: Simon & Schuster, 1938, 31.

Einstein, Albert and Mileva Marić. Einstein Family Correspondence. New York: Christie's Catalogue, 1996.

Eliot, T. S. "Shakespeare and the Stoicism of Seneca." In *Selected Essays, 1917–1932,* 107–20. New York: Harcourt Brace, 1932, 107.

Elkind, David. *The Hurried Child: Growing Up Too Fast Too Soon.* Reading, MA: Addison-Wesley, 1981, 114–15, 132.

Ellis, Bruce J. "The Evolution of Sexual Attraction: Evaluative Mechanisms in Women." In *The Adapted Mind: Evolutionary Psychology and the Generation of Culture,* ed. Jerome H. Barkow, Leda Cosmides, and John Tooby, 267–88. New York: Oxford University Press, 1992.

Ephron, Nora. *Heartburn.* New York: Random House, 1983, 158.

Epictetus. *The Art of Living.* New interpretation by Sharon Lebell. New York: Harper-SanFrancisco, 1995, 10.

Fabes, Richard A., Laura D. Hanish, and Carol Lynn Martin. "Children at Play: The Role of Peers in Understanding the Effects of Child Care." *Child Development* 74 (4) (July/August 2003): 1039–43.

Fernald, Ann. "Human Maternal Vocalizations to Infants as Biologically Relevant Signals: An Evolutionary Perspective." In *The Adapted Mind: Evolutionary Psychology and the Generation of Culture,* ed. Jerome H. Barkow, Leda Cosmides, and John Tooby, 391–428. New York: Oxford University Press, 1992.

Ficino, Marsilio. *The Letters of Marsilio Ficino.* Vol. 2, book 3, letter #51, 63. Translated from the Latin by members of the Language Department of the School of Economic Science. London: Shepheard-Walwyn, 1978.

Fisher, Helen E. *Anatomy of Love: The Natural History of Monogamy, Adultery, and Divorce.* New York: Norton, 1992, 109.

———. *Why We Love: The Nature and Chemistry of Romantic Love.* New York: Henry Holt, 2004, 53, 84, 92, 182–83, 204.

Frankl, Viktor. *Man's Search for Meaning: An Introduction to Logotherapy.* New York: Simon & Schuster, 1959, 45, 139–40, 143.

Frederickson, Doren. "Breastfeeding Study Design Problems: Health Policy, Epidemiologic and Pediatric Perspectives." In *Breastfeeding: Biocultural Perspectives,* ed. Katherine A. Dettwyler and Patricia Stuart-Macadam, 405–18. New York: Aldine de Gruyter, 1995.

Freud, Anna. "Instinctual Anxiety during Puberty." In *The Ego and Mechanisms of Defense,* vol. 2, 152–72. New York: International Universities Press, 1966.

Freud, Sigmund. "The Dissolution of the Oedipus Complex." In *The Standard Edition of the Complete Psychological Works of Sigmund Freud.* Vol. 19. 1961. Reprint, London: Hogarth Press and Institute of Psycho-Analysis, 1968, 171–79.

———. "On the Universal Tendency to Debasement in the Sphere of Love." In *The Standard Edition of the Complete Psychological Works of Sigmund Freud.* Vol. 11, 177–90. 1957. Reprint, London: Hogarth Press and Institute of Psycho-Analysis, 1968.

Friedan, Betty. *The Feminine Mystique.* Introduction by Anna Quindlin. New York: Norton, 2001, 16, 158–59, 250, 342.

Gabbe, Steven, G., Jennifer R. Niebyl, Joe Leigh Simpson, eds. *Obstetrics: Normal and Problem Pregnancies.* 4th ed. New York: Churchill Livingstone, 2002, 124–25, 710–11.

Galst, Liz. "Babies Aren't the Only Beneficiaries of Breastfeeding." *New York Times,* June 22, 2003, 4.

Gardner, Ralph Jr. "Alpha Women, Beta Men." *New York Magazine,* November 17, 2003, 25–29.

Gergen, Kenneth J. *The Saturated Self: Dilemmas of Identity in Contemporary Life.* New York: HarperCollins, 1991, 6.

Gibran, Kahlil. *The Prophet.* New York: Knopf, 1989, 16–17.

Glantz, Kalman, and John K. Pearce. *Exiles from Eden: Psychotherapy from an Evolutionary Perspective.* New York: Norton, 1990, 102, 104, 111, 130, 132, 136, 138.

Glass, Shirley P. *Not Just Friends: Protect Your Relationship from Infidelity and Heal the Trauma of Betrayal.* With Jean Coppock Staeheli. New York: Simon & Schuster, 2003, 1, 3, 15, 28, 205, 233.

God's Word: Today's Bible Translation That Says What It Means. Grand Rapids: World Publishing, 1995.

Godwin, Peter. "The Way We Live Now: 7-25-99; Happily Ever After." *New York Times,* July 25, 1999, Sunday Magazine Desk, Section 6, 13.

Gottman, John M., and Nan Silver. *The Seven Principles for Making Marriage Work.* New York: Crown, 1999, 27–34, 80, 132–33, 150, 161.

Gould, Stephen Jay. *Hen's Teeth and Horse's Toes.* New York: Norton, 1983, 26–27, 28.

Gracián, Baltasar. *The Art of Wordly Wisdom: A Pocket Oracle,* aphorism #130, 73, aphorism #154, 87. Translated by Christopher Maurer. New York: Doubleday, 1992.

Gray, John. *Men Are from Mars, Women Are from Venus: A Practical Guide for Improving Communication and Getting What You Want in Your Relationships.* New York: Harper Collins, 1992, 15–28, 29, 124, 138–40.

Greenspan, Stanley I. "Child Care Research: A Clinical Perspective." *Child Development* 74 (4) (July/August 2003): 1064–68.

Gruen, Arno. *The Betrayal of the Self: The Fear of Autonomy in Men and Women.* New York: Grove Press, 1988, 102.

Hacker, Andrew. *Mismatch: The Growing Gulf between Women and Men.* 2000. Reprint, New York: Scribner, 2003, 2, 9, 55.

Haldane, J. B. S. "Population Genetics." In *New Biology.* Vol. 18, 34–51. London: Penguin, 1955.

Harrison, Linda J., and Judy A. Ungerer. "Maternal Employment and Infant-Mother Attachment Security at 12 Months Postpartum." *Developmental Psychology* 38 (5) (September 2002): 758–73.

Havel, Vaclav. *The Power of the Powerless: Citizens against the State in Central-Eastern Europe.* New York: M. E. Sharpe, 1985, 31.

Havens, Leston. *Coming to Life.* Cambridge: Harvard University Press, 1993, 97.

———. *Learning to Be Human.* A William Patrick Book. Reading, MA: Addison-Wesley, 1994, 22–23, 117.

Hazan, Cindy, and Phillip Shaver. "Romantic Love Conceptualized as an Attachment Process." *Journal of Personality and Social Psychology* 52 (3) (1987): 511–24.

Hazan, Cindy, and Debra Zeifman. "Sex and the Psychological Tether." In *Attachment Processes in Adulthood,* ed. Kim Bartholomew and Daniel Perlman. Vol. 5, *Advances in Personal Relationships,* 151–78. London: Jessica Kingsley, 1994.

Hebbel, Friedrich. "Tandelei." In *Gedichte Und Prosa: Samtliche Werke, Zweiter Band,* 74–75. Sonderausgabe Die Tempel-Klassiker. Wiesbaden: Emil Vollmer Verlag, 1957.

Heimel, Cynthia. "Beware of Mr. Right." In *Here Lies My Heart: Essays on Why We Marry, Why We Don't, and What We Find There,* foreword by Amy Bloom, ed. Deborah Chasman and Catherine Jhee, 17–21. Boston: Beacon Press, 1999.

Heyn, Dalma. *Marriage Shock: The Transformation of Women into Wives.* New York: Random House, 1997, 88, 140.

Hilgard, Ernest R. *Divided Consciousness: Multiple Controls in Human Thought and Action.* New York: Wiley, 1977, 110.

Hillman, James. *The Myth of Analysis: Three Essays in Archetypal Psychology.* New York: Harper, 1972, 117, 123.

Hoagland, Edward. "Strange Perfume." In *Here Lies My Heart: Essays on Why We Marry, Why We Don't, and What We Find There,* foreword by Amy Bloom, ed. Deborah Chasman and Catherine Jhee, 74–96. Boston: Beacon Press, 1999.

Horyn, Cathy. "Recipe for the New Perfect Wedding: A $5000 Cake and Hold the Simplicity." *New York Times,* Sunday, June 6, 2004, National Section, 32.

Hutcherson, Hilda. *What Your Mother Never Told You about Sex.* New York: Putnam, 2002, 259.

Ibsen, Henrik. "A Doll's House." In *Four Great Plays by Henrik Ibsen,* xiv, 1–68. Translated by R. Farquharson Sharp, with an introduction and a preface to each play by John Gassner. New York: Bantam, 1981.

Jain, A., J. Concato, and J. M. Levanthal. "How Good Is the Evidence Linking Breastfeeding and Intelligence?" *Pediatrics* 109 (6) (June 2002): 1044–53.

Jennings, C. Robert. "Mae West: A Candid Conversation with the Indestructible Queen of Vamp and Camp." *Playboy Magazine,* January 1971, 73–82.

Johnstone, Barbara. "Community and Contest: Midwestern Men and Women Creating Their Worlds in Conversational Storytelling." In *Gender and Conversational Interaction,* ed. Deborah Tannen, 62–80. Oxford: Oxford University Press, 1993.

Jones, Ernest. *Sigmund Freud, Life and Work.* Vol. 2, *Years of Maturity, 1901–1919.* London: Hogarth Press, 1967, 468.

Jung, Carl G. "The Stages of Life." In *The Collected Works of C. G. Jung,* ed. Sir Herbert Read, Michael Fordham, Gerhard Adler, and William McGuire, executive editor. Vol. 8: *The Structure and Dynamic of the Psyche,* 387–403, secs. 773, 776. New York: Pantheon, 1969.

Justice, Blair, and Rita Justice. *The Broken Taboo: Sex in the Family.* New York: Human Science Press, 1979, 35–41.

Karbo, Karen. *Generation Ex: Tales from the Second Wives Club.* New York: Bloomsbury, 2001, 12, 20–21, 227.

Keller, Helen. *The Story of My Life.* With a new introduction by Jim Knipfel. New York: Penguin Putnam, 1988, 74.

Kendrick, K. M., F. Levy, and E. B. Keverne. "Importance of Vaginocervical Stimulation for the Formation of Maternal Bonding in Primiparous and Multiparous Parturient Ewes." *Physiology and Behavior* 50 (3) (September 1991): 595–600.

Kennell, John H., and Marshall H. Klaus. "Bonding: Recent Observations That Alter Perinatal Care." *Pediatrics in Review* 19 (1) (January 1998): 4–12.

Keverne, E. B., F. Levy, P. Poindron, and D. R. Lindsay. "Vaginal Stimulation: An Important Determinant of Maternal Bonding in Sheep." *Science* 219 (4580) (January 7, 1983): 81–83.

Kierkegaard, Søren A. *A Kierkegaard Anthology.* Edited by Robert Bretall. Princeton: Princeton University Press, 1946, 108–9, 210–11.

Kipnis, Laura. *Against Love: A Polemic.* New York: Pantheon, 2003, 83–84.

Klass, Perri. "Intimacy." In *Love and Modern Medicine,* 52–67. New York: Houghton Mifflin, 2001.

Klaus, Marshall H., and John H. Kennell. *Bonding: The Beginnings of Parent-Infant At-tachment.* Edited by Antonia W. Hamilton. Rev. ed. New York: New American Library, 1983, 1–2.

———. "Commentary: Routines in Maternity Units: Are They Still Appropriate for 2002?" *Birth* 28 (4) (December 2001): 274–75.

Kotulski, Davina. *Why You Should Give a Damn about Gay Marriage.* Los Angeles: Alyson Publications, 2004, 3, 25, 36–39.

Kramer, Peter. *Should You Leave?* New York: Penguin, 1999, 55, 251.

Krasnow, Iris. *Surrendering to Marriage: Husbands, Wives, and Other Imperfections.* New York: Hyperion, 2001, 3–4, 14.

Kubie, Lawrence S. "Psychoanalysis and Marriage: Practical and Theoretical Issues." In *Neurotic Interaction in Marriage,* ed. Victor W. Eisenstein, 10–43. New York: Basic Books, 1956.

Lagemann, John Kord. "Why Young Mothers Are Always Tired." *Redbook Magazine* 113 (5) (September 1959): 42–43, 100–101.

Laing, R. D. *The Politics of Experience.* New York: Pantheon, 1967, 74.

Langlois, Judith, and Lynn Liben. "Child Care Research: An Editorial Perspective." *Child Development* 74 (4) (July/August 2003): 969–75.

Law and Order. Dick Wolf, creator and executive producer, 1990–2004. NBC. Television dramatic series, season 14, episode 4315, "Married with Children," aired February 4, 2004.

Lawrence, D. H. *Women in Love.* London: Penguin, 1995, 331–32.

Lawrence, Ruth A. "Breastfeeding Is More Than Just Good Nutrition." In *Breastfeeding: Biocultural Perspectives,* ed. Katherine A. Dettwyler and Patricia Stuart-Macadam, 395–404. New York: Aldine de Gruyter, 1995.

Le Boeuf, Burney J. "Male-Male Competition and Reproductive Success in Elephant Seals." *American Zoology* 14 (1974): 163–76.

LeDoux, Joseph. *The Emotional Brain: The Mysterious Underpinnings of Emotional Life.* 1996. Reprint, New York: Simon & Schuster, 1998, 69, 79, 168–69, 174, 175.

Leonhardt, David. "It's a Girl (Will the Economy Suffer?)" *New York Times,* Sunday, October 26, 2003, Section 3: Money and Business, 1, 11.

Littman, Heide, Sharon vanderBrug Medendorp, and Johanna Goldfarb. "The Decision to Breastfeed: The Importance of Father's Approval." *Clinical Pediatrics* 33 (4) (April 1994): 214–19.

Love, John M., et al. "Child Care Quality Matters: How Conclusions May Vary with Context." *Child Development* 74 (4) (July/August 2003): 1021–33.

Lucassen, P. L., W. J. Assendelft, et al. "Systematic Review of the Occurrence of Infantile Colic in the Community." *Archives of the Diseases in Childhood* 84 (5) (May 2001): 398–403.

Lyall, Sarah. "In Europe, Lovers Now Propose: Marry Me, A Little." *New York Times,* February 15, 2004, Sunday National Section, 3.

Maccoby, Eleanor E., and Catherine C. Lewis. "Less Day Care or Different Day Care?" *Child Development* 74 (4) (July/August 2003): 1069–75.

Maher, Bill. *Real Time with Bill Maher.* HBO, February 27, 2004. Television program.

Marsak, Leonard M., trans. "Discourse Concerning the Ancients and Moderns." In *The Achievement of Bernard le Bovier de Fontenelle*. Part III, 1688, *The Sources of Science* #76, 1–8. New York: Johnson Reprint Corporation, 1970.

Maushart, Susan. *Wifework: What Marriage Really Means for Women*. New York: Bloomsbury, 2001, 8, 14, 50, 65, 80, 123, 183, 222, 239.

Mazur, Allan, and Alan Booth. "Testosterone and Dominance in Men." *Behavioral and Brain Sciences* 21 (1998): 353–97.

McCrone, John. "'Right Brain' or 'Left Brain': Myth or Reality." *New Scientist* 163 (2193) (July 3, 1999): 26–30.

Mead, Margaret. "Marriage in Two Steps." *Redbook* 127 (July 1966): 48–49, 84, 86.

Micozzi, Marc S. "Breast Cancer, Reproductive Biology, and Breastfeeding." In *Breastfeeding: Biocultural Perspectives*, ed. Katherine A. Dettwyler and Patricia Stuart-Macadam, 347–84. New York: Aldine de Gruyter, 1995.

Miller, Alice. *For Your Own Good: Hidden Cruelty in Child-Rearing and the Roots of Violence*. Translated by Hunter Hannum and Hildegarde Hannum. New York: Farrar, Straus & Giroux, 1990, 116.

Miller, Geoffrey. *The Mating Mind*. New York: Random House, 2001, 70.

Miller, Michael Vincent. *Intimate Terrorism: The Crisis of Love in an Age of Disillusion*. New York: Norton, 1995, 28, 70, 85, 87, 115, 145–46.

Minkoff, H., and F. A. Chervenak. "Elective Primary Cesarean Delivery." *New England Journal of Medicine* 348 (10) (March 6, 2003): 946–50.

Moats, David. *Civil Wars: A Battle for Gay Marriage*. Orlando: Harcourt, 2004, 16, 150–51, 249–50.

Mona Lisa Smile. Directed by Mike Newell, produced by Paul Schiff, Deborah Schindler and Elaine Goldsmith-Thomas, and written by Lawrence Konner and Mark Rosenthal. Columbia Pictures, 2003.

Moore, Thomas. *Care of the Soul: A Guide for Cultivating Depth and Sacredness in Everyday Life*. New York: HarperCollins, 1992, 38.

———. *Soul Mates: Honoring the Mysteries of Love and Relationship*. New York: HarperCollins, 1994, 35, 79, 109, 139, 201.

Morrell, Virginia. "Rise and Fall of the Y Chromosome." *Science* 263 (5144) (January 14, 1994): 171–72.

Mueller, William R. "I'm a Congregationalist, You Know." *The Christian Century* 93 (1976): 476–77.

Murray, Sandra L., and John G. Holmes. "A Leap of Faith? Positive Illusions in Romantic Relationships." *Personality and Social Psychology Bulletin* 23 (6) (June 1997): 586–604.

———. "The (Mental) Ties That Bind: Cognitive Structures That Predict Relationship Resilience." *Journal of Personality and Social Psychology* 77 (6) (1999): 1228–44.

National Institute of Child Health and Human Development Early Child Care Research Network. "Does Amount of Time Spent in Child Care Predict Socioemotional Adjustment during the Transition to Kindergarten?" *Child Development* 74 (4) (July/August 2003): 976–1005.

"National Vital Statistics Report: Births, Marriages, Divorces and Deaths: Provisional Data for November 2003," vol. 52, no. 20, May 11, 2004, www.cdd.gov/nchs.

Neiswender Reedy, Margaret, James E. Birren, and K. Warner Schai. "Age and Sex Difference in Satisfying Love Relationships across the Adult Life Span." *Human Development* 24 (1981): 52–66.

Nesse, Randolph M., and George C. Williams. *Why We Get Sick: The New Science of Darwinian Medicine.* New York: Random House, 1995, 68–69, 94–95, 186.

Nietzsche, Friedrich. "Sensuality Hastens Growth of Love." In *Beyond Good and Evil: Prelude to a Philosophy of the Future,* trans. Walter Kaufmann. *Epigrams and Interludes,* #120, 86. New York: Random House, 1966.

Nock, Stephen. "The Problem with Marriage." *Society* 36 (5) (1999): 20–27.

Nunberg, Geoffrey. "Wed the People? (In Order to Form a More Perfect Gay Union)." *New York Times,* Sunday, February 22, 2004, Week in Review Section, 7.

Odier, Charles. "General Considerations of Affective Relationships." In *Anxiety and Magic Thinking,* trans. Marie-Louise Schoelly and Mary J. Sherfey, 189–208. New York: International Universities Press, 1956.

O'Donnell, Rosie, "Perspectives," *Newsweek,* March 8, 2004, 21.

Ohman, Arne, and Susan Mineka. "Fears, Phobias, and Preparedness: Toward an Evolved Module of Fear and Fear Learning." *Psychological Review* 108 (3) (July 2001): 483–522.

Orwell, George. "Inside the Whale." In *A Collection of Essays by George Orwell,* 215–56. Garden City, NY: Doubleday, 1954.

Paul, Pamela. *The Starter Marriage and the Future of Matrimony.* New York: Random House, 2002, xvii–xviii, 42–43, 74, 157, 172, 208.

Peck, M. Scott. *The Road Less Traveled: A New Psychology of Love, Traditional Values, and Spiritual Growth.* 25th Anniversary Edition. New York: Simon & Schuster, 2002, 109, 167, 264.

Perrin, Ellen C., and the Committee on Psychosocial Aspects of Child and Family Health (American Academy of Pediatrics). "Technical Report: Coparent or Second-Parent Adoption by Same-Sex Parents." *Pediatrics* 102 (2) (February 2002): 341–44.

Petrie, Marion, Tim Halliday, and Carolyn Sanders. "Peahens Prefer Peacocks with Elaborate Trains." *Animal Behavior* 41 (1991): 323–31.

Phillips, David, Camilla A. Van Voorhees, and Todd E. Ruth. "The Birthday: Lifeline or Deadline?" *Psychosomatic Medicine* 54 (5) (September–October 1992): 532–42.

Plato. "Phaedrus." In *Selected Dialogues of Plato,* #244–45, 111–97. Translated by Benjamin Jowett, revised and with an introduction by Hayden Pellicia. New York: The Modern Library, 2001.

———. "The Symposium." In *Selected Dialogues of Plato,* #189–93, 199–277. Translated by Benjamin Jowett, revised and with an introduction by Hayden Pellicia. New York: The Modern Library, 2001.

Pollitt, Katha. "Healthy, Wealthy, and Wise." In *Here Lies My Heart: Essays on Why We Marry, Why We Don't, and What We Find There,* foreword by Amy Bloom, ed. Deborah Chasman and Catherine Jhee, 1–5. Boston: Beacon Press, 1999.

Quinn, P. J., et al. "The Effect of Breastfeeding on Child Development at 5 Years: A Cohort Study." *Journal of Paediatric Child Health* 37 (5) (October 2001): 465–69.

Raleigh, Michael J., Michael T. McGuire, Gary L. Brammer, Deborah B. Pollack, and Arthur Yuwiler. "Serotonergic Mechanisms Promote Dominance Acquisition in Adult Male Velvet Monkeys." *Brain Research* 559 (1991): 181–90.

Rauch, Jonathan. *Gay Marriage: Why It Is Good for Gays, Good for Straights, and Good for America.* New York: Henry Holt, 2004, 7, 31–32, 35, 43, 67, 84, 178.

Reijneveld, Sijmen A., Emily Brugman, and Remy A. Hirasing. "Excessive Infant Crying: The Impact of Varying Definitions." *Pediatrics* 108 (4) (October 2001): 893–97.

Ridley, Matt. *Nature via Nurture: Genes, Experience, and What Makes Us Human.* New York: HarperCollins, 2003, 1–2, 4.

———. "Swallows and Scorpionflies Find Symmetry Beautiful." *Science* 257 (July 17, 1992): 327–28.

Rinpoche, Sogyal. *The Tibetan Book of Living and Dying.* Edited by Patrick Gaffney and Andrew Harvey. 1991. Reprint, New York: HarperCollins, 1994, 34, 46.

Russell, Bertrand. *An Outline of Intellectual Rubbish: A Hilarious Catalogue of Organized and Individual Stupidity.* Girard, KS: Haldeman-Julius Publications, 1943, 22.

Salk, Lee. "The Role of the Heartbeat in the Relations between Mother and Infant." *Scientific American* 228 (5) (May 1973): 24–29.

Sandburg, Carl. "The People, Yes." In *Rainbows Are Made: Poems by Carl Sandburg,* 8. Selected by Lee Bennett Hopkins. San Diego: Harcourt Brace, 1982.

Sander, Jennifer "Gin." *Pamper Yourself: Wear More Cashmere, 151 Luxurious Ways to Pamper Your Inner Princess.* Gloucester, MA: Fair Winds Press, 2003.

Schiffrin, Deborah. "Jewish Argument as Sociability." *Language in Society* 13 (3) (1984): 311–35.

Schlessinger, Laura C. *The Proper Care and Feeding of Husbands.* New York: HarperCollins, 2004, 87, 160.

Seneca. "Epistule Four: On the Terrors of Death." In *Seneca Epistules,* trans. Richard M. Gummere, 1–65. Loeb Classical Library, 1917. Reprint, Cambridge: Harvard University Press, 2002.

Sex and the City. Produced by Michael Patrick King, directed by Tim Van Patten, written by Jenny Bicks. HBO. Television series, episode 83, "A Woman's Right to Shoes."

Shands, Harley C., and Jacob E. Finesinger. "A Note on the Significance of Fatigue." *Pschosomatic Medicine* 14 (4) (1952): 309–14.

Shands, Harley C., Jacob E. Finesinger, and Arthur L. Watkins. "Clinical Studies on Fatigue States." Paper presented at the meeting of the Boston Society of Psychiatry and Neurology, November 13, 1946. *Archives of Neurology and Psychiatry* 60 (2) (1948): 210–14.

Sheehy, Gail. *Menopause: The Silent Passage.* New York: Simon & Schuster, 1998, 141.

Shorter, Edward. *From Paralysis to Fatigue: A History of Psychosomatic Illness in the Modern Era.* New York: Free Press, 1993, 74–75, 79, 83–84, 86.

Sieratzki, J. S., and B. Woll. "Why Do Mothers Cradle Babies on Their Left?" *The Lancet* 347 (9017) (June 22, 1996): 1746–48.

Smith, Russell F. W. "Discussion: Linguistics in Theory—and in Practice." *ETC: Journal of Semantics* 10 (1) (Autumn 1952): 46–49.

Solomon, Marion. *Lean on Me: The Power of Positive Dependency in Intimate Relationships.* New York: Simon & Schuster, 1994, 53–54, 248–51.

Steinberg, Michael. "Symphony No. 45 in f-sharp Minor, Farewell." In *The Symphony: A Listener's Guide,* 200–202. New York: Oxford University Press, 1995.

Stern, Daniel N. *The Interpersonal World of the Infant: A View from Psychoanalysis and Developmental Psychology.* New York: Basic Books, 1985, 142.

Stevenson, Robert Louis. *Virginibus Puerisque and Other Papers by Robert Louis Stevenson.* Harmondsworth, 1881. Reprint, London: Penguin, 1949, 25–26.

Storey, Anne E., Carolyn J. Walsh, Roma L. Quinton, and Katherine E. Wynne-Edwards. "Hormonal Correlates of Paternal Responsiveness in New and Expectant Fathers." *Evolution and Human Behavior* 21 (2000): 79–95.

Storr, Anthony. *Solitude: A Return to Self.* New York: Ballantine, 1988, 187.

Stuart-Macadam, Patricia, and Katherine A. Dettwyler, eds. *Breastfeeding: Biocultural Perspectives.* New York: Aldine de Gruyter, 1995.

Suzuki, Shunryu. *To Shine One Corner of the World: Moments with Shunryu Suzuki.* Edited by David Chadwick. New York: Broadway Books, 2001, 51.

Tannen, Deborah. *You Just Don't Understand: Men and Women in Conversation.* New York: Ballantine, 1990, 48, 76–77, 102, 160, 176–78, 188, 228, 301.

Taylor, Shelley E. *The Tending Instinct: Women, Men, and the Biology of Our Relationships, How Nurturing Is Essential for Who We Are and How We Live.* New York: Henry Holt, 2002, 2, 41.

Theroux, Paul. *My Secret History.* New York: Fawcett Columbine, 1989, 454.

Thornhill, Randy, and Steven W. Gangestad. "Human Facial Beauty: Averageness, Symmetry, and Parasite Resistance." *Human Nature* 4 (3) (1993): 237–69.

———. "Human Fluctuating Asymmetry and Sexual Behavior." *Psychological Science* 5 (1994): 297–302.

Thornhill, Randy, and Karl Grammer. "The Body and Face of Woman: One Ornament That Signals Quality?" *Evolution and Human Behavior* 20 (1999): 105–20.

Todorov, Tzvetan. *Mikhail Bakhtin: The Dialogical Principle,* trans. Wlad Godzich. Vol. 13, *Theory and History of Literature.* Minneapolis: University of Minnesota Press, 1995, 96.

Tolstoy, Leo. *Anna Karenin.* Translated and with an introduction by Rosemary Edmonds. London: Penguin, 1978, 157, 490–91. Reproduced by permission of Penguin Books, Ltd.

Twain, Mark. *Mark Twain's Notebook.* Prepared and with comments by Albert Bigelow Paine. New York: Harper and Brothers, 1935, 235, 397.

Tyler, Anne. *Breathing Lessons.* New York: Berkeley Books, 1988, 188.

Udry, J. Richard, Naomi M. Morris, and Judith Kovenock. "Androgen Effects on Women's Gendered Behavior." *Journal of Biological Science* 27 (3) (July 1995): 359–68.

U.S. Bureau of the Census. *Children's Living Arrangements and Characteristics: March 2002.* Washington, DC: Bureau of the Census, June 2003, 1–20.

van der Hart, Onno. *Rituals in Psychotherapy: Transition and Continuity.* Translated by Angie Pleit-Kuiper. New York: Irvington, 1983, 45.

Viorst, Judith. *Grown-Up Marriage: What We Know, Wish We Had Known, and Still Need to Know about Being Married.* New York: Simon & Schuster, Free Press, 2003, 197.

———. *Suddenly Sixty and Other Shocks of Later Life.* New York: Simon & Schuster, 2000, 38–39, 44–45.

Voltaire. "La Begueule." In *L'Oeuvre de Voltaire,* ed. Guillaume Apolinaire and B. de Villeneuve, 108–14. Paris: Bibliothèque des Curieux, 1923.

Wallerstein, Judith S., and Sandra Blakeslee. *The Good Marriage: How and Why Love Lasts.* New York: Warner Books, 1996, 21–23, 33, 52–53, 74, 262, 296.

———. *What about the Kids? Raising Your Children before, during, and after the Divorce.* New York: Hyperion, 2003, 183, 363.

Warner, Judith. *Perfect Madness: Motherhood in the Age of Anxiety.* New York: Riverhead Books, 2005, 239–57.

Watamura, Sarah E., Bonny Donzella, Jan Alwin, and Megan R. Gunnar. "Morning-to-Afternoon Increases in Cortisol Concentrations for Infants and Toddlers at Child Care: Age Differences and Behavioral Correlates." *Child Development* 74 (4) (July/August 2003): 1006–20.

Watson, John B. *The Psychological Care of Infant and Child.* New York: Norton, 1928, 46.

Wedekind, Claus, Thomas Seebeck, Florence Bettens, and Alexander Paepke. "MHC-Dependent Mate Preference in Humans." Proceedings of the Royal Society of London. *Biology* 260 (1995): 245–49.

Weiskrantz, L., J. Elliott, and C. Darlington. "Preliminary Observations on Tickling Oneself." *Nature* 230 (5296) (April 30, 1971): 598–99.

West, Mae. *Mae West on Sex, Health and ESP.* London: W. H. Allen, 1975, 24, 30.

Wharton, Edith. "Souls Belated." In *Roman Fever and Other Stories,* intro. by Cynthia Griffin Wolff, 87–126. New York: Macmillan, Collier Books, 1993.

White, T. H. *The Once and Future King: The Sword in the Stone.* New York: Putnam, 1987, chap. 21, 182–94, 191–93.

Whitehead, Alfred North. *Dialogues of Alfred North Whitehead.* As recorded by Lucien Price, editor. Boston: Little, Brown, 1954, 199.

Whitehead, Barbara DaFoe. *Why There Are No Good Men Left: The Romantic Plight of the New Single Woman.* New York: Random House, 2003, 6.

Wilson, Glenn. *The Coolidge Effect: An Evolutionary Account of Human Sexuality.* New York: William Morrow, 1982, 36, 125.

Winnicott, D. W. "Primary Maternal Preoccupation." In *Through Pediatrics to Psycho-Analysis,* ed. Donald W. Winnicott, 300–305. New York: Basic Books, 1975.

Wittgenstein, Ludwig. "Philosophical Investigations." In *Deconstruction in Context: Literature and Philosophy,* ed. Mark C. Taylor, 220–41. Chicago: University of Chicago Press, 1986.

Wright, Robert. *The Moral Animal: Why We Are the Way We Are: The New Science of Evolutionary Psychology.* New York: Random House, 1995, 36, 46, 87, 109, 139.

Young, L. J., M. M. Lim, B. Gingrich, and T. R. Insel. "Cellular Mechanisms of Social Attachment." *Hormones and Behavior* 40 (2) (September 2001): 133–38.

Zembo, Cynthia T. "Breastfeeding." *Obstetrics and Gynecology Clinics North America* 29 (1) (March 2002): 51–76.

Zerubavel, Eviatar. *The Fine Line: Making Distinctions in Everyday Life.* New York: Macmillan, Free Press, 1991, 1–3, 6, 34.

Index

adolescents: autonomy, quest for, *142*, 143; clinical examples involving, 141–42; identity formation, *142*, 143, 148, 151–52; individuation, 151–52; marriages, impact on, 3, 141, *142*, *144*, 146; misbehavior, *142*, 144; moodiness, *142*; peers and, *144*, 145, 149; rules for, *135*, 136; sexuality of, 20, 144–45, 147, 148; studies of, 20

aging: biological clocks, 156–57; clinical examples involving, 53–54; health problems and, 188–89; marriage and, 53–54, *154*

American Academy of Pediatrics, 102, 103, 109

animal research: communicative behavior, 117; dominance, 61–62; flight instinct, 129–30; hunting instinct, 126; maternal behavior, 16, 97–98, 126; mate selection, 21; monogamy, 16; sexual behavior, 18, 153–54; stress response, 186

Barash, David P., 16, 44, 46; *The Myth of Monogamy*, 52, 53

Barr, Ronald, 111–12

Barth, John: *Chimera*, 207–8

Barthelme, Donald: "Critique de la Vie Quotidienne," 31, 132

Berger, Peter L., 80

Bernard, Jesse, 182–83, 195

Bible. See Scriptures.

Blakeslee, Sandra: *The Good Marriage*, 8, 94–95, 210, 211; *What about the Kids?* 196

Blum, Deborah, 10, 16, 19, 20, 55, 56, 62, 69, 101, 110, 118, 135; *Sex on the Brain*, 9, 30, 54, 59, 68, 100–101, 121, 126–27

Boszormenyi-Nagy, Ivan, 64, 175, 202

Bradshaw, John, 136, 138

brain: amygdala, 48, 130, 185; analogue versus digital, 66; communication and, 65–66, 72–73, 74–76, 77; cortical, 22, 49, *131*, 205–6; left-brain dominance, 65, 66; love, effects on, 17; mind and, 76–77; men, *76*; perception and, 3, 74, 75–*76*, 205–6; research, 17; right-brain dominance, 65, 66; subcortical, 22–23, 206; visceral, 48, 49, *131*; women, 65, 72–73, 75. *See also* evolution; sex

Campbell, Joseph, 136, 143, 161, 222

Carroll, Lewis: *Through the Looking-Glass*, 7–8, 89

childbirth: anesthesia, *98*; Caesarian, 98, 99; maternal bonding and, *98*, 99;

miscarriages, 117–18; studies of, 97–98, 99; vaginal, 97, *98*. See also infants; pregnancy; reproduction

children: abuse of, 138–39; boundaries for, 136–38; clinical examples involving, 108–9, 121–22, 125–26, 128–29, 134, 136, 139–40, 144; dependency of, *133*, 135–36; fathers and, *100*, 101–2, 105–6, 125–26, *131*; heredity and, 130–31; marriage, effect on, 3, 125; misbehavior, 140–41; mothers and, *102*, 104–5, 106, *107*; nonmaternal care, 107–8; same-sex parents and, 102–3 sexual orientation, 128, *133*; sibling relations, 104, 139–40, 150; studies of, 107–8

Choi, Susan, 11

Chopra, Deepak, 147–48, 156, 157, 184–85, 186, 187, 189

communication: clinical examples involving, 67, 70, 72, 77–78, 79, 80–81, 82–83, 85–86, 88–89; men versus women, 65, 67, 68, 69, 70, 71, 72, 73, 76; studies of, 68, 69; truth, effects of, 83–88. See also brain; men; spouses; women

Congreve, William: *The Way of the World*, 11, 180

Connolly, Cyril, 3, 18, 172, 180, 197

Coolidge, Calvin: "Coolidge Effect" and, 17–18

Cowan, Caroline Pape, 91, 92, 126, 131–32

Cowan, Philip A., 91, 92, 126, 131–32

Coward, Nöel: *Private Lives*, 40–41

Darling, Lynn, 37, 180

Darwin, Charles, 154, 197; *The Expression of the Emotions in Man and Animals*, 23; "This Is the Question," 206–7

Dettwyler, Katherine, 109, 110

De Vries, Peter: *Reuben, Reuben*, 37, 72, 169, 175–76, 196, 201–2

divorce: aftermath of, 193, 218, 219; children and, 92, 203, 218; clinical examples involving, 22; communication and, 203; conditions for, 198, *199*, 201; counseling, 197, 203; mistaken justifications for, 201–2; murder, compared to, 1; remarriage after, 196; women's initiation of, 96, 200. See also spouses

dominance: aggression, contrasted with, 61–62; animals, 19, 61, 63–64; studies of, 61–62

Einstein, Albert, 1–2, 74

emotions: control of, 48–49; cultivation of, *23*; disguising of, 24; "emotional home," 8; physiological basis, 22–23

evolution: brain, 49; females, 32–33; innate fears, 129–30; love and, 45; monogamy, 17; reproduction and, 45–46

Fernald, Ann, 113–14

Fisher, Helen: *Anatomy of Love*, 45; *Why We Love*, 17, 40

Frankl, Viktor, 84, 193

Freud, Sigmund, 10, 31, 96, 206; "Dissolution of the Oedipus Complex," 153

Friedan, Betty, 11; *The Feminine Mystique*, 191, 209

gays, 10, 102–3. See also same-sex marriage

gender: differentiation of, 69, 204; identity, 35, 51, 128; perception and, 80; professional preferences and, 63; social determination of, 24–25, 34–35, 55, 128, *129*. See also children

genes: animals, 126–27; chromosomes, 54, 55, 122; clinical examples involving, 7, 118, 121–22; environment and, 126–27, 129, 131; genetic disorders, *116*, 118–19, 121–23; mate selection and, 120, *121*; studies of, 120–21, 122–23

Glantz, Kalman, 13, 17, 33, 46, 53, 64
Graham, Billy, 1, 3n1
Gray, John, 21–22; *Men Are from Mars, Women Are from Venus,* 12, 68, 201

Hacker, Andrew, 96; *Mismatch,* 102, 198
Haydn, Franz Joseph: *Symphony No. 45,* 222–23
hormones: aggressive behavior and, 56, 57, *58*; animals, 16; cortisol, 108, 156, 184; estradiol, *9,* 20, 30, 56, 59; estrogens, *9,* 12, 18, 59; glucocorticoids, 156; maternal feelings and, *57,* 62–63; oxytocin, 9, 16, 98; paternal feelings and, *58, 59*; progesterone, 18; prolactin, 94; studies of, 16, 57; vasopresin, 16. *See also* neurotransmitters; testosterone
Horyn, Cathy, 2–3

infants: breastfed, 109–10, 127; clinical examples, 95–96, 99–100, 113, 118; colicky, 109, *110,* 111–12; dependency, 135; father, relationship with, 94–95, 101; left-side cradling, *114*–15; marriage, effects on, *93,* 94, *96, 97,* 99–100, 112–13; mother, relationship with, 106, *107,* 113–14, 127; nonmaternal care, 107; sharing parental bed, 112–13; studies of, 107, 109, 110, 111–12, 113–14, 115; tickling, *114,* 116–17, 127. *See also* childbirth; children; pregnancy
infidelity: clinical examples involving, 14, 15–16, 40, 63, 172–73, 174, 176; conditions underlying, 64; midlife, *172*–73, 174, 176; sex and, 14, 18; studies of, 87, 175

Jung, Carl, 160, 167

Karbo, Karen, 200, 202, 218
Kotulski, Davina, 5, 215–16
Krasner, Barbara R., 64, 175, 202
Krasnow, Iris, 203, 209

Lawrence, D. H.: *Women in Love,* 14
LeDoux, Joseph, 22–23, 48, 205–6
lesbians, 10, 100. *See also* same-sex marriage
Lipton, Judith Eve, 16, 46; *The Myth of Monogamy,* 52, 53
love: affectionate, 34, *35,* 37; erotic, 37, 42; maternal, 7, 16, 115–16, 149; objectified, 40, 41; passionate, 31–32, 34, *35*–36; possessive, 42; romantic, 37, 211; sex and, 34, 37, 38, 41, 43, 45; studies of, 17, 43, 45. *See also* marriage; sex; spouses

marriage: cohabitation, compared to, 211–12; counseling, 78, 177, 185, 203; fatigue in, *191*–92; heterogeneity of, 212–13; illness and, 177–79, 185–87, 189, 192–93; incest, 80, 119; infidelity and, 18, 174–75; inherent imperfection of, *200,* 221–22; justifications for, 196, 197–98, 207, *208;* "marriage of companionship," *212,* 213, 214–15; "marriage of parenthood," *212,* 213, 214; "marriage of passion," *212,* 213–14; "MarriageSense," 3; married names, 11, 164; meaning of, 5, 196, 202, *208,* 209, 216; men versus women, views of, 3, 195; mountain climbing, compared to, 216–17; older men and, 53, *55*–56, 131; passion in, 3, *37,* 40; polygamy, 19; prenuptial agreements, 196–97; salvaging, *200, 210*; second, 196, 197, 214; serial, 19, 179; special dates in, 24, *25, 26, 27*; stress, psychological, 177–79, 183, 186–87; studies of, 8, 94, 195, 210, 211; value placed on, 2, 5, 195, 196, 201–2. *See also* infidelity; love; midlife; monogamy; same-sex marriage; spouses
Maushart, Susan, 14, 15, 29, 37, 42, 195, 208
men: aggressive behavior of, 56, 57, *58,* 59, 60; anxiety, proneness to, 26;

clinical examples concerning, 9,
57–59, 60–61, 183, 190–91,
192–93; communication patterns of,
66, 68, 70–71; domestic life and, 13;
fatherhood, 59–60, *100*, 105–6;
genetic predispositions, 18, 19, 54,
55, 129; impotence and, 14;
independence, need for, 10, 32;
marriage, benefits of, *182*–83, 208;
promiscuity of, 19, *45*, 47, *58*;
sexual display, 19, 20, 21; sexual
needs, 16, *30*; sexual revolution
and, 13–14; stress, psychological,
183–84, 190–91; studies of, 26, 57,
60, 62, 100–101; time, sense of,
24, *25*, 26. *See also* hormones;
spouses
midlife: addiction and, 162–63; clinical
examples, 155, 158–59, 160–62, 163,
164–66, 167, 170; health problems,
156, 158, 161, 170–71, 172–73,
186–87, *188*; individuation and, 159,
162; intimacy and, 164–65;
"manopause," 161; marriage and, 3,
154, 155, 161, 163; menopause, 160;
self, sense of, 166–67, 170; spouses
and, 157, *159*, 168 Miller, Michael
Vincent, 7, 29, 79, 199–200; *Intimate
Terrorism*, 198
monogamy: animals and, 14–15, 16, *17*,
52–53; children, benefits for, 15;
sexual libido and, 16–*17*; studies of,
52, 53
Moore, Thomas: *Care of the Soul*, 169;
Soul Mates, 12, 151, 165, 219

narcissism: children and, *100, 102*–3,
104; clinical examples of, 164, 167,
168, 174, 176; modern context of,
169; spouses and, 155, *159*
Nesse, Randolph M., 122, 123, 129–30
neuroses, 167, 168
neurotransmitters, 77; noradrenaline,
56, 57, *58*, 184; serotonin, 56,
58, 61. *See also* hormones;
testosterone

Paul, Pamela, 180, 201, 202, 217; *The
Starter Marriage*, 179
Pearce, John, 13, 17, 33, 46, 53, 64
Peck, M. Scott, 41, 184, 217
personality: genetic influences on, *129*,
131; stages of, 132–33, 144. *See also*
adolescents; narcissism
physical attibutes: marriage and, 153,
154; symmetry of, 20; tallness, 19–20
Plato: "Phaedrus," 148; "The
Symposium," 51
pregnancy: husbands and, 59–60;
marriage, impact on, 3, 91, 93–94,
95; studies of, 59, 93; toxic substances
and, 123. *See also* infants;
reproduction

Rauch, Jonathan, 212, 215; *Gay
Marriage*, 5
reproduction: anatomy and, 46; animals,
46, 47, 52, 53; birth intervals, 44;
clinical examples involving, 51 males
and, 46; sex and, 46–47; sex selection,
53, 54–55. *See also* childbirth;
evolution; genes; sex
Ridley, Matt, 20; *Nature via Nurture*, 7, 126

Salk, Lee, 114–15
same-sex marriage, 3, 5, 100, 103,
215–16
Schlessinger, Laura: *The Proper Care and
Feeding of Husbands*, 108, 204
Scriptures: Adam and Eve, story of, 7,
143, 151; 2 Corinthians, 164; creation
account, 206; Daniel, 81–82; Genesis,
140, 155; 1 Kings, 38, 84–85;
Malachi, 217; Matthew, 105
sex: animals, 46, 47, 153–54; brain and,
18, 49; clinical examples involving,
14, 34, 47–48; libidos, 16; males and,
19; marriage and, 214; passion,
decline of, 16–17, 31–32, 37–38, *60*;
reproduction and, 46; sexual display,
19, 153–54. *See also* adolescents;
infidelity; love; men; reproduction;
spouses; women

Sex and the City (television program), 13, 31, 38

Sheehy, Gail, 161

Solomon, Marion, 132–33

spouses: asymmetric relations, 34–35; cointerdependence, *163*, 171–72; communication between, 65, *67*, 70, *71, 74, 75*, 78–79, 203; conflict, sources of, 132, 139, 141, *142, 144*, 146, 153, 157, 159, 168–69, 174–75, 202–3, 204; differences between, 6, *200*, 204; dominance-submission patterns, 33–34, 51–52, 64; emotional relations, *23*, 134; health issues, 178–79, 183–84, 186–87; idealization of, 209–10; intimacy, *37*, 38, 39, 41, 164, 165, 166; as life-witnesses, 6, 163, 222–23; parenthood and, *92, 93*, 131, *133, 135*, 150; parents, spousal, 7, 8, 39; "psychological hermaphroditism," *204*–5; separated, 193; sexual needs, *43*; sexual passion and, 16–*17*, 31–32, studies of, 126, 131–32, 210; synchronicity of, 217; youth, quest for, 155–56, 157. *See also* infidelity; love; marriage; men; women

Stern, Daniel N., 114, 127

Stevenson, Robert Louis, 6, 163

Tannen, Deborah, 33, 67, 68, 69, 71, 73, 117

Taylor, Shelley E.: *The Tending Instinct*, 182–83

Tay-Sachs disease, 118, 119

temperament, 7–8

testosterone: aggressive behavior and, 56, 57, *58, 59*; decline of, *59, 60*, 63–64; fetal development, influence on, 54; immunological system and, 21; men and, 18, 20, 21, 46, *58, 59, 60*; monogamy, effects of, *17, 59*; sex drive, impact on, 18, 30, 46, 47, *58, 60*; well-being, sense of, *60*, 63; women and, 18, 30, *62. See also* hormones; neurotransmitters

Theroux, Paul: *My Secret History*, 36

Tolstoy, Leo, 102; *Anna Karenin*, 36

Twain, Mark, 15, 222

Tyler, Anne: *Breathing Lessons*, 91–92

United States: children with gay parents, 102; divorce in, 2, 92, 196; marriages, annual, 2; parents, working, 106–7

Viorst, Judith, 39; *Grown-Up Marriage*, 221; *Suddenly Sixty and Other Shocks of Later Life*, 157

Wallerstein, Judith: *The Good Marriage*, 8, 94–95, 210, 211; *What about the Kids?* 196

weddings, 2–3, 179

West, Mae: *Mae West on Sex, Health, and ESP*, 38, 131, 153

Wharton, Edith, 192; "Souls Belated," 37, 213

Whitehead, Barbara DaFoe: *Why There Are No Good Men Left*, 2

Williams, George C., 122, 123, 129–30

women: aggression in, 62; anatomy of, 46, 117–18; attachment, need for, 9, 10, 29; birth control, 120–21; breastfeeding and, *107*, 109–*10*, 111; clinical examples concerning, 9, 12, 41, 155; communication patterns of, 10, 67, 68–*69, 71, 72*, 113–14; conciliatory behavior of, 56, *57*; dependency and, 32–33 depression, proneness to, 26, *181*; genetic predispositions, *9*, 31, 33, 54, *129*; mate selection, 119–21; menstrual cycle, 11, 18, *39*, 43–44, 46; moods of, 12; motherhood, *102*, 104–5, 106, *107*; power over men, 22; single, 2; sexual needs, 18, 29, *30*–31, 43–44; stresses, psychological, 179, 180, *181*–82; studies of, 9, 18, 26, 59, 113–14, 120–21; time, sense of, 24, *26, 27. See also* hormones; infants; midlife; pregnancy; spouses

Wright, Robert, 19, 31, 175, 197

Zerubavel, Eviatar, 75, 76